CALIFORNIA STATE
A
GRANGE

*R*ecipes

*A*re

*N*aturally

*G*ood

*E*ating

EDITORIAL STAFF

Editorial Manager	Mary Jane Blount
Cookbook Editors	Georgia Brazil
	Mary Cummings
	LaNita Stout

Published by
Great American Opportunities, Inc.
P. O. Box 77, Nashville, Tennessee 37202

First Printing: 20,000 Editions

Library of Congress Cataloging in Publication Data
Main entry under title:
California State grange.
    Includes index.
    1. Cookery (Natural foods) 2. Cookery–California.
I. Favorite Recipes Press. II. Title: Grange recipes
are naturally good eating.
TX741.C33 1985   641.5   85-10265
ISBN 0-87197-197-6

CALIFORNIA STATE
A

A special recognition to the CALIFORNIA MILK ADVISORY BOARD for providing this illustration assisting in the success of this cookbook.

GRANGE

A special recognition to the CALIFORNIA HONEY ADVISORY BOARD for providing this illustration assisting in the success of this cookbook.

A special recognition to the CALIFORNIA ALMOND GROWERS EXCHANGE for providing this illustration assisting in the success of this cookbook.

This cookbook has been created by the California State Grange for your enjoyment. Many thanks to all of you who sent in recipes. The response was so great that there wasn't space to include every recipe so the editors at Favorite Recipes Press made the selection in order to include all the Grange chapters that were represented.

Hope you enjoy these Home-Tested Favorite Recipes of the California State Grange.

Joy Beatie, DWA

CALIFORNIA AGRICULTURE

California has led the nation in gross cash farm receipts for the 37th consecutive year. Our California farmers and ranchers received an estimated $14.3 billion for 51.8 million tons of farm products.

Consumers annually spend over $260 billion for the 400 tons of farm-produced foods that are consumed. The cost to assemble, inspect, grade, store, process, package, wholesale and retail tallies over $180 billion. So, it is easy to see that for every dollar generated by the producer (farmer and rancher) three dollars are realized in our economy.

California grows over 200 crops including seeds, flowers and ornamentals. California leads the nation in 48 commercial crop and livestock commodities. A large number are specialty crops in which the "Golden State" accounts for **most** of the U.S. production.

California's "top 20" crop and livestock commodities account for about 78% of the State's gross farm income. Recently, dairy products, cattle and calves, and eggs continued to dominate the livestock industry, while grapes, cotton, hay, nursery products, lettuce, and processing tomatoes were the most important crops. Ranking in value, the 20 leading farm products of California are: milk and cream; cattle and calves; grapes (all); cotton; hay (all); nursery; lettuce; tomatoes (processing); flowers and foliage; eggs (chicken); oranges; almonds; wheat (all); strawberries; rice; chickens; walnuts; potatoes; broccoli; and turkeys. Of these commodities the average American consumer ate an annual average of 148 pounds (retail weight) of beef, veal, pork, lamb and mutton; 61 pounds of chicken and turkey; 84 pounds of fresh fruit (plus 57 pounds of processed fruit and juice); 100 pounds of fresh vegetables (plus 60 pounds of canned or frozen vegetables); 542 pounds of dairy products; and 73 pounds of potatoes.

The membership of the California State Grange, who are supporters of agriculture, have a major challenge as an organization to "spread the word" that city and urban people have as much, or more, to gain from a prosperous agriculture as do farmers and ranchers.

Millions of city jobs are created by farmers who buy the products and services offered by city people. A prosperous agriculture encourages a prosperous economy and a strong foundation for our society which in turn means a strong country.

If anyone wishes to learn more about agriculture, please contact a Grange representative.

CALIFORNIA AGRICULTURE, WE ARE PROUD OF YOU.

California State Grange Headquarters, Sacramento.

COMMITTEE ON WOMEN'S ACTIVITIES

JOY BEATIE
State Director

REGIONAL DIRECTORS

Region 1 . . . . Harriet Sawyer
Region 2 . . . . Fern Whitaker
Region 3 . . . . Leona Greene
Region 4 . . . . Hazel Thompson
Region 5 . . . . .Doris Skow
Region 6 . . . . .Daisy Embree
Region 7 . . . . .Elsie Espinola
Region 8 . . . . .Virginia Davis
Region 9 . . . . Lela Hughes
Region 10 . . . . .Mary Jamerson
Region 11 . . . . .Luella Crandall

Wisteria Hall, Women's Building dedicated in 1955, Sacramento.

CONTENTs

OLD-FASHIONED STRAWBERRY SHORTCAKE

2 c. sifted flour
1 tbsp. baking powder
1/2 tsp. salt
1/4 c. sugar
1/2 c. butter
1 egg, slightly beaten
1/3 c. milk
4 c. sliced fresh strawberries, sweetened

Sift flour, baking powder, salt and sugar into bowl. Cut in butter until crumbly. Beat egg with milk. Add to flour mixture; stir until just moistened. Pat out on floured surface to 1/2-inch thickness. Cut into eight 3-inch rounds. Place on baking sheet. Bake at 450 degrees for 12 to 15 minutes. Cool slightly. Split biscuits. Spoon sliced strawberries between biscuit halves and over top. Garnish with whipped cream and whole strawberries.

VIP

BEEF MARINADE

5 oz. soy sauce
Several drops of liquid smoke
Favorite cut of beef
Garlic salt

Combine soy sauce and liquid smoke in shallow bowl. Sprinkle both sides of beef with garlic salt. Place in marinade. Let stand for 20 minutes or longer. Drain, reserving marinade. Grill to desired degree of doneness, basting occasionally with reserved marinade.
Note: Also good for chicken-fried steak.

David Austin, California State Grange Master

CAKE OF GENOA (GENOISE)

1 c. (about 5) eggs
1 c. sugar
1/2 tsp. salt
1 tsp. vanilla extract
1 1/4 c. sifted flour
Buttercream Filling
Chocolate Frosting

Beat eggs in bowl until light and foamy. Add sugar, salt and vanilla gradually. Beat until thick and pale yellow. Do not underbeat. Sift flour 1/4 at a time over egg mixture; fold in after each addition until well mixed. Pour into 2 greased 8-inch cake pans lined with waxed paper. Bake at 350 degrees for 30 to 35 minutes or until cake tests done. Cool layers in pans; remove. Split each layer into 2 thin layers. Spread Buttercream Filling between layers and over side of cake. Frost top with Chocolate Frosting. Yield: 12-15 servings.

BUTTERCREAM FILLING

3/4 c. sugar
2 tbsp. cornstarch
3 eggs
1 1/2 c. milk
1/2 c. butter, softened
1 tsp. vanilla extract

Combine sugar and cornstarch in saucepan. Add eggs; beat until light anf foamy. Stir in milk. Cook over medium heat until thickened, stirring constantly. Remove from heat; cool to lukewarm. Blend in butter and vanilla. Cool completely.

CHOCOLATE FROSTING

2 tbsp. butter, softened
1 c. sifted confectioners' sugar
1 sm. egg
1 oz. chocolate, melted
1/2 tsp. vanilla extract

Cream butter and confectioners' sugar in bowl. Beat in egg. Add chocolate and vanilla; beat until smooth.

Joy Beatie, California State Grange DWA

BISHOP CHOCOLATE PIE

1 stick butter, softened
1 c. flour
1/4 c. packed brown sugar
1/4 c. chopped nuts
1 pkg. French vanilla instant
*   pudding mix*
1 pkg. chocolate fudge instant
*   pudding mix*
2 c. milk
1 pt. vanilla ice cream, softened
Whipped topping
1 chocolate bar, shaved

Combine butter with flour, brown sugar and nuts in bowl; mix well. Spread on baking sheet. Bake at 350 degrees for 15 minutes. Cool and crumble. Pat into 9 x 13-inch dish. Combine pudding mixes and milk in bowl; mix well. Stir in ice cream. Pour into prepared dish. Chill until firm. Spread whipped topping over pudding layer. Top with shaved chocolate.
Yield: 10-12 servings.

Darlene Andersen, First Lady of National Grange

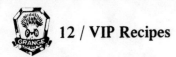

POACHED SALMON STEAKS WITH BROCCOLI

1 med. onion, sliced
6 whole peppercorns
1 tsp. salt
1 bunch broccoli, trimmed
4 salmon steaks

Bring onion, peppercorns, salt and 4 cups water to a boil in shallow pan. Simmer for 15 minutes. Add broccoli. Simmer for 5 to 10 minutes or until stems are tender. Remove with slotted spoon; drain. Arrange on warm serving platter. Place salmon in pan, adding water to cover if necessary. Simmer, covered, for 10 minutes or until fish flakes easily; drain. Arrange on platter with broccoli. Yield: 4 servings.
Note: May substitute other vegetables for broccoli.

Mary R. Buffington
National Director of Women's Activities

APRICOT-CHEESE DELIGHT

1 lg. can apricots, drained,
*   finely chopped*
1 lg. can crushed pineapple, drained
1 lg. package orange gelatin
3/4 c. miniature marshmallows
1/2 c. apricot juice
1/2 c. pineapple juice
1/2 c. sugar
3 tbsp. flour
1 egg, lightly beaten
1/2 c. apricot juice
1/2 c. pineapple juice
2 tbsp. butter
1/2 pt. whipping cream, whipped
3/4 c. shredded Cheddar cheese

Chill apricots and pineapple in refrigerator. Dissolve gelatin in 2 cups boiling water in bowl. Add marshmallows; stir until melted. Stir in 1/2 cup apricot juice, 1/2 cup pineapple juice and chilled fruit. Pour into 9 x 13-inch dish. Chill until firm. Combine sugar, flour, egg and remaining juices in double boiler. Cook until thickened, stirring constantly. Stir in butter; cool. Fold in whipped cream. Spread over congealed layer. Sprinkle with cheese.
Yield: 12 servings.

Marjorie Brown, California State Grange Secretary

CHICKEN CACCIATORE

200 chicken pieces
Flour

5 c. oil
40 med. onions, sliced
40 cloves of garlic, chopped
20 c. tomato sauce
40 c. chopped tomatoes
6 tbsp. plus 2 tsp. each salt, oregano
3 tbsp. plus 1 tsp. celery seed
1 tbsp. plus 2 tsp. pepper
40 bay leaves
5 c. Sauterne

Coat chicken with flour. Brown in hot oil in large skillet; remove chicken to large pans. Saute onions and garlic in skillet. Combine with tomato sauce, tomatoes and seasonings in large bowl. Pour over chicken. Simmer, covered, for 45 minutes. Stir in wine. Simmer, uncovered, until chicken is tender and sauce is thick, turning chicken occasionally. Remove bay leaves. Yield: 100 servings.
Note: Serve with zucchini fried with bacon, tossed green salad and polenta.

Eugene F. Runyon, California State Grange Lecturer

EGGPLANT PARMIGIANA

2 eggs, beaten
1 c. milk
1 eggplant, peeled, sliced 1/4 in. thick
2 c. flour
2 c. bread crumbs
1 1/4 c. olive oil
1 1/2 c. tomato sauce
1/4 c. Parmesan cheese
8 oz. mozzarella cheese, grated

Beat eggs with milk in bowl. Dip eggplant slices into flour, egg mixture and bread crumbs in order listed, coating well. Brown in hot olive oil in skillet; drain. Layer half the tomato sauce, eggplant, Parmesan cheese and mozzarella cheese in 9 x 13-inch baking dish. Repeat layers with remaining ingredients. Bake at 375 degrees until cheese is melted. Yield: 8 servings.

Barbara McGrosso, California State Grange Pomona

FROZEN SALAD

2 c. sour cream
2 tbsp. lemon juice
1/2 c. sugar
1/8 tsp. salt
1   8-oz. can crushed pineapple
2 bananas, sliced
5 kiwi fruit, peeled, sliced
1 can pitted Bing cherries,
*   drained, sliced*

4 drops of red food coloring
1 jar whole maraschino cherries, drained

Combine all ingredients except maraschino cherries in bowl; mix gently. Spoon into lined muffin cups. Top each with maraschino cherry. Freeze until firm. Yield: 24 servings.

Sue Squire, California State Grange Flora

MUSHROOMS FRANCESCO

2 lb. fresh mushrooms
1 bunch parsley, finely chopped
3 cloves of garlic, finely chopped
1 stick butter
Salt to taste
1/4 c. red wine

Saute mushrooms, parsley and garlic in butter in skillet for 5 minutes. Add salt and wine. Simmer for 2 minutes. Serve as appetizer with cheese and crackers. Yield: 8-10 servings.

Peg Maple, National Grange, Advisory Com. WA

CHOCOLATE PUDDING BROWNIES

1 sm. package chocolate pudding and
*   pie filling mix*
2 c. milk
1 2-layer pkg. chocolate cake mix
Chocolate chips
Nuts

Cook pudding mix according to package instructions, using 2 cups milk. Combine with cake mix in bowl; mix well. Pour into greased and floured 10 x15-inch baking pan. Sprinkle with chocolate chips and nuts. Bake at 350 degrees for 30 minutes. Cut into squares when cool. Yield: 12 servings.

Lois Austin, Wife of California State Grange Master

TEX-MEX DIP

2 c. bean dip
3 med. avocados, mashed
2 tbsp. lemon juice
1/2 tsp. salt
1/4 tsp. pepper
1 c. sour cream
1/2 c. mayonnaise
1 pkg. taco seasoning mix
3 med. tomatoes, chopped
1 c. chopped onion
1 lg. can sliced ripe olives, drained

8 oz. Cheddar cheese, grated
Tortilla chips

Spread bean dip in 9 x 13-inch dish. Combine avocados, lemon juice, salt and pepper in bowl; mix well. Spread over bean dip. Combine sour cream, mayonnaise and taco seasoning in bowl; mix well. Spread over avocado mixture. Layer tomatoes, onion, olives and cheese over sour cream. Serve with tortilla chips.

Edna Koster
Wife of Past Master of California State Grange

SUGARLESS CAKE

2 c. raisins
2 eggs
1/2 c. corn oil
1 c. unsweetened applesauce
1 tbsp. liquid sweetener (opt.)
1 3/4 c. flour
1 tsp. soda
1 tsp. pumpkin pie spice

Combine raisins with 2 cups water in saucepan. Cook until water is absorbed; cool. Add eggs, oil, applesauce and sweetener; mix well. Mix in sifted dry ingredients. Pour into greased and floured 8 x 10-inch baking pan. Bake at 350 degrees for 35 minutes. Yield: 10-12 servings.

Ruth A. Quinn
Wife of Past Master of California State Grange

GRANMA SAWYER'S BUTTERHORNS

2 cakes yeast
1 c. milk, scalded
3/4 c. shortening
3/4 c. sugar
1 tsp. salt
2 eggs, lightly beaten
8 c. sifted flour

Dissolve yeast in cooled milk. Cream shortening, sugar and salt in mixer bowl. Beat in eggs, yeast mixture and 1 cup lukewarm water. Add 3 cups flour; beat until smooth. Add remaining flour; mix well. Knead on floured surface until smooth and elastic. Place in greased bowl, turning to grease surface. Let rise in warm place for 2 hours. Roll into large circles on floured surface. Cut into wedges. Roll up from large end. Place on greased baking sheets. Let rise until doubled in bulk. Bake at 325 degrees for 12 minutes or until lightly browned. Yield: 3 dozen.

Harriet Sawyer, Region 1, CWA Director

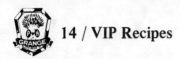

MICROWAVE PEANUT BRITTLE

1 c. sugar
1/2 c. light corn syrup
1 c. roasted salted peanuts
1 tsp. butter
1 tsp. vanilla extract
1 tsp. soda

Combine sugar and corn syrup in 1 1/2-quart glass bowl. Microwave on High for 4 minutes. Stir in peanuts. Microwave for 1 to 5 minutes or until lightly browned. Stir in butter and vanilla. Microwave for 1 to 2 minutes longer. Add soda; mix until foamy. Pour onto greased baking sheet; cool. Break into pieces. Store in airtight container. Yield: 1 pound.

Fern Whitaker, Region 2, CWA Director

PORK CHOP SUPPER

2 3/4-in. thick pork chops
1/3 c. rice
2 tbsp. chopped onion
1 tsp. instant chicken bouillon
1/2 c. chopped apple
1 tbsp. melted butter
1 tbsp. brown sugar
1/4 tsp. cinnamon
1/2 c. sliced apple

Trim pork chops. Render trimmings in skillet. Reserve 2 tablespoons drippings. Discard trimmings and remaining drippings. Brown chops in reserved drippings in skillet over low heat; remove chops. Add rice and onion. Cook until golden brown, stirring constantly. Stir in bouillon and 1 cup water. Bring to a boil. Add chopped apple; mix well. Pour into greased baking dish. Arrange pork chops on top. Bake, covered, at 350 degrees for 30 minutes. Combine remaining ingredients in bowl; mix lightly. Arrange apple slices around pork chops. Bake, uncovered, for 20 minutes longer or until pork chops are tender. Yield: 2 servings.

Hazel Thompson, Region 4, CWA Director

PERSIMMON PUDDING WITH RUM SAUCE

1 c. sugar
1 1/2 c. flour, sifted
2 tsp. soda
1 1/2 tsp. baking powder
Pinch of salt
1/2 tsp. cloves
1 egg, beaten
1/4 c. milk
1 tsp. vanilla extract
1/3 c. melted butter
1 c. persimmon pulp
1 c. raisins
1 c. chopped walnuts
2 eggs, beaten
1 c. sugar
1/2 c. rum
1 c. whipping cream

Combine 1 cup sugar and next 5 dry ingredients in bowl. Beat 1 egg with milk and vanilla in bowl. Add to dry ingredients; mix well. Stir in butter, persimmon pulp, raisins and walnuts. Pour into greased 2-quart casserole. Place in pan of water. Bake at 350 degrees for 2 hours. Combine 2 eggs, 1 cup sugar, rum and whipping cream in saucepan. Bring to a boil, stirring constantly. Serve with hot pudding.
Yield: 4-6 servings.

Doris W. Skow, Region 5, CWA Director

MEATBALLS IN MUSHROOM GRAVY

2 c. croutons
3/4 c. milk
1 lb. ground chuck
1/2 lb. ground pork
1 tbsp. soy sauce
1 tsp. garlic powder
1/2 tsp. onion powder
2 c. beef broth
1 3-oz. can sliced mushrooms
1 tsp. instant onion
1 tbsp. cornstarch

Combine croutons and milk in bowl. Let stand for 5 minutes. Beat until smooth. Add ground chuck, pork, soy sauce and seasonings; mix well. Shape into 60 small balls. Place in greased 2-quart casserole. Combine broth, mushrooms and onion in saucepan. Cook until heated through. Stir in mixture of cornstarch and 1/4 cup cold water. Cook until thickened, stirring constantly. Pour over meatballs. Bake at 350 degrees for 40 minutes. Yield: 20 servings.

Daisy Embree, Region 6, CWA Director

CRANBERRY FRUIT SALAD

    1 8-oz. can crushed pineapple
    2 3-oz. packages lemon gelatin
    1 16-oz. can whole cranberry sauce
    2 apples, finely chopped
    1 c. finely chopped celery

Drain and chill pineapple, reserving juice. Add enough water to reserved juice to measure 2 cups. Bring to a boil in saucepan. Pour over gelatin in bowl, stirring until dissolved. Add 1 cup cold water and pineapple. Chill until partially set. Add remaining ingredients; mix well. Pour into serving dish. Chill until firm. Yield: 9 servings.

Elsie Espinola, Region 7, CWA Director

SOUTHERN PECAN PIE

    1 c. pecans
    1 unbaked 9-in. pie shell
    3 or 4 eggs, well beaten
    1/2 c. sugar
    1/4 c. melted butter
    1/2 tsp. vanilla extract
    1/2 tsp. salt
    1 c. dark corn syrup

Arrange pecans in pie shell. Combine remaining ingredients in bowl; mix well. Pour into pie shell. Bake at 450 degrees for 10 minutes. Reduce temperature to 350 degrees. Bake for 30 minutes longer or until set. Cool before cutting.

Virginia Davis, Region 8, CWA Director

DATE AND PECAN CAKE

    1 c. chopped dates
    2 tsp. soda
    3/4 c. shortening
    2 c. sugar
    2 eggs
    3 c. flour
    1 1/2 c. chopped pecans
    1 sm. jar maraschino cherries, chopped
    1 recipe white frosting
    1 c. coconut
    1 1/2 c. chopped pecans
    1 sm. jar maraschino cherries, chopped

Mix dates with soda and 2 cups boiling water in bowl; set aside. Cream shortening and sugar in mixer bowl until light and fluffy. Add eggs 1 at a time, beating well after each addition. Add flour and date mixture; mix well. Stir in 1 1/2 cups pecans and 1 jar cherries. Pour into greased and floured 9 x 11-inch baking pan. Bake at 350 degrees for 25 to 30 minutes or until cake tests done; cool. Combine white frosting with remaining ingredients; mix well. Frost cooled cake.

Lela Hughes, Region 9, CWA Director

DUMB CAKE

    2 c. flour
    2 c. sugar
    2 eggs
    2 tsp. soda
    1 20-oz. can crushed pineapple
    1/2 tsp. salt
    1/2 c. chopped nuts
    1 pkg. cream cheese, softened
    1 stick butter, softened
    1 16-oz. package confectioners' sugar

Combine first 6 ingredients in mixer bowl; mix well. Stir in nuts. Pour into greased and floured 11 x 15-inch baking pan. Bake at 350 degrees for 45 minutes. Combine cream cheese, butter and confectioners' sugar in bowl. Beat until smooth. Spread on cooled cake. Yield: 20 servings.

Mary Jamerson, Region 10, CWA Director

THREE-RING MARINATED CAULIFLOWER SALAD

    1 med. cauliflower, separated
       into flowerets
    5 med. carrots, thinly sliced diagonally
    1 tsp. fresh lemon juice
    1 lg. red pepper, sliced into rings
    1 lg. green pepper, sliced into rings
    3 sm. onions, sliced into rings
    1 c. cider vinegar
    1 1/2 tsp. sugar
    1 clove of garlic, chopped
    3/4 tsp. oregano
    1/4 tsp. salt

Combine cauliflower and carrots with lemon juice and water to cover in saucepan. Cook until tender-crisp; drain. Mix with peppers and onions in bowl. Combine remaining ingredients in bowl. Pour over vegetables. Chill in refrigerator overnight. Drain vegetables. Arrange on serving plate.

Luella Crandall, Region 11, CWA Director

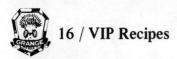

ALL-IN-ONE-DISH SUPPER

4 c. thinly sliced potatoes
1 9-oz. package frozen green
  beans, thawed
3/4 c. shredded cheese
1/3 c. flour
1 tsp. salt
1/8 tsp. pepper
1 15-oz. can tomato sauce
1 lb. ground beef
3/4 c. shredded cheese
1/2 c. dry bread crumbs
1/3 c. milk
1 egg
1/4 c. chopped onion

Combine potatoes, green beans, 3/4 cup cheese, flour and seasonings in bowl; mix well. Spoon into 7 x 12-inch baking dish. Pour half the tomato sauce evenly over top. Bake at 350 degrees for 20 minutes. Mix ground beef, 3/4 cup cheese, bread crumbs, milk, egg and onion in bowl. Shape into 24 meatballs. Arrange over vegetable layer in baking dish. Top with remaining tomato sauce. Bake for 45 to 55 minutes longer or until potatoes are tender.
Yield: 6 servings.

Betty-Jane Gardiner, Connecticut State Grange DWA

EGG SOUFFLE

8 slices bread, trimmed
6 eggs
3 1/2 c. milk
1 tsp. dry mustard
1/2 lb. Monterey Jack cheese, shredded
1/2 lb. sharp Cheddar cheese, shredded

Arrange bread slices in 9 x 13-inch baking dish. Beat eggs in bowl until light and foamy. Add remaining ingredients; mix well. Pour over bread slices. Refrigerate, covered, overnight. Bake at 350 degrees for 50 minutes.
Yield: 12-16 servings.

Marie Thelen, Michigan State Grange DWA

EASY-BAKE POTATOES

6 med. potatoes
1 lg. onion, coarsely chopped
1/4 c. butter
1 clove of garlic, cut into halves
Salt, pepper and celery seed to taste
Paprika to taste

Cut unpeeled potatoes into 1 1/2-inch pieces. Arrange potatoes and onion in single layer in shallow baking dish. Melt butter with garlic in small saucepan; remove garlic. Drizzle butter over potatoes. Sprinkle with salt, pepper and celery seed. Bake, covered, at 400 degrees for 45 minutes. Sprinkle with paprika. Bake, uncovered, for 20 minutes longer or until brown. Yield: 6-8 servings.

Irene Homolka, Oregon State Grange DWA

NOODLE SERVE

1 16-oz. can peas
2 6-oz. cans tuna
1 4-oz. can pimento
1 12-oz. package noodles, cooked
1/2 c. grated Cheddar cheese
3 cans mushroom soup
1/4 c. butter
1/2 c. grated Cheddar cheese

Combine first 7 ingredients and enough water to make of desired consistency in bowl; mix well. Spoon into 9 x 13-inch baking dish. Sprinkle 1/2 cup cheese on top. Bake at 350 degrees for 30 minutes. Garnish with parsley.
Yield: 18 servings.

Mary Richmond, Washington State Grange DWA

ZUCCHINI-OLIVE ENCHILADAS

1 pkg. enchilada sauce mix
1 6-oz. can tomato paste
2 c. shredded zucchini
1 lb. Monterey Jack cheese, grated
1 2 1/2-oz. can sliced ripe
  olives, drained
8 corn tortillas

Prepare enchilada sauce mix with tomato paste and 3 cups water according to package directions. Pour 1 cup sauce into 8 x 12-inch baking dish. Mix zucchini, half the cheese and olives in bowl. Dip tortillas in remaining enchilada sauce. Place 1/2 cup zucchini mixture on each tortilla; roll to enclose filling. Place seam side down in prepared baking dish. Top with remaining enchilada sauce and cheese. Bake at 350 degrees for 25 to 30 minutes or until bubbly. Serve with dollop of sour cream. Yield: 8 servings.
Note: This recipe does not freeze well.

Eleanor K. Grant, Oregon State Grange Exec. Com.

ACCOMPANIMENTS

Solid Iron Power Corn Sheller & Cleaner.

We present a correct engraving of the solid iron Power Corn Sheller and Cleaner on low wagon, for merchant work. In strength, durability and capacity, this Sheller has no equal in the United States. It is built entirely of iron, except the riddle frames, very simple in construction, has not a cog-wheel about it, does not shell against a rest like most shellers, but entirely by friction; has a large fan and extra broad riddles, giving increased cleaning capacities, and enabling the sheller to clean the grain perfectly. It is now in successful operation in nearly every distillery and grist mill in this section of country.

This Sheller may be driven by a Four Horse Lever Power, but for active merchant work, when it is desirable to shell large quantities of corn, it is always run by a Ten Horse Power Portable Threshing Engine.

Capacity, from 2,500 to 3,500 bushels of corn per day.

Price of Sheller, $160. Price of Wagon, $55.00

Main Driving Belt extra.

THE IRON DUKE CORN SHELLER.

In presenting this excellent Sheller to the farmers of the South, little need be said to convince any intelligent man that it is one of the very best machines for shelling corn ever invented. *It shells with great rapidity; takes all the kernels from the cob;* is strong, durable and simple in construction, comprising only a small number of pieces, consequently it is not liable to get out of order. It gives universal satisfaction.

PRICES.

Iron Duke No. 1	$12 00
Iron Duke No. 2	15 00

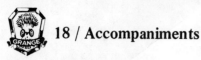

HOT CHEESE PUFFS

3/4 lb. sharp Cheddar cheese, grated
4 1/2 tbsp. flour
1/4 tsp. pepper
1/2 tsp. salt
5 egg whites, stiffly beaten
1/2 c. dried bread crumbs
Oil for deep frying

Combine first 4 ingredients in bowl; mix well. Fold in egg whites gently. Shape by tablespoonfuls into balls. Roll in bread crumbs. Deep-fry in 1 1/2 to 2-inch deep 375-degree oil for 30 seconds or until golden. Drain on paper towel. Serve hot. Yield: 32 puffs.

Edith Sanford, Ripon 511

CRISPY RICE NIBBLERS

2 c. flour
2 c. crisp rice cereal
2 1/2 c. grated Cheddar cheese
2 sticks margarine, softened
1/2 tsp. cayenne pepper
1/4 tsp. salt

Combine all ingredients in bowl. Mix well by hand. Shape by teaspoonfuls into balls. Place on baking sheet; flatten. Bake at 350 degrees for 10 to 12 minutes or until lightly browned. Cool on waxed paper. Store in covered container. Yield: 2 dozen.
Note: Good hot or cold with salads or as hors d'oeuvres.

Sadie M. Wautier, Ripon 511

FIREWEED HONEY

30 white clover blossoms
30 red clover blossoms
18 fireweed blossoms
10 c. sugar
1 tsp. alum

Wash blossoms; drain in strainer. Set aside. Combine sugar, 2 1/2 cups water and alum in saucepan. Boil rapidly for 10 minutes. Remove from heat. Add blossoms to syrup. Let stand for 40 minutes. Strain through jelly bag. Pour into hot sterilized jars. Honey will thicken as it cools and ages. Yield: 6 1/2 pints.

Rita Moore, Concow 735

FRESH CRANBERRY SAUCE

4 lg. oranges
1 lemon
6 lg. apples, cored
8 c. fresh cranberries
2 c. sugar

Remove seeds from oranges, lemon and apples. Put all fruit through food grinder. Combine with sugar in bowl; mix well. Pour into shallow dish. Chill for 2 to 3 days before serving. Serve as relish.
Note: May store in refrigerator for several weeks.

Faye Rice, Fairfax 570

SPICED PINEAPPLE

3/4 c. pineapple syrup
1 1/4 c. sugar
1/4 tsp. salt
1/2 c. cider vinegar
8 whole cloves
1 4-in. stick cinnamon
1 29-oz. can pineapple chunks, drained

Combine first 6 ingredients in saucepan; mix well. Simmer for 10 minutes. Add pineapple. Bring to a boil; cool. Chill for 24 hours or longer. Drain. Serve with meats.

Edna Mae Miller, Empire 521

HOW TO CORRECT JAMS AND JELLIES

1 pkg. powdered pectin
1/4 tsp. soda
8 c. soft jelly or jam
1 1/2 c. sugar
1/4 c. lemon juice

Combine 3/4 cup boiling water and pectin in bowl; mix well. Stir in soda. Let stand for 10 minutes or until no longer bubbly. Combine jelly and sugar in saucepan. Bring to a rapid boil, stirring constantly. Add pectin mixture and lemon juice. Boil for 4 minutes. Pour into hot sterilized jars, leaving 1/2-inch headspace; seal.
Note: This method is successful in correcting jams and jellies that fail to jell for any reason.

Ora Dickens, Quartz Hill 697

SUGARLESS JAM

3 c. fruit, mashed
1 pkg. Slim Set

Combine fruit, 1 cup water and Slim Set in saucepan; mix well. Bring to a rolling boil. Boil for 2 minutes, stirring constantly. Pour into hot sterilized jars, leaving 1/2-inch headspace; seal. Store in refrigerator. Yield: 2-3 pints.
Note: Great for diabetics or those on low sugar diets.

Marion Meeks, Bayside 500

FIG JAM

6 1/2 lb. figs, ground
1 29-oz. can crushed pineapple
Juice of 3 lemons
9 c. sugar
1 tbsp. each cinnamon, allspice
*   and cloves*

Combine all ingredients in saucepan; mix well. Cook until thickened, stirring constantly. Pour into hot sterilized jars, leaving 1/2-inch headspace. Seal with paraffin.

Ruth Dean, Loomis 638

BLUSHING PEACH JAM

2 c. mashed peaches
2 tbsp. lemon juice
2 c. red raspberries, crushed
2 tbsp. lemon juice
7 c. sugar
2 bottles of liquid fruit pectin
Several drops of almond extract

Combine peaches and 2 tablespoons lemon juice in bowl; mix well. Combine raspberries and 2 tablespoons lemon juice in bowl; mix well. Let stand for several minutes. Combine fruits and sugar in saucepan. Bring to a rolling boil, stirring constantly. Boil for 1 minute; remove from heat. Stir in liquid pectin; skim. Add flavoring. Pour into hot sterilized jars, leaving 1/2-inch headspace; seal. Yield: 4 pints.
Note: Very old, delicious recipe.

Evelyn Smith, Garberville 514

WILD PLUM PRESERVES

2 lb. sugar
2 lb. wild plums

Combine sugar and plums in saucepan. Let stand for 1 hour. Boil for 5 minutes, stirring constantly. Pour into hot sterilized jars, leaving 1/2-inch headspace. Seal with melted paraffin. Note: Be sure to use equal measurements of plums and sugar.

Bee Weichers, Montgomery 442

ZUCCHINI JAM

6 c. grated seeded peeled zucchini
1/4 c. lemon juice
1 c. drained crushed pineapple
1 pkg. pectin
6 c. sugar
1 6-oz. package apricot gelatin

Combine zucchini and lemon juice in saucepan. Cook for 1 hour, stirring occasionally. Add pineapple, pectin and sugar. Boil for 6 minutes, stirring constantly. Add gelatin. Stir until dissolved. Pour into hot sterilized jars, leaving 1/2-inch headspace; seal.
Note: This jam is quicker, less expensive and tastier than that made with apricots.

Betty Goeringer, Madera 783

GARLIC SPREAD

1 c. mayonnaise
1 c. margarine
1/4 c. grated Romano cheese
4 cloves of garlic, minced
1 tsp. Italian seasoning
1/2 tsp. paprika
1/2 tsp. poppy seed
4 loaves sourdough French bread, split
Dried parsley to taste

Combine first 7 ingredients in bowl; mix well. Spread mixture on bread. Sprinkle with parsley. Place on baking sheet. Cut bread into slices, but not through bottom. Bake at 400 degrees for 15 to 20 minutes or until edges brown.
Note: May store spread in refrigerator for about 1 month.

Marve Handley, Lake Francis 745

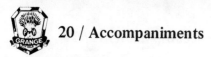

HOMEMADE MUSTARD

3 tbsp. dry mustard
3 tbsp. sugar
3 tbsp. white vinegar
1 egg, beaten

Combine all ingredients in saucepan; mix well. Heat until thickened, stirring constantly. Remove from heat. Beat until smooth.

Betty Loyola, Fort Bragg 672

NO-SALT SEASONING

1 tsp. chili powder
2 tsp. each pepper, oregano
2 tbsp. each garlic powder, dry
*   mustard and onion powder*
3 tbsp. each paprika, poultry seasoning
*   and brewers' yeast*
Celery seed, parsley and dried green
*   pepper to taste (opt.)*

Combine all ingredients in bowl; mix well. Store in containers with shaker tops.

Erva Marie Flint, Lake Francis 745

CRISP PICKLE SLICES

4 qt. medium cucumbers, thinly sliced
6 med. onions, thinly sliced
2 green peppers, chopped
2 cloves of garlic
1/3 c. medium-coarse salt
3 c. sugar
3 c. cider vinegar
1 1/2 tsp. celery seed
2 tbsp. mustard seed

Combine cucumbers, onions, green peppers, garlic and salt in bowl; mix well. Cover with crushed ice; mix thoroughly. Let stand for 3 hours. Drain well. Combine remaining ingredients in bowl; mix well. Combine with cucumber mixture in saucepan. Bring to a boil. Pack in hot sterilized jars, leaving 1/2-inch headspace; seal. Yield: 8 pints.

Pat Saude, San Jose 10

SUN PICKLES

1 clove of garlic
2 tsp. pickling spice
1 dried hot red pepper
1 hot green pepper (opt.)
Fresh dill
Small cucumbers
1 c. salt

Place garlic, pickling spice, peppers and dill in sterilized jar. Add cucumbers, packing tight. Fill each jar with mixture of salt and 1 gallon water, leaving 1/4-inch headspace. Adjust lids to medium tightness. Place in direct sunlight at 70 to 80 degrees outdoor temperature. Let stand for 4 days or until cucumbers become milky in appearance. Do not bring inside at night. Store for 6 weeks before serving.
Note: Pickles will retain crispness for 1 year.

Margaret Bailey, Feather River 448

PICKLED OKRA

4 c. white vinegar
6 tbsp. salt
1 tbsp. celery seed or mustard
    seed (opt.)
2 lb. tender fresh okra
5 hot red or green peppers
5 cloves of garlic

Combine first 3 ingredients and 1/2 cup water in saucepan. Bring to a boil. Pack okra into five hot sterilized 1-pint jars. Place 1 pepper and 1 clove of garlic into each jar. Pour hot liquid into jars, leaving 1/2-inch headspace; seal. Let stand for 8 weeks before using.

June Dodson, Quartz Hill 697

ZUCCHINI CHUNK PICKLES

4 qt. zucchini chunks
6 med. onions, cut into chunks
2 sweet green peppers, cut into chunks
2 sweet red peppers, cut into chunks
3 cloves of garlic, chopped
1/3 c. salt
1 1/2 tsp. celery seed
2 tbsp. mustard seed
1 cinnamon stick
1 bay leaf (opt.)
1 tsp. pickling spice
3 c. white vinegar
3 c. sugar
1 1/2 tsp. turmeric

Layer vegetables and ice cubes in bowl, sprinkling each layer with salt. Let stand for 4 hours. Drain. Do not rinse. Place in saucepan. Tie celery and mustard seed, cinnamon, bay leaf and pickling spice in cheesecloth bag. Combine vinegar, sugar, turmeric and spice bag in saucepan. Bring to a boil. Pour over vegetables. Bring to a boil. Spoon into hot sterilized jars, leaving 1/2-inch headspace; adjust lids. Process in hot water bath for 10 minutes for 1-pint jars or 20 minutes for 1-quart jars. Store for 1 month before serving.

Della McNaught, Clearlake 680

CORN RELISH

8 c. fresh cut corn
2 c. chopped cabbage
1 1/2 c. chopped celery
1 1/2 c. chopped green pepper
1 3/4 c. chopped onion
2 c. cider vinegar
1/3 c. fresh lemon juice
1 c. sugar
2 tbsp. salt
2 1/2 tsp. whole celery seed
5 tsp. dry mustard
1/8 tsp. cayenne pepper
1 tsp. turmeric

Combine vegetables, vinegar, lemon juice, sugar, salt and 1/2 cup water in large saucepan. Simmer for 25 minutes, stirring frequently. Add spices. Simmer for 15 minutes or until thickened, stirring frequently. Spoon into hot sterilized 8-ounce jars, leaving 1/2-inch headspace; seal. Let stand for 6 weeks or longer before using. Yield: 7 cups.

Photograph for this recipe on opposite page.

QUICK AND EASY CORN RELISH

1/2 c. sugar
1/2 c. vinegar
2 tsp. minced dried onion
1/2 tsp. salt
1/4 tsp. celery seed
2 12-oz. cans Mexicorn, drained
3 tbsp. oil

Combine first 5 ingredients in saucepan; cover. Bring to a boil. Simmer for 2 minutes. Add to mixture of corn and oil; mix well. Let stand, covered, until cool. Chill for several hours. Drain before serving. Yield: 3 cups.
Note: May store, covered, in refrigerator for 3 weeks.

Lydia Blesch, Apple Valley 593

MICROWAVE CRANBERRY AND GINGER RELISH

2 12-oz. packages cranberries
1 20-oz. can juice-pack
    pineapple chunks
2 c. packed brown sugar
1/2 c. dark seedless raisins
1 tbsp. minced ginger
1 tsp. salt
1/2 tsp. cinnamon

Combine all ingredients in 4-quart glass casserole. Microwave, covered, on High for 25 minutes or until cranberries pop and mixture thickens, stirring every 5 minutes. Serve warm or cold.

Estelle Flowerdew, Loomis 638

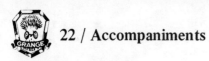

CUCUMBER RELISH

4 c. ground unpeeled cucumbers
1/2 c. ground sweet red peppers
1 c. ground green peppers
3 c. ground onions
3 c. finely chopped celery
1/4 c. salt
3 1/2 c. sugar
2 c. white vinegar
1 tbsp. celery seed
1 tbsp. mustard seed

Combine vegetables and salt in bowl; mix well. Add cold water to cover. Let stand for 4 hours. Drain well, pressing out excess liquid. Combine remaining ingredients in saucepan. Bring to a boil, stirring until sugar is dissolved. Add vegetables. Simmer for 10 minutes. Pack into hot sterilized jars, leaving 1/2-inch headspace; adjust lids. Process in boiling water bath for 10 minutes. Yield: 5-6 pints.

Ella Garrison, El Camino 462

TOMATO RELISH

2 lb. tomatoes, chopped
2 lg. green peppers, chopped
2 lg. onions, chopped
1 tsp. dry mustard
1 tsp. celery seed
1/4 c. vinegar
1/4 c. oil
2 tsp. (about) salt

Combine all ingredients in bowl; mix well. Chill for several hours.

Ann McManus, Lompoc 646

PICKLE RELISH

25 2 1/2 to 3-in. cucumbers
3 lg. onions, cut into quarters
1 red pepper, cut into 1-in. pieces
1 green pepper, cut into 1-in. pieces
3 stalks celery, chopped
1/3 c. salt
1 tbsp. mustard seed
1 tbsp. celery seed
2 c. vinegar
2 c. sugar

Grind vegetables coarsely. Combine with salt in bowl; mix well. Let stand for 3 hours. Drain well. Combine remaining ingredients in saucepan. Bring to a boil. Add vegetables. Return to a boil. Pack into hot sterilized jars, leaving 1/4-inch headspace; adjust lids. Process in boiling water bath for 10 minutes. Yield: 8 pints.

Francies C. Frost, Lake Francis 745

DILL-ZUCCHINI RELISH

6 lb. zucchini
6 lg. onions, cut into chunks
4 red Anaheim chilies, seeded, chopped
1/2 c. salt
2 c. white distilled vinegar
1 c. sugar
2 tsp. dry mustard
2 tsp. celery seed
2 lg. cloves of garlic, minced
1 c. chopped fresh dill

Put vegetables through food chopper with medium blade. Combine with mixture of 1 quart water and salt in bowl. Add enough additional water to cover. Let stand, covered, for 4 hours or marinate in refrigerator overnight. Drain, rinse and drain again. Combine remaining ingredients in saucepan; mix well. Add vegetables. Bring to a boil over medium heat, stirring constantly. Simmer for 20 minutes or until mixture is reduced to 4 quarts. Spoon into hot sterilized 1-pint jars, leaving 1/4-inch headspace; adjust lids. Process in simmering water bath for 15 minutes. Yield: 8 pints.

Myrtle Wolf, Lake Francis 745

ZUCCHINI RELISH

10 c. chopped zucchini
4 c. chopped onions
1 red pepper
5 tbsp. salt
4 1/2 c. sugar
2 1/2 c. vinegar
1 tsp. nutmeg
1 tsp. turmeric
2 tsp. mustard
2 tsp. cornstarch
1/2 tsp. pepper

Grind first 3 ingredients together. Mix with salt in bowl. Let stand overnight. Drain and rinse. Combine with remaining ingredients in saucepan. Cook for 30 minutes. Pour into hot sterilized jars, leaving 1/2-inch headspace; seal.

Ethel Cantwell, Sacramento 12

bREADs

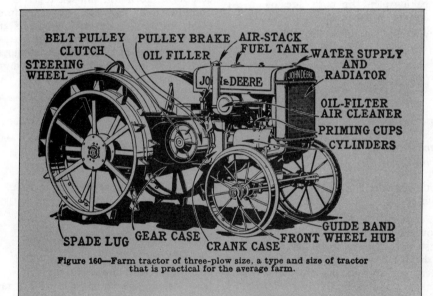

Figure 160—Farm tractor of three-plow size, a type and size of tractor that is practical for the average farm.

Labels in figure:
BELT PULLEY
CLUTCH
STEERING WHEEL
PULLEY BRAKE
OIL FILLER
AIR-STACK
FUEL TANK
WATER SUPPLY AND RADIATOR
JOHN DEERE
OIL-FILTER
AIR CLEANER
PRIMING CUPS
CYLINDERS
SPADE LUG
GEAR CASE
CRANK CASE
GUIDE BAND
FRONT WHEEL HUB

BEER BREAD

3 c. self-rising flour
3 tbsp. sugar
1   12-oz. can beer

Combine all ingredients in bowl; mix well. Let stand for 20 to 30 minutes. Pour into greased loaf pan. Bake at 375 degrees for 1 hour or until bread tests done. Serve hot or warm.

Jan Griffith, Humboldt 501

BUTTERMILK BISCUITS

2 c. flour
3 tbsp. baking powder
1/4 tsp. soda
Buttermilk
1/4 c. oil

Combine dry ingredients in bowl; mix well. Add enough buttermilk to make soft dough. Knead lightly on floured surface until smooth. Roll to 1-inch thickness; cut with biscuit cutter. Pour oil in baking pan. Dip both sides of biscuits in oil; arrange in pan. Bake at 450 to 500 degrees for 20 minutes or until browned.

Lois Short, Manton 732

CORNMEAL SPOON BREAD

2 c. milk
1 c. yellow cornmeal
1 c. milk
3 eggs, separated
1 tbsp. butter
1 tsp. salt
1 tsp. baking powder
1 tbsp. butter

Combine 2 cups milk and cornmeal in saucepan. Cook over low heat until milk is absorbed, stirring constantly; remove from heat. Add 1 cup milk, slightly beaten egg yolks, 1 tablespoon butter, salt and baking powder. Fold stiffly beaten egg whites gently into mixture. Pour into greased baking dish. Bake at 350 degrees for 45 minutes. Dot with 1 tablespoon butter. Spoon hot bread out of baking dish to serve. Yield: 6 servings.

Lois Robison, Rosedale 565

WINONA'S INDIAN CORN CAKES

2 lb. cut fresh corn
1/4 c. flour
Salt to taste
1 tbsp. shortening

Mash corn in bowl. Add flour and salt; mix well. Drop by tablespoonfuls into medium-hot shortening in skillet. Fry until brown on both sides. Yield: Ten 4-inch corn cakes.
Note: Corn cakes are usually served with honey for breakfast. Smaller corn cakes can be served as snacks or appetizers.

Patrie Butler, Lake Earl 577

SAUSAGE CORN BREAD

1 lb. pork sausage, crumbled
1 c. sifted flour
2 1/2 tsp. baking powder
3 tbsp. sugar
1 c. yellow cornmeal
1 tsp. salt
1 c. milk
1 egg, beaten

Cook sausage in skillet until almost cooked through, stirring until crumbly. Drain, reserving 3 tablespoons drippings. Sift flour, baking powder, sugar, cornmeal and salt together 3 times. Combine milk, egg and reserved drippings in bowl; mix well. Add dry ingredients and half the sausage; mix well. Pour into greased 7 x 11-inch baking pan. Sprinkle remaining sausage over top. Bake at 425 degrees for 30 minutes or until brown. Yield: 6-8 servings.

Clara Watson, Loma Rica 802

SAVORY DUMPLINGS

1 tsp. butter, softened
1 c. fine bread crumbs
1 c. flour
4 tsp. baking powder
1 tsp. salt
1/2 c. dried currants
1 egg, beaten
2/3 c. milk
2 tsp. grated onion

Mix butter with bread crumbs in bowl. Sift in flour, baking powder and salt. Add currants and mixture of remaining ingredients, stirring just until moistened. Drop by spoonfuls into simmering stew. Steam, tightly covered, for 20 minutes.
Note: Dumplings are especially good with stewed chicken.

Betty Conroy, Rubidoux 611

SPAETZLE

3 c. sifted flour
1 tsp. salt
3 eggs, beaten

1 tbsp. melted butter
1/2 to 3/4 c. milk

Sift flour and salt together in bowl. Add eggs, butter and enough milk to make stiff dough. Cut off small pieces of dough with sharp knife. Drop into boiling salted water in saucepan. Cook for 6 to 8 minutes or until cooked through. Remove with slotted spoon; drain in colander.

Agnes McKeever, American River 172

STRIP DUMPLINGS

1 c. flour
1 1/2 tsp. baking powder
1/4 tsp. soda
1/4 tsp. salt
1/2 c. buttermilk
Broth

Mix first 5 ingredients together in bowl in order listed. Knead on floured surface until smooth. Roll out 1/4 inch thick; cut into strips. Drop into boiling broth in saucepan. Simmer, covered, for 12 minutes or until cooked through. Yield: 8-10 servings.
Note: May use chicken, beef or vegetable broth.

Melba Grigsby, Fairfax 570

CLAIRE'S COFFEE CAKE

1/4 c. shortening
3/4 c. sugar
1 egg
1 1/2 c. flour
2 tsp. baking powder
1/2 tsp. salt
1/2 c. milk
1/2 c. packed brown sugar
1 1/2 tsp. cinnamon

Cream shortening and sugar in bowl until light and fluffy. Add egg; mix well. Sift flour, baking powder and salt together. Add to creamed mixture alternately with milk, beating well after each addition. Pour into greased 8 x 8-inch baking pan. Sprinkle with mixture of brown sugar and cinnamon. Bake at 375 degrees for 25 to 35 minutes or until cake tests done.

Claire Latter, Los Angeles Pomona 37

CHERRY COFFEE CAKE

1 c. margarine, softened
1 3/4 c. sugar
4 eggs
1 tsp. vanilla extract

3 c. flour
1 1/2 tsp. baking powder
1/2 tsp. salt
1 can cherry pie filling

Cream margarine and sugar in bowl until light and fluffy. Add eggs, 1 at a time, beating well after each addition. Mix in vanilla. Add sifted dry ingredients; mix well. Reserve 1 cup batter. Pour remaining batter into greased and floured 11 x 17-inch baking pan. Spread pie filling evenly over batter. Drop reserved batter by teaspoonfuls over pie filling. Bake at 350 degrees for 30 to 35 minutes or until cake tests done. Garnish with confectioners' sugar or whipped topping. Yield: 16-20 servings.

Margaret Millerick, Rincon Valley 710

RHUBARB-STRAWBERRY COFFEE CAKE

1   13-oz. package frozen unsweetened rhubarb, cut in 1-in. pieces, thawed
1   16-oz. package frozen sliced sweetened strawberries, thawed
2 tbsp. lemon juice
1 c. sugar
1/3 c. cornstarch
3 c. flour
1 c. sugar
1 tsp. each soda, baking powder
1 tsp. salt
1 c. butter
1 c. buttermilk
2 eggs, slightly beaten
1 tsp. vanilla extract
3/4 c. sugar
1/2 c. flour
1/4 c. butter

Combine rhubarb and strawberries in saucepan. Cook, covered, for 5 minutes. Add lemon juice and mixture of 1 cup sugar and cornstarch. Cook for 4 to 5 minutes or until thickened and bubbly, stirring constantly; cool. Combine 3 cups flour, 1 cup sugar, soda, baking powder and salt in bowl. Cut in 1 cup butter until crumbly. Add mixture of buttermilk, eggs and vanilla; stir to moisten. Spoon half the batter into greased 9 x 13-inch baking pan. Spread fruit filling over batter. Spoon remaining batter in mounds over filling. Combine remaining 3/4 cup sugar and 1/2 cup flour in bowl. Cut in 1/4 cup butter until crumbly. Sprinkle over batter. Bake at 350 degrees for 40 to 45 minutes or until brown. Yield: 12-15 servings.

Thelma Buhler, Prunedale 388

OLD-FASHIONED CAKE DOUGHNUTS

1 egg, beaten
1 tbsp. margarine, melted
1/2 c. milk
2 c. flour
2 tsp. baking powder
1/4 tsp. salt
1/2 tsp. cinnamon
1 tsp. nutmeg
Oil for deep frying
1/2 c. sugar

Combine egg, margarine and milk in bowl. Stir in flour, baking powder, salt and spices to form dough. Roll 1/2 inch thick on floured surface; cut with doughnut cutter. Deep-fry in hot oil until golden brown. Cool on wire racks. Place doughnuts in bag with sugar; shake to coat. Yield: 15 servings.

Dortha Holloway, DeSabla 762

POTATO DOUGHNUTS

2 eggs, well beaten
1 c. sugar
2 tbsp. oil
1 c. mashed potatoes
1 c. sour milk
3 c. flour
4 tsp. baking powder
1 tsp. each salt, soda and nutmeg
Oil for deep frying

Beat eggs with sugar in bowl until foamy. Add oil, potatoes and milk; mix well. Stir in sifted dry ingredients. Chill in refrigerator. Roll 1/2 inch thick on floured surface; cut with doughnut cutter. Deep-fry in medium-hot oil until golden brown.

Ivadell Carpenter, McArthur 420

APPLESAUCE LOAF

1/2 c. butter, softened
1 c. sugar
1 egg
1 1/4 c. applesauce
1 1/2 c. flour
1 1/2 tsp. soda
1 tsp. cinnamon
1/2 tsp. nutmeg
1/8 tsp. cloves
Salt to taste
1/2 c. raisins
1/2 c. chopped nuts
Confectioners' sugar

Cream butter and sugar in mixer bowl until light and fluffy. Add egg and applesauce; mix well. Add sifted dry ingredients; mix well. Stir in raisins and nuts. Pour into greased and floured 5 x 9-inch loaf pan. Bake at 350 degrees for 1 hour and 10 minutes or until bread tests done. Cool in pan for 10 minutes. Remove to wire rack to cool completely. Sprinkle with confectioners' sugar.

Emeline Frace, San Marcos 633

APRICOT-NUT BREAD

1 c. apricot nectar
3/4 c. chopped dried apricots
1/2 c. golden raisins
2 c. flour
1 tbsp. baking powder
1/2 tsp. salt
1 c. sugar
1 egg, beaten
1/3 c. milk
2 tbsp. oil
1/2 c. apricot nectar
1/2 c. chopped almonds

Combine 1 cup apricot nectar, apricots and raisins in saucepan. Bring to a boil. Remove from heat; cool. Mix dry ingredients in bowl. Add mixture of egg, milk, oil and 1/2 cup apricot nectar; mix just until moistened. Stir in raisin mixture and almonds. Pour into 2 greased and floured loaf pans. Bake at 350 degrees for 1 hour or until loaves test done. Cool in pan for 10 minutes. Remove to wire racks to cool completely. Let stand, wrapped, overnight before serving. Yield: 2 loaves.
Note: Bread freezes well.

Merle Milosevich, Bear Creek 530

LUCY'S BANANA BREAD

1 1/2 c. sugar
1/2 c. shortening
3 eggs, separated
1 c. mashed banana
1/4 c. sour cream
1 c. chopped walnuts
1 tsp. soda
1 1/2 c. flour
1 tsp. baking powder
1/2 tsp. salt

Cream sugar and shortening in bowl until light and fluffy. Add egg yolks, banana, sour cream and walnuts; mix well. Mix soda with 1/4 cup water. Add to creamed mixture alternately with sifted dry ingredients; mix well. Fold stiffly beaten egg whites gently into mixture. Pour into 4 greased and floured small loaf pans. Bake at 300 degrees for 40 to 50 minutes or until loaves test done. Yield: 4 small loaves.

Lucy M. Killette, Tulare 198

APPLE-BANANA-NUT BREAD

1/2 c. margarine, softened
1 c. sugar
2 eggs
2 c. sifted flour
1 tsp. soda
1/2 tsp. salt
2 bananas, mashed
2 sm. apples, peeled, chopped
1/2 c. chopped nuts (opt.)

Cream margarine and sugar in bowl until light and fluffy. Add eggs, 1 at a time, beating well after each addition. Add sifted dry ingredients to creamed mixture; mix well. Stir in bananas, apples and nuts. Pour into greased loaf pan. Bake at 350 degrees for 1 hour. Cool in pan for 10 minutes. Remove to wire rack to cool overnight.
Note: May rewarm slices and serve with butter.

Julia R. Hurst, North Shore 822

ORANGE-BANANA BREAD

1/2 c. margarine, softened
2/3 c. packed brown sugar
2 eggs
1/2 c. whole wheat flour
1 1/2 c. unbleached flour
1/4 c. rice flour
1/2 tsp. soda
1/2 tsp. (scant) salt
1 tsp. allspice
1/4 c. orange juice
3 med. bananas, mashed
1 1/2 tsp. finely grated orange rind
1/2 to 1 c. chopped dates
3/4 c. chopped walnuts

Cream margarine and brown sugar in bowl until light and fluffy. Add eggs 1 at a time, beating well after each addition. Add dry ingredients alternately with orange juice and bananas, mixing well after each addition. Stir in orange rind, dates and walnuts. Pour into greased 5 x 9-inch loaf pan. Bake at 350 degrees for 1 hour or until bread tests done. Cool on wire racks. Let

stand overnight to improve flavor. Serve plain or toasted with cream cheese or peanut butter.

Grace Capen, American River 172

BANANA-NUT BREAD

1 c. sugar
1/2 c. shortening
3 lg. bananas, mashed
2 eggs
2 c. sifted flour
1 tsp. soda
1/3 tsp. salt
1/3 c. chopped nuts

Cream sugar and shortening in bowl until light and fluffy. Add bananas and eggs; mix well. Add sifted dry ingredients; mix well. Stir in nuts. Pour into greased and floured small bread pan. Bake at 350 degrees for 1 hour or until bread tests done.

Frieda Cook, Elk Grove 86

SPICY ORANGE-NUT BREAD

1 c. ground orange rind
2 tbsp. sugar
2 1/4 c. flour
2 1/4 tsp. baking powder
3/4 tsp. salt
1/4 tsp. (heaping) cinnamon
1 c. sugar
2/3 c. milk
3 tbsp. oil
2 eggs
1/2 tsp. orange extract
1/4 tsp. vanilla extract
2 drops each of almond and lemon extract
3/4 c. chopped nuts
1/2 tsp. cinnamon
2 tbsp. sugar

Combine orange rind with 2 tablespoons sugar and 1/2 cup water in saucepan. Cook, covered, over low heat until rind is tender and water is absorbed. Remove from heat; cool. Sift flour, baking powder, salt, 1/4 teaspoon cinnamon and 1 cup sugar together into bowl. Add milk, oil, eggs and flavorings; beat at low speed just until mixed. Stir in cooled orange rind and nuts. Pour into 2 greased loaf pans. Sprinkle with mixture of 1/2 teaspoon cinnamon and 2 tablespoons sugar. Bake at 350 degrees for 45 to 50 minutes or until bread tests done.
Yield: 2 loaves.

Kelly Covert, DeSabla 762

BOSTON BROWN BREAD

3 1/2 c. whole wheat flour
1/2 c. cornmeal
1 c. all-purpose flour
4 tsp. soda
1 1/2 tsp. salt
4 c. buttermilk
1 c. molasses
1 1/2 c. raisins

Combine dry ingredients in bowl in order listed. Stir in buttermilk, molasses and raisins; mix well. Pour into 6 greased 1-pound cans. Let stand for 30 minutes. Bake at 350 degrees for 40 to 45 minutes or until bread tests done. Yield: 6 small loaves.

Mina Spruit, Encinitas 634

GRAHAM NUT BREAD

1 3/4 c. graham flour
1 c. whole wheat flour
1 tsp. soda
1 tsp. salt
1 c. packed brown sugar
1 egg, beaten
1 1/2 c. sour milk
1 tbsp. melted shortening
1/2 c. raisins
1/2 c. chopped nuts

Combine dry ingredients in bowl. Add egg, milk and shortening; mix well. Stir in raisins and nuts. Pour into greased and floured loaf pan. Bake at 375 degrees for 1 hour.

Jean Gregor, San Dimas 658

OLD-FASHIONED NUT BREAD

1/4 c. butter, softened
1 c. packed dark brown sugar
2 eggs
1 c. buttermilk
2 c. flour
1 tsp. soda
1/2 c. chopped nuts

Cream butter and brown sugar in bowl until light and fluffy. Beat eggs with buttermilk in small bowl. Add to creamed mixture alternately with mixture of flour and soda, mixing well after each addition. Stir in nuts. Pour into greased loaf pan. Let stand for 30 minutes. Bake at 350 degrees for 1 hour.

Pearl Hungerford, Thermalito 729

LOQUAT BREAD

3 eggs
1/2 c. oil
2 c. flour
1 1/2 c. sugar
2 tsp. baking powder
1/4 tsp. each cinnamon, allspice
1/2 tsp. salt
2 c. chopped loquats
1/2 c. chopped walnuts
1/2 c. flaked coconut
1/2 tsp. vanilla extract

Mix eggs and oil in bowl. Add dry ingredients; mix well. Stir in loquats, walnuts, coconut and vanilla. Pour into loaf pan lined with greased and floured waxed paper. Bake at 350 degrees for 45 minutes.

Emma Michalk, Farmersville 637

PERSIMMON BREAD

2/3 c. shortening
2 2/3 c. sugar
4 eggs
2 c. persimmon pulp
3 1/3 c. flour
1/2 tsp. baking powder
2 tsp. soda
1 tsp. salt
1 tsp. each allspice, cinnamon
1/2 tsp. nutmeg
1 c. chopped nuts
1 c. chopped dates
1/2 c. chopped raisins

Cream shortening and sugar in bowl until light and fluffy. Add eggs and persimmon; mix well. Add sifted dry ingredients; mix well. Stir in nuts, dates and raisins. Pour into 3 greased and floured 1-pound coffee cans. Bake at 350 degrees for 1 hour and 10 minutes. Let stand overnight before slicing for best flavor. Yield: 3 loaves.

Mary Boyd, Rio Linda 403

PERSIMMON-DATE-NUT BREAD

6 tbsp. butter, softened
1 c. sugar
2 eggs
1 tsp. soda
1 c. persimmon pulp
2 c. flour
1 tsp. baking powder

1/2 tsp. salt
1/2 tsp. each cinnamon, cloves
2 tbsp. grated orange rind
1 c. each chopped dates, nuts

Cream butter and sugar in bowl until light and fluffy. Add eggs 1 at a time, beating well after each addition. Stir in mixture of soda and persimmon. Add next 5 dry ingredients; mix well. Stir in orange rind, dates and nuts. Pour into greased loaf pan. Bake at 350 degrees for 1 hour or until bread tests done.
Note: May bake in 2 small loaf pans, reducing temperature to 325 degrees.

Rena Webb, Mt. Vernon 453

POPPY SEED LOAF

1/4 c. butter, softened
1 c. sugar
2 eggs
1 tsp. grated orange rind
2 c. flour
2 1/2 tsp. baking powder
1/2 tsp. salt
1/4 tsp. nutmeg
1 c. milk
1/3 c. poppy seed
1/2 c. each chopped nuts, golden raisins
1/2 c. butter, softened
1/4 c. apricot jam
1 tsp. grated lemon rind
1 tbsp. lemon juice

Cream 1/4 cup butter and sugar in bowl until light and fluffy. Add eggs 1 at a time, beating well after each addition. Add orange rind and sifted dry ingredients alternately with milk, mixing well after each addition. Stir in poppy seed, nuts and raisins. Pour into greased and floured loaf pan. Bake at 350 degrees for 1 hour or until toothpick inserted in center comes out clean. Cool in pan for 10 minutes. Remove to wire rack to cool completely. Combine remaining ingredients in bowl; mix well. Serve with bread slices.

Hilda A. Krull, DeSabla 762

SEVEN-UP-DATE-NUT LOAF

1 c. chopped dates
1 7-oz. bottle of 7-Up
1 tsp. soda
1 c. sugar
1 tbsp. butter

1 egg
1 1/2 c. flour
1/2 c. chopped walnuts
1 tsp. vanilla extract
Pinch of salt

Bring dates and 7-Up to a boil in saucepan. Stir in soda; cool. Add remaining ingredients; mix well. Pour into greased 5 x 9-inch loaf pan. Bake at 350 degrees for 1 hour.
Yield: 8-10 servings.

Ida Sordello, Mt. Hamilton 469

SWEET POTATO-BANANA BREAD

1/2 c. orange juice
3/4 c. raisins
3 c. mashed cooked sweet potatoes
3 ripe bananas, mashed
1/2 c. honey
3 eggs, beaten
3/4 c. oil
3 c. whole wheat flour
1 1/2 tsp. baking powder
1 tbsp. soda
1 tsp. salt
3/4 tsp. each nutmeg, cinnamon,
   cloves and ginger
1 c. chopped nuts

Heat orange juice in saucepan. Add raisins. Let stand for several minutes to plump. Combine sweet potatoes, bananas, honey, eggs and oil in bowl. Add sifted dry ingredients; mix well. Stir in raisins and nuts. Pour into greased and floured loaf pans. Bake at 350 degrees for 45 minutes or until bread tests done.

Theresa Heuschkel, Jacinto 431

BISCUITY MUFFINS

1 3/4 c. flour
2 1/2 tsp. baking powder
1/2 tsp. salt
2 tbsp. sugar
1 egg
3/4 c. milk
1/3 c. melted margarine

Combine first 4 ingredients in bowl; mix well. Beat egg and milk in bowl. Add dry ingredients and margarine. Mix until just moistened. Fill 10 greased muffin cups 2/3 full. Bake in preheated 400-degree oven for 25 minutes.

Nina McBride, Western Yolo 423

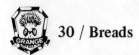

ALWAYS READY SIX-WEEK BRAN MUFFINS

1 16-oz. box Raisin Bran
5 c. flour
2 tsp. salt
3 c. sugar
5 tsp. soda
4 eggs, beaten
1 qt. buttermilk
1 c. melted shortening

Combine first 5 ingredients in bowl; mix well. Add eggs, buttermilk and shortening; mix well. Store, covered, in refrigerator for 6 weeks or less. Fill greased muffin cups 3/4 full. Bake at 425 degrees for 15 minutes or until muffins test done.

Virginia Peterson, Ceres 520

HONEY-PECAN BRAN MUFFINS

1/4 c. honey
4 doz. pecan halves
1 1/4 c. bran
1 c. milk
1 egg, beaten
3 tbsp. oil
3/4 c. flour
2 tbsp. sugar
1 tbsp. baking powder
1/2 tsp. salt

Spoon 1 teaspoon honey into each of 12 greased muffin cups. Place 4 pecan halves in each. Combine bran and milk in bowl; mix well. Let stand for 5 minutes. Add egg and oil. Sift in dry ingredients; mix until just moistened. Fill prepared muffin cups 2/3 full. Bake at 400 degrees for 25 minutes. Yield: 1 dozen.

Ruth Johnson, Loomis 638

LOW-CALORIE MUFFINS

2 c. All-Bran
1/2 c. honey
1 1/2 c. milk
1 egg, beaten
1 c. flour
1 tsp. soda
1/2 tsp. salt
1/2 c. raisins (opt.)

Combine first 3 ingredients in bowl; mix well. Let stand for 15 minutes. Add egg; mix well. Sift in dry ingredients; mix until blended. Stir in raisins. Fill greased muffin cups 2/3 full. Bake at 400 degrees for 20 minutes. Yield: 1 dozen. Note: There is no sugar or shortening in these muffins.

Janet Cameron, Berry Creek 694

MUFFINS FOR MANY

1 c. margarine
2 c. chopped dates
5 tsp. soda
4 eggs, beaten
1 c. sugar
1 qt. buttermilk
5 c. flour
1 tsp. salt
3 1/2 c. All-Bran
2 c. 40% Bran flakes

Combine margarine, dates and 2 cups water in saucepan. Bring to a boil; cool. Stir in soda. Combine eggs, sugar and buttermilk; mix well. Add to date mixture; mix well. Combine flour, salt and cereals in large bowl. Add date mixture; mix well. Store, tightly covered, for 24 hours to 3 weeks. Fill greased muffin cups 2/3 full. Bake at 425 degrees for 20 minutes.

Liz Higgs, Rio Linda 403

NUTRITIOUS MUFFINS

1 c. All-Bran
1/2 c. wheat germ
1/2 c. bran
2 c. buttermilk baking mix
1/4 c. oil
2 eggs
1 c. milk
1 c. raisins
1 c. chopped walnuts

Combine all ingredients in bowl in order listed. Mix until just moistened. Fill greased muffin cups 2/3 full. Bake at 350 degrees for 20 minutes. Yield: 16 servings.

Bobbie Williams, French Camp-Lathrop 510

APPLE MUFFINS

1 c. thinly sliced apple
1 tsp. nutmeg
1 tsp. cinnamon

2 tbsp. sugar
2 1/3 c. flour
5 tsp. baking powder
1/2 tsp. salt
1/4 c. sugar
1/4 c. melted butter
1 egg, beaten
1 c. milk

Combine apple, nutmeg, cinnamon and 2 table-spoons sugar in bowl; mix well. Sift flour, bak-ing powder, salt and 1/4 cup sugar into large bowl. Combine butter, egg and milk in small bowl; mix well. Add to flour mixture, stirring until just moistened. Fill greased muffin cups 1/2 full. Top with apple mixture. Bake at 400 degrees for 20 minutes or until muffins test done.

Carole Reeves, Van Duzen 517

DATE-NUT MUFFINS

1   8-oz. package pitted dates,
    coarsely chopped
1/4 c. oil
1/2 tsp. vanilla extract
1 c. flour
1/2 c. sugar
1/3 c. coarsely chopped walnuts
1/2 tsp. soda

Combine dates, 3/4 cup boiling water, oil and vanilla in bowl. Mix flour, sugar, walnuts and soda in bowl. Add to date mixture; stir until just mixed. Fill greased muffin cups 2/3 full. Bake at 375 degrees for 25 minutes or until golden brown. Remove from pan immediately.

Beulah Gentert, Quartz Hill 697

FRENCH BREAKFAST PUFFS

2 1/2 tbsp. butter, softened
1/2 c. sugar
2 1/2 tbsp. (rounded) shortening
1 egg
1 1/2 c. sifted flour
1 1/2 tsp. baking powder
1/2 tsp. salt
1/4 tsp. nutmeg
1/2 c. milk
6 tbsp. butter, melted
1/2 c. sugar
1 tsp. cinnamon

Cream 2 1/2 tablespoons butter, 1/2 cup sugar, shortening and egg in mixer bowl until light and fluffy. Sift flour, baking powder, salt and nut-meg together. Add to creamed mixture alter-nately with milk, beating well after each addi-tion. Fill greased muffin cups 2/3 full. Bake at 350 degrees for 20 minutes or until browned. Dip muffins in melted butter then in mixture of 1/2 cup sugar and cinnamon. Yield: 1 dozen.

Mary Lou Moses, Montgomery 442

PEANUT-BACON MUFFINS

1 egg, lightly beaten
1 c. milk
2 tbsp. soft Fleischmann's margarine
1/2 c. chopped Planters cocktail peanuts
1/4 c. crumbled crisp-fried bacon
1 3/4 c. flour
1/4 c. packed light brown sugar
1 tbsp. baking powder

Combine egg, milk and margarine in large bowl; mix well. Add peanuts and bacon; mix well. Sift in flour, brown sugar and baking powder; mix about 15 strokes. Fill muffin cups greased on bottoms only 2/3 full. Bake at 400 degrees for 25 minutes or until golden brown. Cool on wire racks. Yield: 10 muffins.

Photograph for this recipe below.

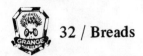

ZUCCHINI MUFFINS

1 c. unbleached flour
1 c. whole wheat flour
1 tbsp. baking powder
1 tsp. cinnamon
3/4 tsp. salt
2 eggs
3/4 c. milk
1/3 c. oil
1/3 c. honey
1 c. coarsely grated zucchini
2/3 c. raisins
1/4 c. nuts (opt.)

Combine first 5 ingredients in bowl. Mix eggs, milk, oil and honey in bowl. Add to dry ingredients; mix until just moistened. Stir in zucchini, raisins and nuts. Fill greased muffin cups 2/3 full. Bake at 375 degrees for 20 minutes or until golden brown. Yield: 1 dozen.

Mae O. Greeley, Ripon 511

BLUEBERRY-COTTAGE CHEESE PANCAKES

1 c. flour
1/4 c. sugar
2 eggs
Pinch of salt
2 c. low-fat cottage cheese
Margarine
1   12-oz. package frozen blueberries
2 tsp. lemon juice
2 tbsp. cornstarch
1 pt. sour cream

Combine first 5 ingredients in bowl. Mix until just blended. Mixture will be thick and lumpy. Brown by spoonfuls in margarine in skillet. Combine blueberries, lemon juice, cornstarch and 1/2 cup water in saucepan. Bring to a boil. Cook until thickened, stirring constantly. Serve over pancakes. Top with sour cream.
Yield: 2-4 servings.
Note: Delicious for a Sunday brunch or holiday breakfast.

Esther Blesch, Apple Valley 593

MELVA'S OATMEAL PANCAKES

1 c. oats
1 c. whole wheat flour
1/2 c. wheat germ
1 tsp. soda
1/4 tsp. salt
1 tbsp. brown sugar

2 eggs
2 c. buttermilk
1/4 c. oil

Combine first 6 ingredients in bowl. Mix eggs, buttermilk and oil in bowl. Add to dry ingredients. Mix until blended. Bake on medium-hot griddle until golden brown on both sides.
Yield: 16 pancakes.

Melva Simpson, Whitethorn 792

PAT'S OATMEAL PANCAKES

1 1/2 c. oats
1/2 c. flour
4 tsp. baking powder
1/2 tsp. salt
1 egg
1 tbsp. oil
1 tbsp. molasses
3/4 c. milk

Combine oats, flour, baking powder, salt, egg, oil, molasses, 3/4 cup warm water and milk in bowl in order listed; mix well. Let stand for 10 minutes. Bake on hot griddle until brown on both sides. Yield: 3-4 servings.

Pat Svelmoe, Julian 643

SOUTHERN PEANUT PANCAKES

1 3/4 c. milk
1 egg
3 tbsp. Planters oil
1 1/2 c. flour
2 tbsp. sugar
2 tsp. baking powder
1/2 tsp. salt
1 1/4 c. whole kernel corn
1/4 c. chopped Planters cocktail peanuts

Blend milk, egg and oil in large bowl. Add flour, sugar, baking powder and salt; beat until smooth. Stir in corn and peanuts. Pour about 3 tablespoons batter onto hot greased griddle. Brown on both sides, turning once. Repeat with remaining batter. Serve with maple syrup. Yield: 20 pancakes.

Photograph for this recipe on page 31.

GERMAN POTATO PANCAKES

1 lb. potatoes, peeled, grated
1 onion, grated (opt.)
1 egg, beaten
1/2 tsp. salt

1/4 tsp. pepper
1/2 tsp. baking powder
2 tbsp. milk
Flour

Combine potatoes and onion in bowl. Let stand for 10 minutes; drain. Add egg; mix well. Add remaining ingredients and enough flour to bind ingredients; mix well. Drop by spoonfuls into hot oil in skillet. Brown on both sides. Serve with meat or fish.
Note: Omit onion and pepper and serve as dessert with sour cream, sugar or applesauce.

Mary M. Starsiak, Thermalito 729

OVEN-BAKED PANCAKE WITH SAUSAGE

3 eggs, beaten
3 tbsp. melted butter
1 1/2 c. milk
1 3/4 c. sifted flour
4 tsp. baking powder
1 1/2 tbsp. sugar
1 tsp. salt
2   1-lb. packages brown and serve
    sausage links
3 tbsp. sugar
2 tsp. cornstarch
3 c. apricot nectar
2 tbsp. lemon juice

Combine first 3 ingredients in bowl; mix well. Sift flour, baking powder, 1 1/2 tablespoons sugar and salt together. Add to egg mixture. Beat until smooth. Pour into greased 10 x 15-inch baking pan. Arrange sausages over top. Bake at 450 degrees for 15 minutes. Cut into serving portions. Combine remaining ingredients in saucepan; mix well. Cook over low heat for 5 minutes or until thickened, stirring constantly. Serve with pancake.

Terrie Null, Rio Linda 403

LIGHT-AS-A-FEATHER WAFFLES

2 c. biscuit mix
1 egg, well beaten
1/2 c. oil
1 1/3 c. club soda

Combine biscuit mix and egg; mix well. Add oil and soda; mix until blended. Bake in hot waffle iron until golden. Yield: 6 servings.

Ellen V. Weber, Lake Francis 745

PUMPKIN-NUT WAFFLES

2 c. sifted cake flour
1/2 tsp. salt
1/4 tsp. nutmeg
4 tsp. baking powder
3/4 tsp. cinnamon
3 eggs, separated
1 3/4 c. milk
1/2 c. melted shortening
1/2 c. pumpkin
3/4 c. chopped pecans

Sift dry ingredients together into bowl. Combine beaten egg yolks, milk, shortening and pumpkin in bowl; mix well. Stir into dry ingredients. Fold stiffly beaten egg whites into batter gently. Pour 1/6 of the batter onto hot waffle iron. Sprinkle with 3 tablespoons pecans. Bake until browned. Repeat with remaining ingredients. Serve with butter and maple syrup. Yield: 6 servings.

Loretta Myers, Ceres 520

CARDAMOM COFFEE BREAD

2 pkg. dry yeast
2 tbsp. sugar
2 c. milk, scalded
3 c. flour
3/4 c. margarine, softened
3/4 c. sugar
1 egg
1 egg yolk
1/2 tsp. cardamom
1 1/2 tsp. salt
3 1/4 c. flour
1 egg, slightly beaten
1/4 c. sugar
2 tbsp. chopped almonds

Combine yeast, 2 tablespoons sugar and lukewarm milk in bowl. Stir until yeast is dissolved. Add 3 cups flour. Beat until smooth. Let rise, covered, until doubled in bulk. Add margarine, 3/4 cup sugar, 1 egg and egg yolk, cardamom and salt; mix well. Add 3 cups flour; mix well. Knead in 1/4 cup flour until dough is smooth and elastic. Place in greased bowl, turning to grease surface. Let rise, covered, for 1 hour or until doubled in bulk. Divide into 6 portions. Roll each into 18-inch rope. Braid 3 ropes together; pinch ends to seal. Repeat with remaining dough. Place on greased baking sheet. Brush with beaten egg. Sprinkle with 1/4 cup sugar and almonds. Let rise until doubled in bulk. Bake at 350 degrees for 30 minutes or until browned.

Linda Thruston, Wyandotte 493

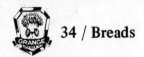

ANGEL BISCUITS

1 cake yeast, crumbled
5 c. flour
1 tsp. soda
1 tsp. baking powder
1 tsp. salt
3 tbsp. sugar
3/4 c. shortening
2 c. buttermilk

Dissolve yeast in 1/2 cup lukewarm water. Sift dry ingredients into bowl. Cut in shortening until crumbly. Stir in yeast and buttermilk until all flour is moistened. Roll desired amount of dough 1/2 inch thick on floured surface. Cut with biscuit cutter. Place on baking sheet. Let rise for 45 minutes. Bake at 400 degrees for 12 minutes.

Vina J. Weathers, Capay 461

FROZEN BISCUITS

2 pkg. dry yeast
5 c. flour
1 tsp. salt
1 tsp. soda
4 tsp. (heaping) baking powder
1/4 c. sugar
1 c. shortening
2 c. buttermilk

Dissolve yeast in 1/2 cup warm water. Sift dry ingredients into bowl. Cut in shortening until crumbly. Add yeast and buttermilk; mix well. Knead 20 to 30 times on floured surface. Roll to 1/2-inch thickness. Cut with biscuit cutter. Place on baking sheet lined with waxed paper. Store, tightly wrapped, in freezer. Place on unlined baking sheet. Bake at 400 degrees for 15 minutes or until browned. Yield: 3 1/2 dozen. Note: Do not thaw before baking.

George Ryan, Humboldt 501

GRANGE BOWKNOTS

1/2 c. shortening
1/3 c. sugar
1 tsp. salt
1 1/4 c. milk, scalded
1 pkg. dry yeast
2 eggs, well beaten
1/4 c. prune juice
5 c. flour

Combine first 3 ingredients and lukewarm milk in bowl. Add yeast. Stir until dissolved. Add eggs and juice; mix well. Add flour; mix well. Let rise, covered, until doubled in bulk. Knead on floured surface until smooth and elastic. Place in greased bowl, turning to grease surface. Let rise for 2 hours. Roll to 1/2-inch thickness. Cut into 1/2 x 10-inch strips. Shape into bowknots on baking sheet. Let rise, covered, until doubled in bulk. Bake at 400 degrees for 15 minutes. Serve with jam and butter or frost with favorite icing.

Leah B. Noriel, Cloverdale 456

RAISIN-OATMEAL BREAD

1 c. quick-cooking oats
2 tbsp. shortening
1 tbsp. salt
1/2 c. honey
2 env. dry yeast
5 1/2 c. sifted flour
1 1/2 c. raisins

Combine oats and 2 cups boiling water in bowl. Add shortening. Let stand for 1 hour. Stir in salt and honey. Dissolve yeast in 1/3 cup lukewarm water. Add to oats mixture. Stir in 4 cups flour and raisins. Add enough remaining flour to make stiff dough. Knead on floured surface until smooth and elastic. Let rise, covered, until doubled in bulk. Knead until smooth. Shape into 2 loaves; place in greased loaf pans. Let rise, covered, until doubled in bulk. Bake at 350 degrees for 50 minutes or until bread tests done.

Phoebe Andreas, Elbow Creek 733

POP-OFF BREAD

1 pkg. dry yeast
1 tbsp. sugar
1/8 tsp. ginger
1 lg. can evaporated milk
2 tbsp. oil
2 tbsp. sugar
2 tsp. salt
4 to 4 1/2 c. flour
1 tbsp. butter, melted

Combine first 3 ingredients and 1/2 cup warm water in large bowl. Let stand for 15 minutes. Add remaining ingredients except butter; mix well. Pour into greased 2-pound coffee can. Let rise, covered with lid, for 1 1/2 to 2 hours or until lid pops off. Bake at 350 degrees for 1 hour. Cool on wire rack for 10 minutes. Brush with butter. Remove from can. Cool.

Libby Griffith, Manton 732

A special recognition to the CLING PEACH ADVISORY BOARD for providing this illustration assisting in the success of this cookbook.

This page is in special recognition to the LINDSAY OLIVE GROWERS for providing a monetary donation along with an illustration depicting their commodity. Their generous donation has assisted in the success of this new California State Grange Cookbook.

BASQUE SHEEPHERDER BREAD

1/2 c. margarine
1/2 c. sugar
1 1/2 tsp. salt
2 pkg. dry yeast
9 1/2 c. flour

Combine margarine, sugar, salt and 3 cups very hot water in bowl. Stir until margarine is melted. Cool to lukewarm. Stir in yeast. Let stand for 15 minutes or until bubbly. Add 5 cups flour; beat well. Add remaining flour; mix well. Knead on floured surface until smooth and elastic. Place in greased bowl, turning to grease surface. Let rise until doubled in bulk. Punch dough down. Place in greased medium-sized Dutch oven. Cover with greased lid. Let rise until lid lifts slightly. Bake, covered, at 375 degrees for 12 minutes. Bake, uncovered, for 30 minutes or until bread tests done.

Harvey Johnson, Fieldbrook 771

WHEAT BREAD

2 pkg. dry yeast
6 c. whole wheat flour
2/3 c. oil
2/3 c. honey
1 tbsp. salt
2 tbsp. molasses
6 c. whole wheat flour

Dissolve yeast in 1/2 cup warm water. Combine 6 cups whole wheat flour and 5 cups warm water in mixer bowl. Beat at medium speed for 3 to 5 minutes or until smooth. Add oil, honey, salt and molasses. Beat at medium speed until well mixed. Add yeast and 6 cups flour gradually; mix well. Knead on floured surface for 10 minutes. Place in greased bowl, turning to grease surface. Let rise until doubled in bulk. Shape into loaves; place in greased loaf pans. Let rise until doubled in bulk. Bake at 350 degress for 30 minutes. Yield: 4 loaves.

Helen McKeague, Sisquoc 651

OLIVE PEASANT BREAD

1 pkg. dry yeast
1 egg
1 tbsp. butter, softened
1 tsp. each basil, oregano
1 tsp. garlic salt
1 tbsp. sugar
1 1/4 c. coarsely chopped ripe olives
3/4 c. Parmesan cheese

3 1/2 to 4 c. flour
1 egg, beaten
1/4 c. Parmesan cheese

Dissolve yeast in 1 cup hot water in bowl. Stir in 1 egg and butter. Add seasonings, olives, 3/4 cup cheese and enough flour to make stiff dough; mix well. Knead on floured surface for 10 minutes or until smooth and elastic. Place in lightly greased bowl, turning to grease surface. Let rise, covered, in warm place for 1 1/2 hours or until doubled in bulk. Shape into 10-inch loaf on greased baking sheet. Let rise for 30 minutes or until doubled in bulk. Slash top 3 times. Brush with beaten egg; sprinkle with 1/4 cup cheese. Bake at 350 degrees for 25 minutes or until golden brown. Cool slightly before serving.
Note: May be used as pizza base.

Iva B. Sanders, Bennett Valley 16

HERB BREAD

2 c. milk
2 tsp. French's herb seasoning
4 tsp. caraway seed
1 tsp. aniseed
1/4 c. sugar
2 pkg. dry yeast
3 c. sifted flour
1 tbsp. salt
1/3 c. shortening
3 eggs
4 to 4 1/2 c. flour
Butter, melted
1 egg, beaten
Aniseed and caraway seed

Combine first 4 ingredients in saucepan. Heat to boiling point. Mix with sugar in large bowl. Cool to lukewarm. Dissolve yeast in 1/4 cup warm water. Add yeast and 3 cups flour to milk mixture; mix well. Add salt, shortening and eggs 1 at a time, mixing well after each addition. Mix in 4 to 4 1/2 cups flour to make stiff dough. Knead on floured surface until smooth and elastic. Place in greased bowl, turning to grease surface. Let rise until doubled in bulk. Divide into 2 portions. Shape 1 portion into three 14-inch ropes. Braid on greased baking sheet to form loaf, tucking ends under. Brush with beaten egg; sprinkle with mixture of aniseed and caraway seed. Bake at 375 degrees for 40 to 50 minutes or until loaf tests done. Shape remaining dough into long rope. Coil in greased round baking pans. Proceed as with braid.

Photograph for this recipe on page 38.

THREE-WHEAT SOURDOUGH BREAD

3 1/2 to 4 c. all-purpose flour
1 c. whole wheat flour
1/2 c. cracked wheat
2 tsp. salt
1 pkg. dry yeast
1 1/4 c. milk
1/4 c. honey
2 tbsp. margarine
1 1/2 c. sourdough starter
1 tsp. soda
1/2 c. sunflower seed

Mix flours in bowl. Combine 1 1/2 cups flour mixture, salt and yeast in mixer bowl. Heat milk, 1/4 cup water, honey and margarine in saucepan until very warm. Add to dry ingredients gradually. Beat for 2 minutes. Add starter, soda and 1 cup flour mixture. Beat for 2 minutes. Stir in remaining flour mixture, sunflower seed and enough additional all-purpose flour to make stiff dough. Knead on floured surface for 8 to 10 minutes or until smooth and elastic. Place in greased bowl, turning to grease surface. Let rise until doubled in bulk. Shape into 2 loaves; place in loaf pans. Let rise until doubled in bulk. Bake at 375 degrees for 35 minutes. Yield: 2 loaves.

Mary Krick, Trinity Valley 618

SWEDISH RYE BREAD

1 pkg. dry yeast
2 c. sifted all-purpose flour
1 c. dark molasses
1/4 c. melted shortening
2 c. sifted rye flour
10 c. sifted all-purpose flour
1 tbsp. salt
2 tsp. aniseed

Dissolve yeast in 4 cups warm water in bowl. Let stand for 5 minutes. Add 2 cups all-purpose flour, molasses and shortening; mix well. Let rise in warm place until bubbly. Stir in rye flour, 10 cups all-purpose flour, salt and aniseed. Knead on floured surface until smooth and elastic. Place in greased bowl, turning to grease surface. Let rise, covered with damp cloth, for 3 hours or until doubled in bulk. Shape into loaves; place in greased 5 x 11-inch loaf pans. Let rise until doubled in bulk. Bake at 375 degrees for 40 minutes or until bread tests done. Yield: 3-4 loaves.

Margaret Toombs, Ripon 511

GRANNY'S DILLY BREAD

2 pkg. dry yeast
1 c. small curd cottage cheese
2 eggs, well beaten
1/4 c. oil
1/4 c. sugar
1/2 c. flour
1 tbsp. salt
3 tbsp. dillseed
2 tbsp. dried onion
2 to 2 1/2 c. flour

Dissolve yeast in 3/4 cup warm water. Heat cottage cheese in double boiler over hot water. Combine cheese, eggs, oil and sugar in bowl; beat well. Stir in yeast; beat well. Add mixture of 1/2 cup flour, salt, dillseed and onion; beat well. Add 2 to 2 1/2 cups flour gradually, beating well after each addition. Knead 30 times or more on floured surface. Place in greased bowl, turning to grease surface. Let rise until doubled in bulk. Shape into loaf; place in greased loaf pan. Let rise until doubled in bulk. Bake at 325 degrees for 40 minutes.

Edna Todd, Chico 486

SPONGE-METHOD WHITE BREAD

1 tsp. sugar
2 cakes yeast, crumbled
2 c. sifted flour
2 tbsp. light brown sugar
1 tbsp. salt
3 tbsp. butter, melted
7 to 7 1/2 c. flour, sifted

Combine sugar and yeast with 1 cup lukewarm water in bowl; stir until dissolved. Add 2 cups flour; mix well. Let stand, covered, in warm place for 6 to 8 hours or until light and spongy. Beat until smooth. Add brown sugar, salt, butter and 2 cups lukewarm water; mix well. Stir in enough flour to make stiff dough. Knead on floured surface until smooth. Let rise, covered, for 15 minutes. Knead until smooth and elastic. Place in greased bowl, turning to grease surface. Let rise, covered, until doubled in bulk. Shape into 3 loaves; place in greased loaf pans. Let rise

until doubled in bulk. Bake at 375 degrees for 15 minutes. Reduce temperature to 350 degrees. Bake for 30 minutes longer or until loaves test done.

Note: If crusty top is desired, brush with mixture of 1 egg beaten with 1 teaspoon water before baking.

Elizabeth Kondor, Escalon 447

BUTTERMILK ROLLS

1 c. buttermilk
2 tbsp. sugar
2 tbsp. shortening
2 tbsp. butter
1 1/2 tsp. salt
1/4 tsp. soda
1 cake yeast
2 3/4 c. sifted flour
Melted butter

Heat buttermilk in saucepan to lukewarm. Remove from heat. Add next 6 ingredients. Stir until yeast is dissolved. Stir in flour. Knead on floured surface until smooth. Place in bowl. Let rise, covered, until doubled in bulk. Shape into rolls; place in greased baking pan. Brush with butter. Let rise until doubled in bulk. Bake at 425 degrees for 15 minutes. Yield: 1 dozen.

Floy Fry, Orland 432

QUICK BEER ROLLS

1 c. milk
1/2 c. butter
1/4 c. packed brown sugar
1 c. beer
2 pkg. dry yeast
2 eggs
6 c. unbleached flour

Heat first 3 ingredients in saucepan until butter is melted. Add beer. Cool to lukewarm. Add yeast; stir to dissolve. Add eggs; mix well. Pour into mixer bowl. Add 4 cups flour gradually. Beat for 5 minutes or longer. Add remaining flour; mix well. Knead until no longer sticky. Shape into rolls. Place in greased baking pans. Let rise for 45 minutes or until doubled in bulk. Bake at 400 degrees for 15 to 20 minutes or until light golden brown. Remove from pans immediately. Yield: 4 dozen.

Ann Feutz, Berry Creek 694

FRENCH CRESCENTS

1 cake yeast
1 tbsp. shortening
2 tbsp. sugar
1 tsp. salt
3/4 c. milk, scalded
1 egg, well beaten
2 1/2 c. flour
Butter, softened
1 1/2 c. sifted confectioners' sugar
1/4 tsp. almond extract
Pinch of salt
1/2 c. chopped almonds

Dissolve yeast in 1/4 cup lukewarm water. Combine shortening, sugar, 1 teaspoon salt and milk in large bowl. Cool to lukewarm. Blend in egg and yeast. Add flour; mix until smooth. Place in greased bowl. Chill, covered, for 1 hour or longer. Roll 1/4 inch thick on floured surface. Spread generously with butter. Fold corners to center, overlapping slightly. Fold in half. Chill, wrapped in waxed paper, for 30 minutes. Repeat rolling, buttering, folding and chilling 2 times. Divide dough into 3 portions. Roll each into 1/8-inch thick circles. Cut each into 8 wedges. Roll from wide end. Place point side down on greased baking sheet. Shape into crescents. Let rise in warm place for 1 1/2 hours or until doubled in bulk. Bake at 400 degrees for 12 minutes or until browned. Combine remaining ingredients and enough water to make of spreading consistency in bowl; mix well. Spread over crescents. Yield: 3 dozen.

Evelyn Rusk, Garberville 514

QUICK DINNER ROLLS

2 pkg. dry yeast
2 c. warm milk
1/4 c. melted margarine
2 eggs
1/2 c. sugar
2 tsp. salt
7 to 7 1/2 c. flour

Dissolve yeast in 1/2 cup warm water in bowl. Add milk, margarine and eggs; mix well. Add sugar, salt and enough flour to make stiff dough. Shape into rolls; place in greased baking pan. Let rise, covered, until doubled in bulk. Bake at 350 degrees for 12 minutes or until browned. Yield: 2 dozen.

Marjorie Meadows, Anderson 418

OATMEAL ROLLS

1/3 c. shortening
1/3 c. packed brown sugar
1 tsp. salt
1 c. oats
1 egg, beaten
1 pkg. dry yeast
3/4 c. instant nonfat dry milk powder
4 c. sifted flour

Combine 1 1/2 cups boiling water, shortening, brown sugar, salt and oats in large bowl. Cool to lukewarm. Add egg and yeast; mix well. Sift in milk powder and 2 cups flour; beat until smooth. Mix in remaining flour gradually. Knead on floured surface until smooth and elastic. Let rise, covered, until doubled in bulk. Punch dough down. Let rest for 10 minutes. Shape into 1 1/2-inch balls. Arrange 1 inch apart in 2 greased 8-inch square baking pans. Let rise, covered, until doubled in bulk. Bake at 375 degrees for 25 minutes or until brown.

Photograph for this recipe on opposite page.

REFRIGERATOR ROLLS

1 cake yeast, crumbled
1/2 c. sugar
1 tsp. salt
1 egg, beaten
3 1/2 c. flour, sifted
3 tbsp. shortening, melted
3 1/2 c. flour, sifted

Combine first 3 ingredients and 2 cups lukewarm water in bowl. Add egg; mix well. Add 3 1/2 cups flour; mix well. Stir in shortening. Add 3 1/2 cups flour; mix well. Let rise until doubled in bulk. Punch dough down. Store, tightly covered, in refrigerator. Shape into rolls; place in greased baking pan. Let rise until doubled in bulk. Bake at 425 degrees for 20 minutes or until browned.

Frances Johnson, Bear Creek 530

REFRIGERATOR YEAST ROLLS

1 pkg. dry yeast
1 egg
1/4 c. sugar
4 c. self-rising flour
1 tsp. salt
3/4 c. shortening

Dissolve yeast in 2 cups warm water in bowl. Add remaining ingredients; mix well. Store, covered, in refrigerator for 2 weeks or less. Shape into rolls; place in greased baking pan. Bake at 400 degrees for 20 minutes.
Yield: 2 1/2 dozen.

Vivian Clow, Rio Linda 403

SWEET ROLL DOUGH

2 pkg. dry yeast
1 1/2 c. lukewarm milk
1/2 c. sugar
2 tsp. salt
2 eggs
1/2 c. shortening
7 to 7 1/2 c. flour

Dissolve yeast in 1/2 cup warm water in bowl. Add milk, sugar, salt, eggs, shortening and half the flour; mix well. Add enough remaining flour to make stiff dough. Knead on floured surface until smooth and elastic. Place in greased bowl, turning to grease surface. Let rise in warm place until doubled in bulk. Punch dough down. Let rise again. Shape into rolls. Place in greased baking pan. Let rise until doubled in bulk. Bake at 400 degrees for 12 minutes or until browned.

Juanita Schooler, Independent 470

MY MOM'S SWEET BUNS

1 c. sugar
1/2 c. shortening
1 tsp. salt
2 pkg. dry yeast
3 c. flour
4 eggs, beaten
3 c. (or more) flour

Combine sugar, shortening, salt and 1 cup boiling water in mixer bowl; mix well. Add yeast and 3 cups flour; beat well. Add eggs; mix well. Add remaining flour; mix well. Knead on floured surface until smooth and elastic. Place in greased bowl, turning to grease surface. Let rise in warm place until doubled in bulk. Shape into buns; place in greased baking pan. Let rise until doubled in bulk. Bake at 350 degrees for 15 minutes. Reduce temperature to 325 degrees. Bake for 20 minutes longer or until golden brown. Yield: 2 dozen.

Eva Fagundes, Los Banos 79

YEAST WAFFLES

1 pkg. yeast
1/2 c. warm milk
2 eggs
3 c. flour
1 tbsp. sugar (opt.)
1/2 c. oil
1 tsp. salt
2 c. milk

Dissolve yeast in 1/2 cup warm milk in bowl. Add remaining ingredients; mix well. Chill overnight. Bake in hot waffle iron until browned. Note: May store in refrigerator for 2 weeks.

Shirley Young, French Camp-Lathrop 510

CHEESE-TOPPED SOURDOUGH BREAD PLUS

2 sticks butter, softened
1 loaf French bread, split
1 1/2 c. grated Cheddar cheese
2 4-oz. cans green chilies,
* finely chopped*

Spread butter on bread halves. Sprinkle with cheese and chilies. Place bread halves together; wrap in foil. Bake at 325 degrees for 10 to 15 minutes or until heated through. Cut into serving pieces. Yield: 6 servings.

Barbara Davis, Little Lake 670

STICKY BREAD

2 loaves frozen white bread dough
1 c. packed brown sugar
1/2 c. butter
2 tbsp. corn syrup
1 tsp. cinnamon
1/2 c. chopped pecans

Thaw bread dough in refrigerator overnight. Knead on floured surface until smooth and elastic. Cut into 1-inch pieces. Combine brown sugar, butter, syrup and cinnamon in saucepan. Heat until ingredients are blended. Layer half the dough and syrup in greased bundt pan. Repeat layers. Sprinkle with pecans. Let rise for 30 to 40 minutes or until doubled in bulk. Bake at 350 degrees for 30 minutes. Cool for several minutes. Turn carefully onto serving plate. Serve warm with butter.

Charlene Stone, Montgomery 442

PIZZA SPREAD

1 lb. Cheddar cheese, shredded
1 4-oz. can chopped olives
1 4-oz. can chopped green chilies
1 can tomato sauce
1/2 c. oil
1/2 sm. onion, chopped
1 tsp. vinegar
Garlic salt to taste
1 tsp. Worcestershire sauce
Dash of Tabasco sauce
Salt and pepper to taste
1 loaf French bread, split

Combine cheese, olives, green chilies, tomato sauce, oil, onion and seasonings in bowl; mix well. Spread on bread. Place on baking sheet. Bake at 400 degrees for 5 minutes.

Iva Proctor, Chico 486

STUFFED CHEESE ROLLS

2 doz. hard rolls
1 lb. sharp Cheddar cheese, shredded
1/2 c. olive oil
1 8-oz. can tomato sauce
2 hard-boiled eggs, chopped
1 can chopped olives
1 can chopped pimento
5 green onions, chopped
1/2 green pepper, chopped
Salt and pepper to taste

Slice tops from rolls. Remove soft centers from roll bottoms. Combine remaining ingredients in bowl; mix well. Spoon into rolls; replace tops. Wrap in foil. Bake at 300 degrees for 30 minutes.

Marie Pedro, Berryessa 780

STUFFED ROLLS

1 med. onion
1 lb. Tillamook cheese
1 c. chopped ripe olives
1 green pepper (opt.)
Pickles (opt.)
1 8-oz. can tomato sauce
1/2 c. oil
3 doz. rolls, split, soft center removed

Grind onion, cheese, olives, green pepper and pickles together. Combine ground ingredients, tomato sauce and oil in bowl; mix well. Fill rolls; wrap in foil. Bake at 300 degrees for 30 minutes.

Ethel Brookshire, Santa Cruz-Live Oak 503

cAKEs

WILCOX & GIBBS' SEWING MACHINES.

WILLCOX & GIBBS SEWING MACHINE.

In connection with our large and valuable assortment of improved machinery for farm and household, we have been induced to accept the agency of a Sewing Machine, the *superior merits* of which will commend it to our friends, and prove a *real blessing* in every family. With several years practical experience with Sewing Machines of various patterns, including the most popular now in use, we unhesitatingly pronounce the WILCOX & GIBBS as the most perfect machine for family use we have ever seen, and recommend to our customers to give it a trial before purchasing any other pattern. WE WARRANT THEM FOR FIVE YEARS, and to give *perfect satisfaction*.

ANGEL FROTH SPONGE CAKE

3 eggs, separated
1 1/4 c. sugar
1 tsp. grated orange rind
1 tsp. each orange, lemon extract
1 1/2 c. cake flour
1/4 tsp. salt
1 tsp. baking powder

Combine 3/4 cup cold water and egg yolks in 1-quart mixer bowl. Beat until bowl is full. Combine sugar, orange rind and flavorings in large mixer bowl. Add egg yolks. Beat for 4 minutes. Fold in sifted flour, salt and baking powder. Fold in stiffly beaten egg whites gently. Pour into ungreased tube pan. Bake at 350 degrees for 50 to 60 minutes or until cake tests done. Invert on funnel to cool.

Irene Faoro, Rincon Valley 710

CHERRY ANGEL FOOD CAKE

1 jar maraschino cherries
1 angel food cake mix
1/2 c. chopped walnuts
1 pkg. vanilla instant pudding mix
1 3/4 c. milk
1 carton whipped topping

Drain and chop cherries, reserving juice. Prepare cake mix according to package directions, using cherry juice for part of liquid. Fold in chopped cherries and walnuts gently. Pour into ungreased tube pan. Bake using package directions. Prepare pudding mix with milk according to package directions. Fold in whipped topping. Chill for 15 to 20 minutes. Frost cooled cake.

Kenneth Von Hoorebeke, Rohner 509

BERNIECE'S APPLE CAKE

4 c. chopped peeled apples
2 c. sugar
2 eggs, beaten
1 c. oil
1/2 tsp. vanilla extract
3 c. flour
1 tbsp. soda
1 tsp. salt
1 tsp. cinnamon
1 tsp. nutmeg
3/4 c. chopped nuts
1 c. packed brown sugar
1/2 c. margarine
1/2 c. milk
1/4 tsp. vanilla extract

Combine apples and sugar in bowl. Let stand for 1 hour. Beat eggs with oil and 1/2 teaspoon vanilla in large bowl. Sift in mixture of flour, soda, salt and spices; mix well. Add apples and nuts; mix well. Pour into greased bundt pan. Bake at 350 degrees for 1 hour or until cake tests done. Combine brown sugar, margarine and milk in saucepan. Bring to a boil. Boil for 5 minutes, stirring constantly. Stir in 1/4 teaspoon vanilla. Spread over warm cake.

Berniece T. McGraw, Lompoc 646

APPLE BLOSSOM MOIST CAKE

2 eggs, beaten
1 1/2 c. oil
3 c. flour
2 c. sugar
1 tsp. salt
1 1/2 tsp. soda
3/4 tsp. each cinnamon, nutmeg
and allspice
1 tsp. vanilla extract
1 can unsweetened sliced pie
apples, drained

Combine eggs and oil in bowl. Add sifted dry ingredients; mix well. Mix in vanilla. Add apples; mix gently. Pour into greased and floured 10-inch tube pan. Bake at 350 degrees for 1 1/2 hours or until cake tests done.

Marilyn L. Fricke, Copper Mountain 814

APPLE-WALNUT UPSIDE-DOWN CAKE

3 med. cooking apples, peeled, cored
3 tbsp. butter
1/2 c. packed brown sugar
9 maraschino cherries
1/2 c. shortening
1/2 c. sugar
1 egg
2 c. flour
1 tsp. soda
1 tsp. each cinnamon, ginger
1/4 tsp. cloves
1/4 tsp. salt
1/2 c. molasses
1/2 c. walnuts

Slice 9 thick rings from apples. Chop enough remaining apples to measure 1 cup; set aside. Melt butter in 9 x 13-inch baking pan. Add brown sugar. Arrange apple rings in pan; place cherries in centers. Cream shortening and sugar

in bowl until light and fluffy. Add egg; beat well. Add sifted dry ingredients. Add molasses and 1/2 cup hot water; mix well. Fold in chopped apples and walnuts. Pour into prepared pan. Bake at 350 degrees for 40 to 50 minutes or until cake tests done. Cool on wire rack for 5 minutes. Invert on serving plate. Serve with whipped cream.
Yield: 15-20 servings.

Florence Goff, Whitethorn 792

WHOLE GRAIN APPLE CAKE

2 eggs, beaten
1 c. sugar
1 c. packed brown sugar
1/2 c. oil
1 c. chopped walnuts
4 c. chopped tart apples
2 c. whole wheat flour
1/4 c. toasted wheat germ
2 tsp. soda
1 1/2 tsp. cinnamon
1 tsp. salt
1/2 tsp. nutmeg

Beat eggs, sugars and oil in bowl. Add walnuts and apples; mix well. Add mixture of sifted dry ingredients; mix gently until well blended. Pour into greased 9 x 13-inch baking dish. Bake at 350 degrees for 50 minutes or until cake tests done.

Marie Lengyel, Rough and Ready 795

EASY APPLESAUCE CAKE

1 c. sugar
1 2/3 c. flour
1 1/2 tsp. soda
1/2 tsp. salt
3 tbsp. cocoa
1/2 c. margarine
1 1/2 c. applesauce
1 tsp. vanilla extract
1 egg, beaten

Combine first 5 ingredients in bowl. Cut in margarine until crumbly. Add mixture of applesauce and vanilla; mix well. Add egg; mix well. Pour into greased and floured baking pan. Bake at 350 degrees for 45 minutes.

Louise Aldrich, Humboldt 501

HILDA'S APPLE CAKE

4 c. chopped apples
2 c. sugar

1/2 c. oil
2 eggs
2 tsp. vanilla extract
2 c. flour, sifted
2 tsp. soda
1 tsp. salt
2 tsp. cinnamon
1 c. chopped nuts

Combine first 5 ingredients in bowl in order listed; mix well. Sift together dry ingredients. Add with nuts to apple mixture; mix well. Pour into greased and floured 9 x 13-inch baking pan. Bake at 350 degrees for 45 minutes.

Hilda M. Sonniksen, San Bernardo 506

GLADYS' FRESH APPLE CAKE

2 c. coarsely grated apple
1 egg, beaten
1 c. sugar
1 tsp. salt
1 tsp. soda
1 tsp. cinnamon
1/2 tsp. nutmeg
1/4 c. oil
1 c. chopped walnuts
1 c. raisins
1 c. sifted flour

Combine all ingredients except flour in bowl; mix well. Add flour; mix well. Pour into greased 8-inch round baking pan. Bake at 350 degrees for 45 minutes. Serve with whipped cream or ice cream. Yield: 12 servings.

Gladys B. Bollman, Airport 820

IRENE'S FRESH APPLE CAKE

1 1/3 c. oil
3 eggs
2 tsp. vanilla extract
3 c. flour
2 c. sugar
1 tsp. baking powder
1 tsp. soda
1 tsp. salt
1 c. chopped nuts
3 c. chopped apples

Mix oil, eggs and vanilla in bowl. Sift in mixture of flour, sugar, baking powder, soda and salt; mix well. Stir in nuts and apples. Pour into greased and floured bundt pan. Place in cold oven. Bake at 350 degrees for 1 1/4 hours or until cake tests done. Yield: 24 servings.

Irene Cardoza, Atascadero 563

APRICOT DELIGHT CAKE

2 eggs, beaten
1 can cherry pie filling
1 c. oil
2 c. sugar
2 c. flour
1 tsp. soda
1 tsp. salt
1 tsp. cinnamon
1 tsp. vanilla extract
1 c. chopped apricots
1 c. chopped walnuts

Beat eggs in large bowl. Add pie filling and oil; mix well. Add remaining ingredients; mix well. Pour into greased and floured 9 x 13-inch baking pan. Bake at 350 degrees for 1 hour or until cake tests done. Yield: 15-20 servings.

Esther Galle, Fort Bragg 672

CRUNCHY APRICOT CAKE

4 c. chopped apricots
1 tbsp. cornstarch
1 tbsp. sugar
1 tsp. almond extract (opt.)
1 2-layer pkg. yellow cake mix
1 egg
1/2 c. coconut
1/2 c. nuts
1/2 c. butter, melted

Combine first 4 ingredients in 9 x 13-inch baking pan. Combine cake mix with egg and 1/3 cup water in mixer bowl; mix well. Spread over apricot mixture. Top with coconut and nuts. Drizzle butter over all. Bake at 350 degrees for 40 minutes or until cake tests done. Serve warm or cold. Yield: 15-20 servings.

Gerry Langford, Manton 732

ELLEN'S BANANA-NUT CAKE

4 firm bananas
1/2 c. shortening
1 1/4 c. sugar
2 eggs
1 c. chopped nuts
1/3 c. milk
2 tsp. vanilla extract
1 1/2 c. flour
1 tsp. each soda, salt and
    baking powder

Slice bananas lengthwise into quarters; cut into 1/2-inch pieces. Cream shortening and sugar in bowl until light and fluffy. Add eggs; mix well. Add bananas, nuts, milk and vanilla; mix well. Add sifted dry ingredients; mix well. Pour into prepared 9 x 13-inch cake pan. Bake at 350 degrees for 40 to 60 minutes or until cake tests done.

Ellen M. Kalles, Danville 85

KATHERINE'S BANANA-NUT CAKE

2 1/2 c. flour
1 1/4 tsp. soda
1/8 tsp. salt
1/2 c. shortening
1 c. sugar
1/2 c. packed brown sugar
1 to 2 tsp. vanilla extract
3 eggs
1 c. mashed banana
1/4 c. orange juice
1/2 c. buttermilk
1/2 c. finely chopped nuts

Combine flour, soda and salt. Cream shortening, sugars and vanilla in bowl until light and fluffy. Add eggs and banana; mix lightly. Add flour mixture alternately with orange juice and buttermilk, mixing well after each addition. Do not overbeat. Fold in nuts. Pour into greased and floured 9 x 13-inch cake pan. Bake at 350 degrees for 45 minutes or until cake tests done.

Katherine H. Warren, Rosedale 565

WON'T-LAST CAKE

3 eggs, beaten
1 1/3 c. oil
1 1/2 tsp. vanilla extract
1 8-oz. can crushed pineapple
2 c. chopped bananas
3 c. flour
2 1/2 c. sugar
1 tsp. salt
1 tsp. soda

Combine eggs, oil, vanilla, pineapple and bananas in bowl; mix well. Add sifted dry ingredients; mix well. Pour into greased and floured 9 x 13-inch baking pan. Bake at 350 degrees for 1 hour or until cake tests done.

Valerie Dobbins, Goat Mountain 818

CARROT CAKE

3 eggs, beaten
1 3/4 c. sugar
1 1/3 c. oil
2 1/2 c. flour
2 tsp. each soda, cinnamon
1 1/2 tsp. salt
2 tsp. vanilla extract
1 c. chopped walnuts
1/3 c. flaked coconut
1 sm. can juice-pack crushed
  pineapple, well drained
2 c. grated carrots
1/2 c. butter
1 tsp. vanilla extract
1/2 tsp. soda
1 c. sugar
1 tbsp. light corn syrup
1/2 c. buttermilk

Beat eggs and 1 3/4 cups sugar in bowl. Add oil and next 4 sifted dry ingredients; mix well. Add 2 teaspoons vanilla, walnuts, coconut, pineapple and carrots; mix well. Pour into greased and floured 9 x 13-inch baking pan. Bake at 350 degrees for 45 minutes. Combine remaining ingredients in saucepan; mix well. Boil for 5 minutes, stirring constantly. Prick top of cake. Pour cooked mixture over top.
Yield: 12-15 servings.

Joan L. Sauer, San Jose 10

POPULAR MICROWAVE CARROT CAKE

1 1/4 c. sugar
1 c. oil
1 tsp. vanilla extract
3 eggs
1 1/2 c. flour
3/4 tsp. salt
1 1/2 tsp. soda
2 1/2 tsp. cinnamon
2 1/4 c. grated carrots
1/2 c. chopped nuts
1 16-oz. package confectioners' sugar
1/4 c. milk
1/4 tsp. vanilla extract
1/4 c. butter

Blend sugar, oil and 1 teaspoon vanilla in large mixer bowl. Add eggs; beat well. Add mixture of sifted flour, salt, soda and cinnamon; mix well. Fold in carrots and nuts. Pour into greased 8 x 12-inch glass baking pan. Microwave on High for 13 to 15 minutes, turning dish 1/2 turn after 8 minutes. Let stand to cool. Combine confec-

tioners' sugar with milk and 1/4 teaspoon vanilla in 1 1/2-quart casserole; mix well. Top with butter. Microwave on High for 2 minutes. Blend until smooth. Spread over cooled cake.

Jean Clark, Kingsburg 679

TWENTY-FOUR CARROT CAKE

3 eggs, slightly beaten
1 c. grated carrots
2 c. sugar
1 c. oil
1 c. crushed pineapple, drained
1 c. chopped nuts
2 c. flour
1 tsp. soda
2 tsp. baking powder
1 tsp. salt
2 tsp. cinnamon
1 tsp. vanilla extract
1 c. coconut
2 tbsp. melted butter
1/2 c. packed brown sugar
1/3 c. cream
1 c. coconut
1 c. chopped nuts

Combine first 6 ingredients in large bowl; mix well. Add next 5 dry ingredients; mix well. Stir in vanilla and coconut. Pour into prepared 9 x 13-inch baking pan. Bake at 350 degrees for 45 minutes. Combine melted butter and remaining ingredients in bowl; mix well. Spread over hot cake. Broil for 2 to 3 minutes or until golden.
Yield: 15 servings.

May Brouhard, Stanislaus-Mountain View 558

BERINGER VINEYARDS' MALVASIA CAKE

1 2-layer pkg. yellow cake mix
1 sm. package instant vanilla pudding mix
6 eggs
3/4 c. oil
1 c. Malvasia Bianca wine
1 tsp. nutmeg

Combine all ingredients in mixer bowl in order listed. Mix at medium speed for 5 minutes. Pour into greased 10-inch tube pan. Bake at 350 degrees for 1 hour or until cake tests done. Cool in pan for 5 minutes. Turn onto wire rack to cool completely. Garnish with confectioners' sugar. This cake keeps well for several days.

Ethel Plecker, Waterford 553

BRAZIL NUT CAKE

2 c. ground Brazil nuts
1 c. sugar
1/4 tsp. salt
6 eggs, separated

Mix nuts with sugar and salt. Beat egg yolks in bowl until foamy. Beat in nut mixture. Fold in stiffly beaten egg whites gently. Pour into 3 greased 8-inch layer pans. Bake at 350 degrees for 30 minutes. Frost as desired.
Note: To obtain 2 cups ground nuts you will need at least 1/2 pound shelled nuts.

Lelia T. Helms, Encinitas 634

BOURBON CAKES

2 c. red candied cherries
1 1/2 c. golden seedless raisins
2 c. Bourbon
1 1/2 c. butter, softened
2 1/3 c. sugar
2 1/3 c. packed brown sugar
6 eggs, separated
4 1/2 c. sifted flour
2 tsp. nutmeg
1 tsp. baking powder
4 c. pecans
1/2 c. flour

Combine first 3 ingredients in bowl. Let stand, covered, overnight. Drain, reserving liquid. Cream butter and sugars in large bowl until light and fluffy. Add egg yolks; beat well. Sift 4 1/2 cups flour with nutmeg and baking powder. Add to creamed mixture with reserved liquid, beating well after each addition. Fold in stiffly beaten egg whites gently. Fold in fruit and mixture of pecans and 1/2 cup flour. Pour into 2 greased and waxed paper-lined star-shaped baking pans. Bake at 275 degrees for 3 1/2 hours or until cakes test done. Cool. Remove from pans.
Note: May use loaf pans.

Lois Wyland, Dow's Prairie 505

CHERRY DUMP CAKE

1 20-oz. can cherry pie filling
1 20-oz. can crushed pineapple
1 2-layer pkg. yellow cake mix
1 stick margarine
1 c. chopped nuts

Combine pie filling and crushed pineapple in bowl; mix well. Spread in ungreased 9 x 13-inch baking dish. Sprinkle cake mix over fruit. Dot with margarine. Top with nuts. Bake at 350 degees for 45 to 60 minutes. Yield: 15 servings.

Marilyn Reynolds, Elk Creek 441

DONALD'S DUMP CAKE

1 lg. can crushed pineapple
1 can cherry pie filling
1 2-layer pkg. white cake mix
1/2 c. chopped nuts
1 stick margarine, sliced

Layer ingredients in order listed in 9 x 13-inch baking pan. Do not mix. Bake at 350 degrees for 1 hour.

Donald R. Fulton, Banner 627

LEONA'S CHERRY CAKE

2 21-oz. cans cherry pie filling
1 lg. can crushed pineapple, drained
1 c. chopped walnuts
1 2-layer pkg. white cake mix
1 c. melted butter

Layer pie filling, pineapple, walnuts and cake mix in 9 x 13-inch baking dish. Drizzle melted butter over top. Mix gently. Bake at 350 degrees for 35 minutes. Serve with whipped topping. Yield: 24 servings.

Leona M. Boatright, Windsor 410

MARIE'S DUMP CAKE

1 can cherry pie filling
1 med. can crushed pineapple
1 2-layer pkg. yellow cake mix
2 sticks butter, melted
1 can coconut
1 c. chopped walnuts

Layer ingredients in order listed in 9 x 13-inch baking pan. Bake at 350 degrees for 1 hour or until cake tests done. Serve with whipped cream.

Dotty Greene, Alturas 406

BUTTERMILK COCOA CAKE

2 sticks margarine
3 tbsp. cocoa
2 c. flour
2 c. sugar
1/2 tsp. salt

2 eggs, beaten
1 tsp. soda
1/2 c. buttermilk
1 tsp. vanilla extract
1 tsp. cinnamon
1 stick butter
2 tbsp. cocoa
6 tbsp. buttermilk
1 16-oz. package confectioners' sugar
1 tsp. vanilla extract
Walnuts

Heat margarine, 3 tablespoons cocoa and 1 cup water in saucepan until margarine is melted. Pour over mixture of flour, sugar and salt in large bowl; mix well. Add eggs, soda, 1/2 cup buttermilk, 1 teaspoon vanilla and cinnamon; mix well. Pour into prepared 11 x 17-inch baking pan. Bake at 350 degrees for 20 minutes or until cake tests done. Combine butter, 2 tablespoons cocoa and 6 tablespoons buttermilk in saucepan. Heat until blended. Add confectioners' sugar and 1 teaspoon vanilla; mix well. Pour over hot cake. Sprinkle walnuts over top.

Doris Silva, Mount Hamilton 469

EDITH'S CHOCOLATE CAKE

3 c. flour
2 c. sugar
2/3 c. cocoa
2 tsp. soda
1 tsp. salt
1 c. oil
2 tsp. vinegar
2 tsp. vanilla extract

Mix first 5 ingredients in bowl. Add mixture of oil, 2 cups water, vinegar and vanilla all at once; mix well by hand. Batter will be thin. Pour into prepared 9 x 13-inch baking pan. Bake at 350 degrees for 30 minutes or until cake tests done. Ice with favorite chocolate frosting.
Yield: 24 servings.
Note: This cake is rich, moist and keeps well. It is especially good if split and filled with whipped cream and slivered almonds.

Edith Benyo, Capay 461

COOKIE SHEET CAKE

1/2 c. shortening
2 tbsp. margarine
3 tbsp. cocoa
2 c. flour
2 c. sugar

1 tsp. salt
1/2 c. buttermilk
1 tsp. soda
2 eggs, beaten

Combine first 3 ingredients and 1 cup water in large saucepan. Bring to a boil, stirring constantly, until well blended. Remove from heat. Add remaining ingredients; mix well. Pour into greased 10 x 15-inch baking pan. Bake at 350 degrees for 10 to 16 minutes or until cake tests done.
Note: May frost with cooked coconut-pecan frosting if desired.

Mary Victorine, Tulelake 468

NAMELESS CAKE

3/4 c. shortening
1 1/2 c. sugar
3 eggs, well beaten
1 3/4 c. sifted flour
1/2 tsp. baking powder
1/2 tsp. soda
1/2 tsp. salt
3/4 tsp. nutmeg
1 tsp. cinnamon
2 tbsp. cocoa
3/4 c. buttermilk
1 tsp. lemon extract
1 tsp. vanilla extract
1/2 c. chopped nuts
Mocha Icing

Cream shortening and sugar in bowl until light and fluffy. Add eggs; mix well. Add sifted dry ingredients alternately with buttermilk, mixing well after each addition. Add flavorings and nuts; mix well. Pour into 2 prepared 9-inch cake pans. Bake at 350 degrees for 30 minutes. Cool. Spread Mocha Icing between layers and over top and side of cake.

MOCHA ICING

6 tbsp. butter, softened
1 egg yolk
3 c. confectioners sugar
4 1/2 tsp. cocoa
1 tsp. cinnamon
1 1/2 tbsp. hot coffee

Cream butter in bowl. Blend in egg yolk. Add sifted confectioners' sugar, cocoa and cinnamon alternately with hot coffee, mixing well after each addition. Beat until smooth, adding additional coffee if necessary to make of spreading consistency.

Ruth Heard, Airport 820

CHERRY CHOCOLATE CAKE

> 1 2-layer pkg. chocolate cake mix
> 3 eggs
> 1 can cherry pie filling
> 1 c. sugar
> 5 tbsp. butter
> 1/3 c. milk
> 1 6-oz. package semisweet
>   chocolate chips

Combine cake mix, eggs and pie filling in bowl; mix well. Pour into greased and floured 9 x 13-inch baking pan. Bake at 350 degrees for 35 to 40 minutes or until cake tests done. Combine sugar, butter and milk in small saucepan. Bring to a boil, stirring constantly. Cook for 1 minute, stirring constantly. Remove from heat; stir in chocolate chips until smooth. Spread over cooled cake. Yield: 12-14 servings.

Roma Gardiner, Palermo 493

CREAM-FILLED CUPCAKES

> 4 1/2 c. flour
> 3 c. sugar
> 3/4 c. cocoa
> 1 tsp. soda
> 1/2 tsp. salt
> 1 c. oil
> 3 tbsp. vinegar
> 1 tbsp. vanilla extract
> 2 8-oz. packages cream cheese, softened
> 2 eggs
> 2/3 c. sugar
> 3/8 tsp. salt
> 1 12-oz. package chocolate chips

Combine first 8 ingredients and 3 cups water in bowl; mix well. Blend cream cheese, eggs, 2/3 cup sugar and 3/8 teaspoon salt in bowl. Stir in chocolate chips. Fill greased muffin cups 3/4 full with batter. Add 1 spoonful cream cheese mixture to each. Bake at 375 degrees for 20 minutes. Yield: 48 cupcakes.

Margaret M. Evans, Montgomery 442

MISSISSIPPI MUD

> 2 sticks margarine
> 3 tbsp. cocoa
> 2 c. flour
> 2 c. sugar
> 1/2 tsp. salt
> 2 eggs
> 1/2 c. buttermilk
> 1 tsp. soda
> 1 tsp. vanilla extract
> 1 stick margarine
> Dash of salt
> 1 tsp. vanilla extract
> 7 1/2 tsp. cocoa
> 6 tbsp. milk
> 1 16-oz. package confectioners' sugar
> 1/2 c. chopped walnuts

Combine 2 sticks margarine, 3 tablespoons cocoa and 1 cup water in saucepan. Bring to a boil. Add to mixture of flour, sugar and 1/2 teaspoon salt in bowl; mix well. Blend eggs, buttermilk, soda and 1 teaspoon vanilla in small bowl. Stir into batter. Pour into greased and floured large oblong cake pan. Bake at 350 degrees for 30 minutes. Combine 1 stick margarine, dash of salt, 1 teaspoon vanilla, 7 1/2 teaspoons cocoa and milk in saucepan. Bring to a boil. Stir in confectioners' sugar and walnuts. Pour over hot cake. Yield: 16-20 servings.

Daisy Rathbun, Greenhorn 384

RED VELVET CAKE

> 2 1/2 c. sifted flour
> 1 1/2 c. sugar
> 2 tbsp. cocoa
> 1 tsp. salt
> 1 tsp. soda
> 1 tsp. baking powder
> 2 c. oil
> 2 eggs
> 1 c. buttermilk
> 1 oz. red food coloring
> 1 tsp. vinegar
> 1 tsp. vanilla extract
> 1 c. chopped nuts
> 1 8-oz. package cream cheese, softened
> 1 stick margarine, softened
> 1 16-oz. package confectioners' sugar
> 1 tsp. vanilla extract
> 1 c. chopped nuts

Combine first 6 ingredients in mixer bowl. Add oil and eggs; beat until smooth. Add buttermilk, food coloring, vinegar, 1 teaspoon vanilla and 2 tablespoons water. Beat for 2 minutes. Stir in 1 cup nuts. Pour into prepared 9 x 13-inch baking pan. Bake at 350 degrees for 30 minutes or until cake tests done. Blend cream cheese and margarine in bowl. Add confectioners' sugar and vanilla; mix until smooth. Stir in 1 cup nuts. Spread over cooled cake.

Marguerite Jones, DeSabla 762

WALNUT COCOA CAKE

1/2 c. shortening
3/4 c. sugar
2 eggs
1/2 c. honey
2 tsp. grated orange rind
2 c. sifted cake flour
1/3 c. cocoa
1 tsp. soda
1/2 tsp. salt
1/4 tsp. each cinnamon, nutmeg
2/3 c. buttermilk
3/4 c. finely chopped California walnuts
Cocoa-Orange Icing
1/2 c. chopped walnuts

Cream shortening and sugar in bowl until light and fluffy. Beat in eggs 1 at a time. Add honey in a thin stream. Add 2 teaspoons orange rind; beat until very light and creamy. Sift flour with 1/3 cup cocoa, soda, salt and spices. Add to creamed mixture alternately with buttermilk, mixing well after each addition. Stir in finely chopped walnuts. Pour into 2 greased and floured 9-inch cake pans. Bake at 350 degrees for 25 to 30 minutes or until cake tests done. Cool in pans for 5 minutes. Invert onto wire racks to cool completely. Spread Cocoa-Orange Icing between cooled layers and over top and side of cake. Pat 1/2 cup chopped walnuts around side.

COCOA-ORANGE ICING

1/2 c. melted butter
1/4 c. cocoa
1 16-oz. package confectioners' sugar
1/4 c. light cream
1/2 tsp. vanilla extract
1/2 tsp. grated orange rind

Blend butter and cocoa in bowl. Add confectioners' sugar and enough cream to make of spreading consistency. Stir in vanilla and orange rind.

Photograph for this recipe above.

DATE SURPRISE CAKE

1 1/2 c. chopped dates
3/4 tsp. soda
1 c. sugar
1/2 c. oil
2 eggs, beaten
1 1/2 c. flour
1/2 tsp. soda
1/2 tsp. salt
1 8-oz. package butterscotch chips
1/2 c. chopped nuts
1/3 c. sugar

Mix first 4 ingredients with 1 1/2 cups boiling water in large bowl. Combine eggs, flour, 1/2 teaspoon soda and salt in bowl; mix well. Add to date mixture; mix well. Pour into greased and floured 8-inch square baking pan. Sprinkle butterscotch chips, nuts and 1/3 cup sugar over top. Bake at 350 degrees for 45 minutes or until cake tests done. Serve with whipped cream or ice cream.

Arline Carpenter, Alpine 665

ROSANNE'S DATE CAKE

2 tbsp. butter, softened
1 c. sugar
1 egg
1 c. chopped dates
1 tsp. soda
1 1/3 c. flour
1/2 tsp. salt
1/2 tsp. vanilla extract
1/2 c. chopped nuts

Cream butter and sugar in bowl until light and fluffy. Add egg; beat well. Pour 1 cup hot water over dates in bowl. Stir in soda. Add date mixture to creamed mixture; mix well. Add sifted flour and salt; mix well. Stir in vanilla and nuts. Pour into prepared 8-inch square baking pan. Bake at 350 degrees for 40 minutes. Serve with whipped cream if desired.
Note: This recipe dates from the 1930's.

Rosanne Milner, Pilot Hill 1

FRUIT COCKTAIL PUDDING CAKE

2 eggs
1 tsp. vanilla extract
1 c. sugar
2/3 c. sifted flour
1/4 tsp. salt
2 tsp. baking powder
1 30-oz. can fruit cocktail,
*   well drained*
1 c. flaked coconut

Beat eggs and vanilla in large bowl until light and fluffy. Add sugar gradually, beating until thick and lemon colored. Sift in flour, salt and baking powder; mix well. Add 1 1/4 cups fruit cocktail; reserve remaining fruit for garnish. Pour batter into buttered 9-inch square baking pan. Sprinkle coconut over top. Bake at 350 degrees for 35 to 40 minutes or until cake tests done. Cut into squares. Serve warm or cold with whipped cream and reserved fruit.

Viola M. Brock, Ojai Valley 659

BUNCH-OF-FRUIT CAKE

3 c. flour
2 c. sugar
1 tbsp. baking powder
1 1/2 tsp. salt
1 1/4 c. oil
1 c. crushed pineapple
1 tsp. vanilla extract
3 eggs

2 c. chopped apples
1 8-oz. package chopped dates
1 3 1/2-oz. can coconut
1 c. nuts
1 c. miniature marshmallows
1 c. confectioners' sugar
3 to 4 tsp. fruit juice

Combine first 8 ingredients in large mixer bowl. Beat at medium speed for 3 minutes. Stir in apples, dates, coconut, nuts and marshmallows. Pour into greased and floured 10-inch bundt pan. Bake at 325 degrees for 1 1/2 hours or until cake tests done. Cool in pan for 30 minutes or longer. Invert onto serving plate. Blend confectioners' sugar and fruit juice. Drizzle over cake.

Cecilia E. Like, Loma Rica 802

CALIFORNIA FRUITCAKES

2 c. chopped dried apricots
1 1/2 c. shortening
1 1/2 c. sugar
8 eggs
2 c. white seedless raisins
2/3 c. sliced candied cherries
2/3 c. sliced candied pineapple
2 c. coarsely chopped walnuts
4 c. flour
1 tsp. salt

Boil apricots in water using package directions for 1 minute; cool. Cream shortening and sugar in large bowl until light and fluffy. Beat eggs until thick and light. Add eggs to creamed mixture; mix well. Stir in fruits and walnuts. Sift in flour and salt; mix well. Pour into 2 greased and floured glass loaf pans. Cover with glass lids. Bake at 350 degrees for 1 1/4 hours.

Ora E. Wilsey, Fort Bragg 672

GRANDMA'S FRUITCAKES

2 1/2 c. butter, softened
4 c. packed light brown sugar
6 eggs
1 tbsp. each vanilla and lemon extracts
8 c. flour
2 c. coffee
2 c. molasses
4 tsp. soda
1/2 lb. citron
1 lb. raisins
1 lb. currants
1 c. walnuts

Cream butter and brown sugar in large bowl until light and fluffy. Add eggs and flavorings; mix well. Add flour alternately with mixture of coffee, molasses and soda, mixing well after each addition. Add citron, raisins, currants and walnuts; mix well. Pour into 4 prepared loaf pans. Bake at 300 degrees for 1 1/2 hours.

Ramona Bacoccini, Hangtown 464

LIGHT FRUITCAKE

1 c. butter, softened
2 c. sugar
6 extra-large eggs
3 c. flour
1 tsp. baking powder
1 c. wine
16 oz. candied cherries
16 oz. candied pineapple
1 lb. white raisins
1 lb. pecans
1/2 c. flour

Cream butter and sugar in bowl until light and fluffy. Add eggs 1 at a time, beating well after each addition. Sift 3 cups flour and baking powder together. Add to creamed mixture alternately with wine, mixing well after each addition. Mix fruit and pecans with 1/2 cup flour. Add to batter; mix well. Pour into greased and floured 10-inch tube pan. Bake at 250 degrees for 3 hours.

Allie Thomas, Scott Valley 386

PERSIMMON FRUITCAKES

2 c. persimmon pulp
2 tsp. soda
1/2 c. margarine, softened
2 c. sugar
2 eggs
3 c. flour
1 tbsp. baking powder
1 tsp. salt
1 tsp. each cinnamon, nutmeg
1 c. milk
1 tsp. vanilla extract
2 c. candied fruit
1 c. chopped dates
2 c. chopped walnuts

Mix persimmon pulp and soda; set aside. Cream margarine and sugar in large bowl until light and fluffy. Beat in eggs. Add mixture of flour, baking powder, salt and spices alternately with milk, mixing well after each addition. Mix in vanilla. Add pulp, fruit and walnuts; mix well. Pour into 4 prepared 3 1/2 x 7-inch loaf pans. Bake at 350 degrees for 1 hour or until cakes test done. Serve with rum sauce if desired.

Estelle Fraters, Lompoc 646

PRUNE FRUITCAKE

2 eggs
1 1/2 c. sugar
3/4 c. oil
1 c. buttermilk
2 1/2 c. (or more) flour
1 tsp. baking powder
1 tsp. salt
1 tsp. soda
1 tsp. each cinnamon, nutmeg
1/2 tsp. allspice
1 pkg. glazed fruit
1 c. nuts
1 c. raisins
1 c. chopped prunes, cooked

Combine eggs, sugar and oil in bowl; mix well. Add buttermilk and sifted flour, baking powder, salt, soda and spices; mix well. Stir in remaining ingredients. Pour into large greased and floured tube pan. Bake at 350 degrees for 45 to 50 minutes or until cake tests done.

Lillian Conway, Mt. Lassen 417

TEXAS FRUITCAKE

1 c. pitted dates
1 c. golden raisins
1 c. red candied cherries
1/2 c. candied orange rind
1/2 c. candied citron
2 rings green pineapple
2 rings red pineapple
1 c. whole walnuts
1 1/4 c. flour
1 1/4 c. sugar
1 tsp. baking powder
1/2 tsp. salt
6 eggs
1 1-oz. bottle of rum flavoring

Do not chop fruit or walnuts. Combine in large bowl. Add mixture of flour, sugar, baking powder and salt; mix well. Beat eggs with rum flavoring. Pour over fruit mixture; mix well. Spoon into greased angel food cake pan. Bake at 300 degrees for 2 hours or until cake tests done.

Margaret Thomson, El Camino 462

NO-BAKE CHERRY FRUITCAKE

1 lg. box vanilla wafers, finely ground
1 can sweetened condensed milk
1   12-oz. package red candied
*   cherries, sliced*
1 c. chopped nuts

Combine all ingredients in large bowl. Mix with wooden spoon, then by hand until all crumbs are mixed. Pack into lightly buttered loaf pan.
Note: This fruitcake is ready to eat immediately or will keep a long time if tightly wrapped and hidden. This fruitcake may be habit forming.

June Ryan, Humboldt 501

CURRANY GINGERBREAD

2 c. sifted flour
2 tsp. baking powder
3/4 tsp. salt
1/4 tsp. soda
3/4 tsp. ginger
3/4 tsp. cinnamon
1/8 tsp. cloves
1/2 tsp. shortening
2/3 c. sugar
2 eggs
1/2 c. crushed Wheat Chex
2/3 c. dark molasses
1/2 c. currants
1/4 c. chopped nuts

Sift first 7 ingredients together. Cream shortening and sugar in bowl until light and fluffy. Beat in eggs. Add cereal, molasses and sifted ingredients; mix well. Stir in 3/4 cup boiling water, currants and nuts; mix well. Pour into 9-inch square pan, buttered on bottom only. Bake at 350 degrees for 45 minutes or until gingerbread tests done. Yield: 9 servings.

Photograph for this recipe on opposite page.

HONEY GINGERBREAD

1/2 c. shortening
1 c. sugar
2 or 3 eggs
1 c. honey
3 c. flour
1 tsp. soda
1/2 tsp. each salt, ginger
1 tsp. cinnamon
1/4 tsp. cloves
1 c. sour milk

Cream shortening and sugar in mixer bowl until light and fluffy. Add eggs 1 at a time, beating well after each addition. Add honey in a thin stream, beating constantly. Add sifted dry ingredients alternately with sour milk, mixing well after each addition. Pour into greased and floured 9 x 13-inch baking pan. Bake at 350 degrees for 40 minutes or until toothpick inserted in center comes out clean. Serve warm with whipped cream or lemon sauce.
Yield: 16 servings.

Lois E. Park, Millville 443

MARSHMALLOW GINGERBREAD

1/2 c. melted shortening, cooled
1 c. molasses
1 egg, well beaten
2 1/2 c. flour
1 tsp. baking powder
1 1/2 tsp. each salt, soda
1 tsp. ginger
1/2 tsp. each cloves, cinnamon
1 c. sour milk
Marshmallows

Combine shortening, molasses and egg in bowl; mix well. Add sifted dry ingredients alternately with sour milk, mixing well after each addition. Pour into greased and floured baking pan. Bake at 350 degrees for 25 to 30 minutes or until gingerbread tests done. Remove from pan; cool partially. Split horizontally into 2 layers. Return bottom layer to pan. Arrange marshmallows over bottom layer. Top with remaining layer. Bake at 350 degrees for 3 minutes just before serving. Serve with whipped cream.

Irma Altimus, Greenhorn 384

LEMON CAKE DELIGHT

1   2-layer pkg. lemon cake mix
1   6-oz. package lemon gelatin
1   9-oz. carton whipped topping

Prepare and bake cake mix in 9 x 13-inch baking pan according to package directions. Prepare gelatin according to package directions. Cut cake in half lengthwise then into thirds crosswise. Pour gelatin over hot cake. Chill for 3 hours or until firm. Spread whipped topping over top. Cut into serving pieces. Serve immediately. Yield: 18 servings.

Allen Van Halder, Sunnyvale 416

LEMON LOAF CAKE

1 2-layer pkg. yellow cake mix
1 pkg. lemon gelatin
3/4 c. oil
4 eggs
1 1/2 c. confectioners' sugar
1/4 c. lemon juice
1 tsp. grated lemon rind

Combine cake mix and gelatin in mixer bowl. Add 3/4 cup water, oil and eggs. Beat at medium speed for 3 minutes. Pour into 9 x 13-inch baking pan, greased on bottom only. Bake at 350 degrees for 30 to 35 minutes or until cake tests done. Prick with fork. Pour mixture of confectioners' sugar, lemon juice and rind over hot cake.

Mary Shields, Encinitas 634

ENGLISH LEMON CAKE

3 sticks margarine, softened
2 c. sugar
6 eggs, beaten
1 2-oz. bottle of lemon extract
4 c. flour
1 tsp. baking powder
2 c. chopped walnuts
2 1/2 c. white raisins

Combine first 4 ingredients in mixer bowl; beat well. Sift in flour and baking powder gradually, mixing well by hand. Fold in walnuts and raisins. Pour into greased and floured tube pan. Bake at 275 degrees for 1 hour. Reduce temperature to 250 degrees. Bake for 30 minutes longer or until cake tests done.

Virginia Bresciani, Feather River 440

FIG JAM CAKE

1 c. sugar
1/2 c. butter
3 eggs
2 c. fig jam
2/3 c. milk
2 1/2 c. flour
1 tsp. each cloves, cinnamon
1 tsp. soda
1 tsp. baking powder
1 tsp. vanilla extract
Walnuts
Raisins

Cream first 3 ingredients in bowl until light and fluffy. Add jam and milk; mix well. Add remaining ingredients; mix well. Pour into prepared 9 x 13-inch baking pan. Bake at 325 degrees for 1 hour. Yield: 20 servings.

Emily Bjelland, Copper Mountain 814

GUMDROP CAKE

1 c. butter, softened
2 c. sugar
2 eggs
1 1/2 c. applesauce
3 1/2 c. flour
1 tsp. cinnamon
1/4 tsp. nutmeg
1 lb. white raisins
1 to 2 lb. gumdrops
1 c. chopped walnuts
1/2 c. flour

Combine butter, sugar, eggs and applesauce in bowl; mix well. Sift in 3 1/2 cups flour and spices; mix well. Mix raisins, gumdrops and walnuts with 1/2 cup flour. Add to batter; mix well. Pour into prepared baking pan. Bake at 350 degrees for 2 hours.

Lillian Russell, Alpine 665

ITALIAN CREAM CAKE

1 stick margarine, softened
1/2 c. shortening
2 c. sugar
5 eggs, separated
2 c. flour
1 tsp. soda
1 c. buttermilk
1 tsp. vanilla extract
1 8-oz. can coconut

Cream margarine, shortening and sugar in bowl until light and fluffy. Add egg yolks; beat well. Add mixture of sifted flour and soda alternately with buttermilk, beating well after each addition. Stir in vanilla and coconut. Fold in stiffly beaten egg whites gently. Pour into 2 greased and floured 9-inch cake pans. Bake at 350 degrees for 30 minutes or until cake tests done. Cool in pans for 5 minutes. Remove from pans to cool completely. Frost as desired.

Marie Haley, Mt. Lassen 417

MAYONNAISE CAKE

1 tsp. soda
1 c. chopped dates
1 c. chopped walnuts
1 c. sugar
3 tbsp. cocoa
3/4 c. mayonnaise
2 c. sifted flour
1/2 tsp. salt
1 tsp. vanilla extract

Dissolve soda in 1 cup boiling water; pour over dates and walnuts in large bowl. Let stand for several minutes. Sift sugar and cocoa together into bowl. Blend in mayonnaise. Add date mixture; mix well. Sift in flour and salt; mix well. Mix in vanilla. Pour into greased 9-inch round cake pans. Bake at 350 degrees for 25 minutes.

Blanche Covington, Western Yolo 423

MAYONNAISE SPICE CAKE

1 c. chopped dates
1 c. chopped nuts
1 c. mayonnaise
1 c. sugar
1/2 sq. chocolate, melted
1 tsp. vanilla extract
2 c. sifted flour
1 tsp. soda
1 tsp. cinnamon
1/2 tsp. salt

Pour 1 1/4 cups boiling water over dates and nuts in bowl; set aside. Cream mayonnaise and sugar in bowl. Add chocolate and vanilla; mix well. Drain date mixture, reserving liquid. Add reserved liquid alternately with sifted dry ingredients to batter, mixing well after each addition. Add date mixture; mix well. Pour into greased loaf pan lined with greased waxed paper. Bake at 350 degrees for 45 minutes. Cool; remove waxed paper. Frost as desired.

Ruby H. Fulton, Banner 627

MEXICAN SUPREME CAKE

2 c. flour
2 c. sugar
2 eggs
2 tsp. soda
1 tsp. vanilla extract
1 20-oz. can crushed pineapple
1 c. chopped nuts
1 stick margarine, softened

6 oz. cream cheese, softened
2 c. confectioners' sugar
1 tsp. vanilla extract

Combine first 7 ingredients in bowl; mix well. Pour into prepared 9 x 13-inch cake pan. Bake at 350 degrees for 35 minutes or until cake tests done. Cream margarine and cream cheese in bowl until light and fluffy. Add confectioners' sugar and 1 teaspoon vanilla; mix well. Spread over cooled cake. Yield: 15 servings.

Nina Lobaugh, Grover City 746

MAPLE-NUT CAKE

1/3 c. shortening
1 c. packed light brown sugar
2 eggs, separated
1 tsp. vanilla extract
1/2 c. milk
1 1/2 c. sifted flour
1/4 tsp. salt
2 tsp. baking powder
1 c. chopped nuts

Combine shortening, brown sugar, egg yolks, vanilla and milk in bowl; beat well. Add dry ingredients; mix well. Add nuts. Fold in stiffly beaten egg whites gently. Pour into greased and floured loaf pan. Bake at 350 degrees for 35 to 45 minutes or until cake tests done.

Helen Crile, Humboldt 501

WHITE NUT CAKE

1/2 c. butter, softened
1 1/2 c. sugar
2 c. flour
1/2 tsp. salt
1 tsp. (heaping) baking powder
1 c. milk
1 tsp. vanilla extract
1 c. chopped nuts
4 egg whites, stiffly beaten

Cream butter and sugar in bowl until light and fluffy. Sift flour, salt and baking powder together. Add to creamed mixture alternately with milk, mixing well after each addition. Add vanilla. Fold in nuts. Fold in egg whites gently. Pour into prepared 8 x 12-inch baking pan. Bake at 375 degrees for 25 to 30 minutes or until cake tests done.

Margaret R. Scott, San Jose 10

SYRIAN NUTMEG CAKE

2 c. sifted flour
2 c. packed brown sugar
1/2 c. shortening
1 egg
1 tsp. nutmeg
1 c. sour cream
1 tsp. soda
1/2 c. chopped nuts

Combine flour, brown sugar and shortening in bowl; mix until crumbly. Place half the mixture in 9-inch baking pan. Combine remaining mixture with egg, nutmeg and mixture of sour cream and soda; mix well. Pour into prepared baking pan. Sprinkle nuts over top. Bake at 350 degrees for 40 minutes.

Lucy A. Fassett, Quartz Hill 697

OATMEAL CAKE

1 c. oats
1 stick margarine, softened
1 c. sugar
1 c. packed brown sugar
2 eggs
1 tsp. vanilla extract
1 1/3 c. flour
1 tsp. soda
1/4 tsp. each salt and cinnamon
Raisins (opt.)
Nuts (opt.)
6 tsp. margarine, softened
1/4 c. evaporated milk
1/2 c. packed brown sugar
1/2 c. chopped nuts
1 c. coconut
1 tsp. vanilla extract

Pour 1 1/4 cups boiling water over oats in large bowl. Let stand for several minutes. Add 1 stick margarine, sugars, eggs and vanilla; mix well. Add sifted flour, soda, salt and cinnamon; mix well. Stir in raisins and nuts. Pour into prepared 9 x 12-inch baking pan. Bake at 350 degrees for 40 minutes. Combine remaining ingredients in bowl; mix well. Spread over hot cake. Bake until bubbly. Serve warm.

Marion Meeks, Bayside 500

SALTED PEANUT CAKE

3/4 c. (scant) shortening
1 c. sugar
2 eggs, beaten
1 c. sour milk
1 tsp. soda
1 3/4 c. flour
1 c. ground Spanish peanuts
1 tsp. vanilla extract

Cream shortening and sugar in bowl until light and fluffy. Beat in eggs. Add mixture of milk and soda alternately with flour, mixing well after each addition. Add peanuts and vanilla; mix well. Pour into prepared 9 x 13-inch baking pan. Bake at 350 degrees for 25 to 30 minutes or until cake tests done. Frost with caramel icing. Garnish with chopped peanuts.

Maxine F. Halter

PEA PICKING CAKE

1   11-oz. can mandarin oranges
4 eggs
1   2-layer pkg. yellow cake mix
1/2 c. oil
1   12-oz. carton whipped topping
1   20-oz. can crushed pineapple
1 lg. package instant vanilla pudding mix

Drain oranges, reserving liquid. Combine eggs and cake mix in bowl; mix well. Add reserved liquid and oil; mix well. Fold in oranges. Pour into greased and floured 9 x 13-inch cake pan. Bake at 350 degrees for 25 minutes or until cake tests done. Cool. Invert onto cake platter. Combine remaining ingredients in bowl; mix well. Spread over cooled cake. Chill in refrigerator.

Sylvia Clair, Anderson 418

PERSIMMON PUDDING CAKE

2 c. sugar
2 c. flour
4 tsp. baking powder
1 tbsp. soda
1/8 tsp. salt
2 eggs
1 c. milk
1 tsp. vanilla extract
2 c. chopped nuts
2 c. raisins
2 c. persimmon pulp
3 tbsp. butter, melted

Sift all dry ingredients into bowl. Beat eggs, milk and vanilla in bowl. Stir into dry ingredients. Add nuts, raisins and persimmon. Stir in butter. Pour into prepared 9-inch tube pan. Bake at 350 degrees for 45 minutes or until cake tests done. Cool in pan. Serve warm or cold with hot lemon sauce.

Thelma Garvey, Keyes 524

SPICED PECAN CAKE

2 c. coarsely chopped pecans
1/4 c. packed brown sugar
2 tbsp. cinnamon
1 tsp. nutmeg
1/2 stick unsalted butter, softened
2 tbsp. vanilla extract
1 1/2 sticks unsalted butter, softened
1 1/2 c. sugar
2 tsp. vanilla extract
1 c. plus 2 tbsp. milk
3 c. sifted flour
2 tbsp. baking powder
3 egg whites, at room temperature
1 c. sugar
1 tsp. vanilla extract
Pecan Frosting

Toast pecans in shallow baking pan at 425 degrees for 10 minutes, stirring every 2 minutes. Combine next 4 ingredients in bowl; mix well. Stir in hot pecans. Spread in baking pan. Toast for 10 minutes longer, stirring every 2 minutes. Stir in 2 tablespoons vanilla. Toast for 5 minutes longer. Cool. Cream 1 1/2 sticks butter and 1 1/2 cups sugar in bowl until light and fluffy. Add mixture of 2 teaspoons vanilla and milk alternately with mixture of flour and baking powder, mixing well after each addition. Stir in cooled pecans gently. Beat egg whites until soft peaks form. Add 1/2 cup sugar 1 tablespoon at a time, beating until stiff peaks form. Fold gently into batter. Pour into 3 greased and floured 8-inch round cake pans. Bake at 350 degrees for 40 minutes. Cool in pans for 10 minutes. Remove to wire rack to cool completely. Combine remaining 1/2 cup sugar and 1 cup hot water in saucepan. Heat until sugar dissolves, stirring constantly. Bring to a boil; remove from heat. Stir in 1 teaspoon vanilla. Brush over layers. Spread Pecan Frosting between layers and over top and side of cake.

PECAN FROSTING

1 1/2 c. sugar
8 egg yolks, at room temperature
1 1/2 c. margarine, softened
2 1/2 c. confectioners' sugar
4 1/2 tsp. vanilla extract
2 1/2 c. coarsely chopped pecans, toasted

Heat sugar and 3/4 cup water in saucepan until sugar dissolves. Cook to 230 degrees on candy thermometer. Do not stir. Beat egg yolks in mixer bowl for 5 seconds or until blended. Add sugar mixture in a thin stream, beating constantly at low speed until cooled. Add margarine, confectioners' sugar and vanilla 1 at a time, beating well after each addition. Add pecans. Beat until very thick.

Shirley Gray, Waterford 553

PINEAPPLE PUDDING CAKE

1 2-layer pkg. yellow cake mix
1 20-oz. can crushed pineapple
1 c. packed brown sugar
2 sm. packages vanilla instant pudding mix
3 c. milk
2 c. whipped cream
1 c. chopped walnuts

Prepare cake mix using package directions. Pour into greased and floured 10 x 15-inch cake pan. Bake at 350 degrees for 20 minutes. Cool on wire rack for 10 minutes. Pierce warm cake with fork. Combine pineapple and brown sugar in saucepan. Bring to a boil, stirring constantly. Spoon over hot cake. Cool completely. Combine pudding mix and milk in mixer bowl. Beat at low speed until blended. Chill for 5 minutes. Spread over cake. Frost with whipped cream. Sprinkle walnuts over top.

Cherie Hiner, Humboldt 501

POPPY SEED CAKE

2 c. sugar
4 eggs
1 1/2 c. oil
3 c. flour
1 1/2 tsp. soda
1 lg. can evaporated milk
1 2-oz. box poppy seed
1/2 c. chopped nuts

Combine sugar and eggs in bowl; beat well. Add oil; mix well. Add dry ingredients alternately with evaporated milk, mixing well after each addition. Stir in poppy seed and nuts. Pour into well-greased tube pan. Bake at 350 degrees for 1 1/4 hours.

Barbara Wells, Rohner 509

PRUNE-BUTTERMILK CAKE

3 eggs
1 1/2 c. sugar
1 c. oil
1 c. cooked chopped prunes
1 c. buttermilk
1 tsp. vanilla extract
2 c. flour
1 tsp. soda
1 tsp. cinnamon
Nutmeg and cloves to taste (opt.)
1 c. chopped walnuts
Cream Cheese Frosting

Combine eggs and sugar in bowl; beat well. Add oil, prunes, buttermilk and vanilla; mix well. Sift flour, soda and spices into bowl. Add walnuts. Fold gently into prune mixture. Pour into well-greased 9 x 12-inch cake pan. Bake at 325 degrees for 1 hour. Cool. Frost with Cream Cheese Frosting.

CREAM CHEESE FROSTING

1   8-oz. carton whipped cream cheese
1 1/2 c. confectioners' sugar
1 tsp. vanilla extract
2 tbsp. butter, softened

Combine all ingredients in bowl. Beat until smooth.

Elsie Ashley, Sunnyvale 416

PUMPKIN ROLL

3 eggs
1 c. sugar
2/3 c. mashed pumpkin
1 tsp. lemon juice
3/4 c. flour
1/4 tsp. salt
1 tsp. baking powder
1 tsp. each cinnamon, ginger and nutmeg
Confectioners' sugar
1   8-oz. package cream cheese, softened
1/4 c. butter, softened
1 1/2 tsp. vanilla extract
Chopped nuts

Beat eggs in mixer bowl for 5 minutes. Beat in sugar gradually. Stir in pumpkin and lemon juice. Sift next 6 dry ingredients. Fold gently into pumpkin mixture. Spread in greased jelly roll pan. Bake at 350 degrees for 15 minutes. Turn onto towel sprinkled with confectioners'

sugar. Roll as for jelly roll; cool. Blend 1 cup confectioners' sugar and remaining ingredients except nuts in bowl. Unroll cake. Spread with cream cheese mixture; reroll. Roll in nuts.

Leah Knott, Rainbow Valley 689

TOMATO JUICE CAKE

1/2 c. butter, softened
1 c. sugar
1 c. tomato juice
1 tsp. soda
2 c. flour
1 tsp. cloves
1 tsp. cinnamon
1/2 tsp. salt
2 c. raisins
1/2 c. chopped nuts

Cream butter and sugar in bowl until light and fluffy. Add tomato juice and soda; mix well. Sift flour, spices and salt together. Mix a small amount with raisins and nuts. Add remaining sifted dry ingredients to creamed mixture; mix well. Stir in raisins and nuts. Pour into prepared baking pan. Bake at 350 degrees for 1 hour.

Nora Dusablon, Humboldt 501

TOMATO SOUP CAKE

1/2 c. butter, softened
1 1/2 c. sugar
2 eggs, separated
1 c. raisins
1 c. nuts
1 3/4 c. flour
2 tsp. baking powder
1 tsp. each allspice, cinnamon
1 c. canned tomato soup
1/4 tsp. soda

Cream butter and sugar in bowl until light and fluffy. Add egg yolks 1 at a time, beating well after each addition. Stir in raisins and nuts. Add next 4 sifted dry ingredients gradually, mixing well after each addition. Fold in mixture of soup and soda. Fold in stiffly beaten egg whites gently. Pour into 2 greased and floured 9-inch cake pans. Bake at 350 degrees for 1 hour. Frost cooled cake as desired.

Vennie Walker, Ukiah 419

CANDIES & COOKIES

CUTTING TALL STRAIGHT GRAIN.

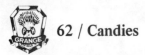

BUCKEYES

1 2-lb. jar peanut butter
1 lb. butter, softened
3 lb. confectioners' sugar
1 12-oz. package chocolate chips
1/2 bar paraffin

Combine peanut butter, butter and confectioners' sugar in bowl. Knead until smooth. Shape into 1-inch balls. Dip in mixture of melted chocolate chips and paraffin, leaving small portion of top uncoated to resemble Buckeyes. Cool on waxed paper.

Maxine Cox, Antelope 161

BURNT SUGAR CANDY

1 c. sugar
1 1/2 c. half and half, scalded
2 c. sugar
Pinch of salt
1/2 c. butter
1 c. chopped nuts

Melt 1 cup sugar in large saucepan. Add half and half. Add 2 cups sugar. Cook until dissolved, stirring constantly. Cook to hard-ball stage. Add salt, butter and nuts. Beat until creamy. Pour onto buttered platter. Cut into pieces when cool.

Myrtle Sturgeon, Los Banos 79

COCONUT ALMOND JOY BALLS

1/2 c. butter, softened
1 1-lb. package confectioners' sugar
1 3-oz. package cream cheese, softened
3 c. coconut
Almonds
1 12-oz. package chocolate chips

Cream butter and confectioners' sugar in bowl until light and fluffy. Add cream cheese and coconut; mix well. Shape into walnut-sized balls around almonds. Melt chocolate chips in double boiler. Dip top half of candy into chocolate. Place in miniature paper liners to cool. Yield: 6 dozen.

Bea Peterson, Los Banos 79

LOUISE'S CHRISTMAS FUDGE

1/2 c. cream
1/2 c. milk
1 tbsp. light corn syrup
1 2/3 c. sugar

1/3 c. packed light brown sugar
1/4 tsp. salt
2 tbsp. butter
1/2 tsp. each almond, vanilla extract
2/3 c. chopped walnuts
1/2 c. chopped candied fruits
1/4 c. chopped candied cherries

Combine first 6 ingredients in heavy saucepan. Bring to a boil, stirring occasionally. Cook over low heat to soft-ball stage or 236 degrees on candy thermometer. Do not stir. Remove from heat. Add butter and flavorings. Cool to lukewarm or 115 degrees. Beat until thick. Add walnuts and fruits; mix well. Pour into buttered 8-inch square dish. Cut into squares when cool. Yield: 1 1/2 pounds.

Louise Gibson, Anderson 418

MYRNICE'S CHRISTMAS FUDGE

4 1/2 c. sugar
1 14 1/2-oz. can evaporated milk
1/2 tsp. salt
1/4 lb. butter
6 2-oz. bars sweet chocolate
2 6-oz. packages semisweet chocolate chips
2 c. chopped nuts
1 7-oz. jar marshmallow creme
1 tsp. vanilla extract

Combine sugar, evaporated milk, salt and butter in saucepan. Bring to a boil. Cook for 10 minutes, stirring constantly. Add remaining ingredients; stir until chocolate is melted and ingredients are well blended. Pour into two 9 x 9-inch buttered pans. Chill until firm. Cut into squares. Yield: 4 pounds.

Myrnice Valentine, Ceres 520

ORANGE CARAMEL FUDGE

3 c. sugar
1 lg. can evaporated milk
1/4 c. butter
1 c. sugar
1/3 to 1/2 c. finely chopped orange rind
1 c. chopped walnuts

Combine first 3 ingredients in large heavy saucepan. Cook over medium heat until sugar is dissolved, stirring frequently. Cook to 234 degrees on candy thermometer, stirring occasionally. Remove from heat. Caramelize 1 cup sugar in skillet. Remove from heat. Stir cooked mixture into caramelized mixture; blend well. Add orange rind and walnuts; beat until mixture begins to thicken. Pour into buttered 8-inch square pan. Cut into squares when cool. Yield: 2 pounds.

Photograph for this recipe on opposite page.

PERSIMMON FUDGE

1 c. pureed persimmon pulp
6 c. sugar
2 1/2 c. milk
1/4 c. light corn syrup
1/2 c. margarine
1 c. (or more) chopped nuts

Combine puree, sugar, milk and corn syrup in saucepan. Cook to soft-ball stage or 230 degrees on candy thermometer. Stir constantly toward end of cooking time to prevent sticking. Cool to lukewarm. Add margarine; beat until thickened. Stir in nuts. Pour into buttered 9 x 13-inch dish. Cut into squares when cool. Yield: 2 pounds.

Pauline Roberts, Golden State 429

PERFECT PEANUT BRITTLE

2 c. salted Spanish peanuts
3 c. sugar
2 c. light corn syrup
1/2 tsp. salt
1 tbsp. butter
2 tsp. soda

Toast peanuts in baking pan at 250 degrees for 10 to 15 minutes or until very hot. Combine sugar, corn syrup and salt in heavy saucepan. Boil until golden brown or extremely brittle when tested in cold water. Stir in butter; remove from heat. Add hot peanuts and soda. Stir until frothy. Spread into thin layer on greased baking sheets. Break into pieces when cool.

Fred Metzger, Vista 609

PECAN PRALINES

1 c. sugar
1 c. packed brown sugar
1/2 c. cream
1/2 tsp. salt
1 c. pecans

Mix first 4 ingredients in saucepan. Stir until sugar is dissolved. Cook over medium heat to soft-ball stage or 236 degrees on candy thermometer. Remove from heat. Stir in pecans. Cool slightly. Drop by spoonfuls onto greased waxed paper to cool completely.

Edna Smith, United Rescue 450

DELICIOUS POPCORN BALLS

1 c. butter
1 c. packed brown sugar
1 c. sugar
1 c. light corn syrup
4 to 8 qt. popped popcorn

Combine first 4 ingredients in saucepan. Cook to soft-ball stage. Pour over popcorn; mix well. Shape into balls with buttered hands.

Arthur Beatie, Anderson 418

CRISPY CARAMEL POPCORN

1 c. packed brown sugar
1/2 c. dark corn syrup
1/2 c. butter
1/2 tsp. salt
1/2 tsp. vanilla extract
3/4 c. popcorn, popped

Combine brown sugar, corn syrup, butter, salt and vanilla in saucepan; mix well. Bring to a boil over medium heat, stirring constantly. Boil for 5 minutes. Remove from heat. Pour over popcorn in large shallow baking pan; stir to coat well. Bake at 250 degrees for 1 hour, stirring every 15 minutes. Remove from oven; stir several times. Cool completely. Store in airtight container.

Ruth Mills, Lompoc 646

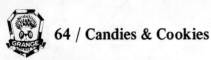

ALMOND TOFFEE

2 sticks butter, melted
1 c. sugar
1 c. slivered almonds
1   6-oz. package chocolate chips
1 c. chopped walnuts

Combine butter and sugar in saucepan. Bring to a boil, stirring constantly. Boil for about 12 minutes or to hard-crack stage, 300 degrees on candy thermometer. Add almonds. Spread on buttered baking sheet. Sprinkle chocolate chips over top. Let stand until chocolate melts. Spread evenly over candy. Sprinkle chopped walnuts over top. Break into pieces when cool.

Joylin Rensted, Ceres 520

ALMOND ROCA

1 lb. butter, melted
2 c. sugar
1 c. slivered almonds
1   11 1/2-oz. package milk
*   chocolate chips*
Chopped almonds

Bring butter to a boil in saucepan. Add sugar and 6 tablespoons water. Cook until bubbly. Add almonds. Cook to 290 degrees on candy thermometer. Pour into buttered jelly roll pan. Cool for 3 to 4 minutes. Sprinkle chocolate chips over top. Let stand until chocolate melts. Spread evenly over surface. Sprinkle with chopped almonds. Press almonds into chocolate with spatula. Break into pieces when cool.

Arlene Stutsman, Ukiah 419

LORRAINE'S SOUR CREAM DELIGHTS

1 c. packed light brown sugar
1/2 c. sugar
1/2 c. sour cream
Pinch of salt
2 c. walnut halves

Combine sugars, sour cream and salt in saucepan. Cook to soft-ball stage. Remove from heat; stir in walnuts. Spread on waxed paper. Separate walnuts. Cool. Store in airtight container.

Lorraine Mason, Empire 521

ORANGE-SUGARED WALNUTS

1 1/2 c. sugar
3 tbsp. orange juice

2 tsp. grated orange rind
3 c. walnut halves

Combine sugar, orange juice and 1/4 cup water in saucepan. Cook to soft-ball stage or 236 degrees on candy thermometer. Add orange rind and walnuts. Stir until mixture is creamy and loses its gloss. Spoon onto waxed paper. Separate walnuts. Cool completely.

Ruth Reiff, Yolo 601

ALMOND ROCA COOKIES

40 saltines
1 c. butter
1 c. packed brown sugar
1   6-oz. package semisweet
*   chocolate chips*
Finely chopped walnuts

Arrange crackers in oiled 10 x 15-inch baking pan. Combine butter and brown sugar in saucepan. Bring to a boil. Cook for 3 minutes. Pour over crackers. Bake at 350 degrees for 5 minutes. Sprinkle chocolate chips over top. Spread to cover evenly. Top with walnuts. Chill in refrigerator. Break crackers apart. Store in airtight container.

Evelyn Brandi, Los Banos 79

ALMOND BUTTER COOKIES

1 c. butter, softened
1 c. sugar
1 c. packed brown sugar
1 c. almond butter
2 eggs
2 3/4 c. flour
2 tsp. soda
1 tsp. vanilla extract

Cream butter, sugar and brown sugar in bowl until light and fluffy. Blend in almond butter. Add eggs; mix well. Sift in flour and soda; mix well. Mix in vanilla. Shape into balls. Place on greased baking sheet. Flatten with fork. Bake at 375 degrees for 10 to 12 minutes or until brown. Yield: 6 dozen.

Nellie Jones, New Era 540

RAISIN BUTTER COOKIES

3/4 c. butter, softened
1/2 c. sugar
1 egg yolk

2 c. flour
1/2 tsp. salt
1 tsp. vanilla extract
2 drops of almond extract
1/4 c. chopped candied cherries (opt.)
3/4 c. raisins

Cream butter with sugar in mixer bowl until light and fluffy. Add egg yolk; mix well. Add mixture of flour and salt; mix well. Stir in remaining ingredients. Drop by teaspoonfuls onto ungreased cookie sheet. Bake at 400 degrees for 8 to 10 minutes or until brown. Cool on cookie sheet. Yield: 3 1/2 dozen.

Edith E. Becker, Elk Grove 86

ROLL BUTTER COOKIES

1 1/2 c. confectioners' sugar
1 c. butter, softened
1 egg
1 tsp. vanilla extract
1/2 tsp. almond flavoring
2 1/2 c. flour
1 tsp. each soda, cream of tartar

Combine confectioners' sugar, butter, egg and flavorings in bowl; mix well. Blend in dry ingredients to form dough. Roll 1/2 inch thick on floured surface. Cut into desired shapes with floured cutter. Place on lightly oiled cookie sheet. Bake at 375 degrees for 6 to 8 minutes or until brown. Yield: 2 dozen.

Sarah L. Peterson, Hessel 750

BIG BATCH COOKIES

1 c. sugar
1 c. packed brown sugar
3 sticks margarine, softened
2 eggs
2 tbsp. vanilla extract
1 tsp. each salt, soda and cream of tartar
2 c. quick-cooking oats
2 c. flour
2 c. crisp rice cereal
1 12-oz. package chocolate chips (opt.)
2 c. chopped walnuts (opt.)

Cream sugar, brown sugar and margarine in mixer bowl until light and fluffy. Add eggs, vanilla, salt, soda and cream of tartar; beat well. Add remaining ingredients 1 at a time, mixing well after each addition. Drop by teaspoonfuls onto ungreased cookie sheet. Bake at 350 degrees for 10 to 20 minutes or until brown. Yield: 9 dozen.

Note: May use varying amounts of chocolate chips, nuts or coconut or add 1/2 teaspoon almond extract.

Mary A. Thornton, Hornbrook 391

COOKIE MIX COOKIES

3 c. Cookie Mix
1 egg
1/2 c. milk
Nuts, raisins and chocolate chips

Combine Cookie Mix, egg and milk in mixer bowl; mix well. Stir in nuts, raisins and chocolate chips as desired. Drop by teaspoonfuls onto cookie sheets. Bake at 350 degrees for 10 to 15 minutes or until brown. Yield: 3 dozen.

COOKIE MIX

2 c. shortening
2 1/2 c. sugar
1 c. packed brown sugar
4 c. flour
4 c. oats
2 tsp. soda

Cream shortening, sugar and brown sugar in mixer bowl until light and fluffy. Add remaining ingredients; mix well. Store, covered, in refrigerator.

Myrtle Buckmaster, Rio Linda 403

FIG-FILLED COOKIES

1 1/2 c. figs
1/2 c. sugar
1 tbsp. butter
1 c. chopped nuts
1 tsp. lemon juice
1 c. shortening
1 c. sugar
1 c. packed brown sugar
3 eggs
3 1/2 c. flour
1 tsp. each salt, soda
1 tbsp. vanilla extract

Combine figs, 1/2 cup sugar, butter, nuts and lemon juice in double boiler. Cook until thick; cool. Cream shortening, 1 cup sugar and brown sugar in mixer bowl until light and fluffy. Add eggs 1 at a time, beating well after each addition. Mix in remaining ingredients to form dough. Roll out on floured surface. Cut with cookie cutter. Spread half the cookies with fig mixture. Top with remaining cookies; seal edges. Place on cookie sheet. Bake at 325 degrees for 15 minutes.

Laura M. Cawley, Greenhorn 384

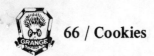

CREAM CHEESE COOKIE CUT-OUTS

1 c. butter, softened
1 3-oz. package cream cheese, softened
1 c. sugar
1 egg yolk
1/2 tsp. vanilla extract
Pinch of salt
2 1/2 c. flour

Cream butter, cream cheese and sugar in mixer bowl until light and fluffy. Beat in egg yolk, vanilla and salt. Add flour gradually, mixing well after each addition. Chill dough for 1 hour or longer. Roll out small amounts of dough at a time; chill unused portion. Cut into desired shapes. Place on greased cookie sheet. Bake at 325 degrees for 10 to 12 minutes or until edges are light brown. Yield: 3 dozen.

Diana Wingfield-Kornbau, Rosedale 565

DATE COOKIES

1 lb. dates, chopped
1/2 c. sugar
1 c. packed brown sugar
1 c. sugar
1 c. butter, softened
3 eggs, beaten
4 c. sifted flour
1 tsp. soda
1/2 tsp. salt
1 tsp. vanilla extract

Combine dates, 1/2 cup sugar and 1 1/2 cups water in saucepan. Cook until thick; cool. Cream brown sugar, 1 cup sugar and butter in mixer bowl until light and fluffy. Beat in eggs. Add remaining ingredients; mix well. Roll out in 2 rectangles 1/2 inch thick on floured surface. Spread with date mixture. Roll as for jelly roll. Chill for several hours to overnight. Cut into slices. Place on cookie sheet. Bake at 375 degrees for 15 minutes or until brown.

Mary Ann Lukenbill, Rio Linda 403

DUNKING COOKIES

2 c. sugar
2 c. packed brown sugar
1 lb. margarine, melted
4 eggs
2 c. Grape Nuts flakes
2 tsp. vanilla extract
4 c. flour
2 tsp. each baking powder, soda
1 12-oz. package chocolate chips

2 c. chopped nuts
1 c. (or more) raisins

Combine sugar, brown sugar and margarine in mixer bowl. Add eggs; mix well. Stir in cereal and vanilla. Add mixture of dry ingredients 1/3 at a time, mixing well after each addition. Stir in chocolate chips, nuts and raisins. Drop by teaspoonfuls onto lightly greased cookie sheet. Bake at 350 degrees for 10 minutes or until brown. Yield: 6 dozen.

Jean Palmer, Pine Creek 770

FORK COOKIES

1 c. shortening
1 c. sugar
1 c. packed brown sugar
3 eggs
1 tsp. vanilla extract
3 1/2 c. flour
2 tsp. soda
1 tsp. cream of tartar
1/2 tsp. cinnamon
Pinch of salt

Cream shortening, sugar and brown sugar in mixer bowl until light and fluffy. Add eggs 1 at a time, beating well after each addition. Mix in vanilla. Add sifted dry ingredients; mix well. Shape by teaspoonfuls into balls. Place on cookie sheet. Flatten with fork. Bake at 350 degrees for 10 minutes. Yield: 3 dozen.

Genevieve Hart, Millville 443

HAWAIIAN COOKIES

1 2-layer pkg. yellow cake mix
1 sm. can crushed pineapple, well drained
1 sm. carton whipped topping
1 egg, beaten
1 c. coconut
1 c. chopped nuts
Confectioners' sugar

Combine cake mix with next 5 ingredients in bowl; mix well. Drop by teaspoonfuls into confectioners' sugar; roll to coat well. Place on ungreased cookie sheet. Bake at 350 degrees for 12 to 15 minutes or until cookies test done.

Marie Miller, DeSabla 762

FRUIT COOKIES

1 c. sugar
1 c. packed brown sugar
1 c. butter, softened
2 eggs, well beaten

1 tsp. each salt, cinnamon, soda and
   baking powder
1 tsp. vanilla extract
1 lb. raisins
2 c. flour

Cream sugar, brown sugar and butter in mixer bowl until light and fluffy. Add remaining ingredients in order listed, mixing well after each addition. Drop by spoonfuls onto cookie sheet. Bake at 350 degrees for 10 minutes. Yield: 7 1/2 dozen.

Pauline Byrne, Airport 820

GINGERSNAPS

3/4 c. shortening
1 c. sugar
1/4 c. molasses
2 eggs
2 c. flour
2 tsp. soda
1 tsp. each cinnamon, cloves and ginger

Cream shortening and sugar in mixer bowl until light and fluffy. Beat in molasses and eggs. Add sifted dry ingredients; mix well. Shape into small balls. Roll in additional sugar. Place on ungreased cookie sheet. Bake at 375 degrees for 15 to 18 minutes or until brown. Yield: 3-4 dozen.

Sarah Patterson, Hangtown 464

HONEY CRISPS

3/4 c. packed brown sugar
1/2 c. margarine, softened
3 tbsp. honey
1 1/2 c. quick-cooking oats
1 2/3 c. (about) flaked coconut
1/2 c. flour

Combine brown sugar, margarine and honey in saucepan. Bring to a boil, stirring to blend well. Pour over mixture of oats, coconut and flour in bowl; mix well. Drop by teaspoonfuls onto greased cookie sheets. Press with fork to flatten slightly. Bake at 350 degrees for 10 minutes or until lightly browned. Store cooled cookies in airtight container. Yield: 4 dozen.

Adeline Stumbaugh, DeSabla 762

GARDEN COOKIES

2 c. sugar
2 1/2 c. shortening

2 eggs
6 c. sifted flour
2 tsp. soda
1 tsp. each allspice, cloves, nutmeg
   and cinnamon
1/2 tsp. salt
1 c. tomato juice
1 c. grated carrots
1 c. chopped spinach
1 c. raisins
1/2 c. chopped nuts

Cream sugar and shortening in mixer bowl until light and fluffy. Add eggs; mix well. Add sifted dry ingredients alternately with tomato juice, mixing well after each addition. Stir in vegetables, raisins and nuts. Drop by spoonfuls onto greased cookie sheet. Bake at 375 degrees for 15 to 20 minutes or until brown. Yield: 8 dozen.

Margaret Conn, Grover City 746

NO-BAKE COOKIES

2 c. sugar
1/3 c. cocoa
1/4 c. margarine
1/2 c. milk
3 c. quick-cooking oats
1/2 c. peanut butter
1/2 tsp. vanilla extract
1/2 c. chopped nuts
1/2 c. coconut
1/2 c. raisins

Combine sugar, cocoa, margarine and milk in saucepan. Bring to a boil. Cook for 1 minute. Stir in remaining ingredients; mix well. Drop by teaspoonfuls onto waxed paper; cool. Yield: 4 dozen.

Dorothy E. White, Antelope 161

MACAROON COOKIES

1 stick margarine, softened
1 c. sugar
1 egg
1 c. baking mix
1 1/2 c. instant potato flakes
2 tsp. coconut flavoring

Cream margarine and sugar in bowl until light and fluffy. Add egg; mix well. Add remaining ingredients; mix well. Drop by teaspoonfuls onto foil-covered cookie sheet. Bake at 325 degrees for 10 minutes.

Ila Bravo, Orchard City 333

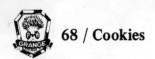

CELESTIAL COOKIES

1 c. shortening
2/3 c. sugar
1 c. packed brown sugar
3 eggs
1 tsp. vanilla extract
2 c. flour
1 tsp. salt
1 tsp. soda
2 c. oats
2 c. cornflakes
1 c. coconut
1 c. semisweet chocolate chips
1 c. chopped nuts

Cream shortening and sugars in bowl until light and fluffy. Add eggs and vanilla; mix well. Sift in flour, salt and soda; mix well. Add remaining ingredients; mix well. Drop by teaspoonfuls onto greased cookie sheet. Bake at 375 degrees for 12 minutes.

Virginia Wann, Oakdale 435

M AND M COOKIES

1/3 c. shortening
1/3 c. butter, softened
1/2 c. sugar
1/2 c. packed brown sugar
1 egg
1 tsp. vanilla extract
1 3/4 c. flour
1/2 tsp. soda
1/4 tsp. salt
3/4 c. chopped nuts
1 6-oz. package M and M's

Cream shortening, butter, sugar and brown sugar in mixer bowl until fluffy. Mix in egg and vanilla. Add sifted dry ingredients; mix well. Stir in nuts and candies. Drop by rounded tea-spoonfuls 2 inches apart onto ungreased cookie sheet. Bake at 375 degrees for 8 to 10 mintues or until lightly browned. Cool slightly on cookie sheet. Remove to wire rack to cool completely. Yield: 4 dozen.

Betty Crile, Humboldt 501

MERINGUE KISSES

2 egg whites
3/4 c. sugar
1/2 tsp. vanilla extract
1/2 c. chopped nuts
1 c. coconut
1 6-oz. package chocolate chips (opt.)
1/2 tsp. food coloring

Beat egg whites in bowl until foamy. Add sugar gradually, beating until stiff peaks form. Blend in vanilla. Fold in nuts, coconut, chocolate chips and food coloring gently. Drop by tea-spoonfuls onto greased cookie sheet. Place in preheated 375-degree oven. Turn off oven. Let stand in closed oven for 5 hours to overnight. Store in airtight container. Yield: 2 dozen.
Note: May bake at 250 degrees for 30 minutes.

Berdie Tomko, Loomis 638

SURPRISE MERINGUES

3 egg whites
1/8 tsp. salt
1/8 tsp. cream of tartar
1 tsp. vanilla extract
3/4 c. sugar
1 6-oz. package chocolate chips
1/3 c. chopped nuts

Beat egg whites, salt, cream of tartar and vanilla in bowl until soft peaks form. Add sugar very gradually, beating until stiff peaks form. Fold in chocolate chips and nuts gently. Drop by rounded teaspoonfuls onto waxed paper-lined baking sheet. Bake at 275 degrees for 25 to 30 minutes or until lightly brown on top.

Betty Van Wyck, Escalon 447

STARLIGHT MINT
SURPRISE COOKIES

1 c. butter, softened
1 c. sugar
1/2 c. packed brown sugar
2 eggs
1 tsp. vanilla extract
3 c. sifted flour
1 tsp. soda
1/2 tsp. salt
1 9-oz. package tiny solid
*   chocolate-mint wafers*
Walnut halves

Cream butter, sugar and brown sugar in mixer bowl until light and fluffy. Add eggs and vanilla; beat well. Add sifted dry ingredients gradually, mixing well after each addition. Chill dough for 2 hours or longer. Shape rounded teaspoon of dough around each chocolate wafer, enclosing it completely. Place on ungreased cookie sheet. Top with walnut half. Bake at 375 degrees for 9 to 10 minutes or until brown. Yield: 150-200 cookies

Louise Miller, Porterville 718

A special recognition to the CALIFORNIA DRIED FIG ADVISORY BOARD for providing this illustration ssisting in the success of this cookbook.

GRAPE GLAZED STEAM PUDDING, recipe on page 97.

LEMON WHIPPER SNAPPERS

1 2-layer pkg. lemon cake mix
1 egg
1 sm. carton whipped topping
1 c. chopped nuts (opt.)
Confectioners' sugar

Combine first 4 ingredients in bowl; mix well. Chill thoroughly. Shape into 1-inch balls. Roll in confectioners' sugar. Place on greased cookie sheet. Bake at 350 degrees for 15 minutes.

Marie Miller, DeSabla 762
Loretta Ellis, Ceres 520

OATMEAL SURPRISE COOKIES

3/4 c. shortening
1/2 c. sugar
1 c. packed brown sugar
1 egg
1 tsp. vanilla extract
1 sm. can crushed pineapple, drained
1 c. flour
3 c. quick-cooking oats
1 tsp. salt
1/2 tsp. soda
1 c. shredded coconut

Cream shortening, sugar and brown sugar in mixer bowl until light and fluffy. Beat in egg, vanilla and 1/4 cup water. Stir in pineapple. Add mixture of dry ingredients; mix well. Stir in coconut. Drop by rounded spoonfuls onto greased cookie sheet. Bake at 350 degrees for 12 to 15 minutes or until golden brown. Yield: 5 dozen.

Naomi Fletcher, Orangevale 354

PEANUT BUTTER-OATMEAL CRUNCHIES

1 c. shortening
2 c. sugar
1/2 c. peanut butter
1/4 c. milk
2 tsp. vanilla extract
3 eggs
1 c. sifted flour
3/4 tsp. baking powder
1 tsp. salt
2 tsp. cinnamon
3 1/2 c. quick-cooking oats
2 c. raisins

Cream shortening, sugar and peanut butter in mixer bowl until fluffy. Add milk, vanilla and eggs; mix well. Stir in mixture of flour, baking powder, salt and cinnamon. Add oats and rai-

sins; mix well. Drop by teaspoonfuls onto greased cookie sheet. Bake at 375 degrees for 12 to 15 minutes or until cookies are lightly browned on edges. Cool on cookie sheet for 2 to 3 minutes. Remove to wire racks to cool completely. Yield: 6 1/2 dozen.

Billie Stenstrom, Lake Frances 745

HONEY-OATMEAL COOKIES

1 c. shortening
3/4 c. honey
1 c. raisins
1/2 c. chopped walnuts
1/2 tsp. each nutmeg, cinnamon
2 c. flour
1 1/2 tsp. soda
2 c. oats
2 eggs, beaten
1 tsp. vanilla extract

Combine first 6 ingredients and 1 cup water in saucepan. Bring to a boil. Cook for 10 minutes; cool. Sift flour and soda together into bowl. Add remaining ingredients; mix well. Stir in cooled raisin mixture. Drop by teaspoonfuls onto greased cookie sheet. Bake at 350 degrees for 10 minutes. Yield: 4 dozen.

Dot Morandi, Banner 627

HONEY-OAT-CORNFLAKE DROP COOKIES

1 1/3 c. margarine, softened
1 c. sugar
1 c. honey
2 eggs
2 tsp. vanilla extract
1 1/2 tsp. salt
1 tsp. soda
4 c. oats
2 c. cornflakes
1 12-oz. package peanut butter chips
1 c. walnuts
1 c. raisins

Cream margarine and sugar in mixer bowl until light and fluffy. Beat in honey, eggs and vanilla. Add remaining ingredients; mix well. Drop by rounded teaspoonfuls onto greased cookie sheet. Bake at 325 degrees for 12 minutes. Cool for several minutes on cookie sheets. Remove to wire racks to cool completely. Yield: 10 dozen.

Marlene Jopson, Meadow Vista 721

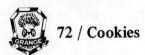

OATMEAL CRUNCHIES

1 c. sifted flour
1/2 c. sugar
1/2 tsp. baking powder
1 tsp. soda
1/4 tsp. salt
1/2 c. packed brown sugar
1/2 c. shortening
1 egg
1 tsp. vanilla extract
3/4 c. quick-cooking oats
1/4 c. chopped walnuts

Sift flour, sugar, baking powder, soda and salt together into mixer bowl. Add brown sugar, shortening, egg and vanilla. Beat to mix well. Stir in oats and walnuts. Shape into small balls. Dip tops in additional sugar. Place 2 inches apart on greased cookie sheet. Bake at 375 degrees for 10 to 12 minutes or until brown. Yield: 3 dozen.

Peggy Striffler, Harbor 775

FAMOUS PEANUT BUTTER COOKIES

1/2 c. butter, softened
1/2 c. shortening
3/4 c. sugar
3/4 c. packed brown sugar
1 c. peanut butter
2 eggs
1 tsp. vanilla extract
2 1/2 c. flour
1 tsp. baking powder
1 1/2 tsp. soda
1 c. crushed whole wheat cereal

Combine butter, shortening, sugar, brown sugar, peanut butter, eggs and vanilla in mixer bowl. Beat for 10 minutes or until very fluffy. Sift flour, baking powder and soda together into bowl. Mix in crushed cereal. Add to peanut butter mixture; mix well. Chill in refrigerator. Shape into 1-inch balls. Place on greased cookie sheet. Flatten with fork in crisscross pattern. Bake at 400 degrees for 9 to 10 minutes or just until set. Yield: 6 dozen.

Kathryn Radueghel, Ripon 511

PERSIMMON COOKIES

1/2 c. butter, softened
1 c. packed brown sugar
3 eggs
1 tsp. soda
1 c. persimmon pulp
2 c. flour
1/2 tsp. cinnamon
1/4 tsp. nutmeg
1 c. shredded coconut
1 c. chopped walnuts
1 c. raisins

Cream butter and brown sugar in mixer bowl until light and fluffy. Add eggs 1 at a time, mixing well after each addition. Dissolve soda in persimmon pulp. Mix into creamed mixture. Add flour and spices; mix well. Stir in remaining ingredients. Drop by teaspoonfuls onto greased cookie sheet. Bake at 350 degrees for 12 to 15 minutes or until light brown. Yield: 3 dozen.

Mary Lee Johnson, Keyes 524

POTATO CHIP COOKIES

1 c. shortening
1 c. sugar
1 c. packed brown sugar
2 eggs
1 tsp. vanilla extract
2 c. flour
1 tsp. soda
1/2 tsp. salt
2 c. oats
2 c. crushed potato chips
1 c. chopped nuts

Cream shortening with sugar and brown sugar in mixer bowl until light and fluffy. Beat in eggs and vanilla. Add sifted flour, soda and salt; mix well. Stir in remaining ingredients. Drop by teaspoonfuls onto greased cookie sheet. Bake at 375 degrees for 10 to 15 minutes or until brown. Yield: 4 dozen.
Note: May add chocolate chips, chopped dates or raisins.

Lois M. Smith, Lake Earl 577

PUDDING COOKIES

1 1/2 c. biscuit mix
1 lg. package desired flavor instant
    pudding mix
1/2 c. oil
2 eggs

Combine baking mix and pudding mix in bowl. Add oil and eggs; mix well. Drop by teaspoonfuls onto ungreased baking sheet. Bake at 350 degrees for 10 to 12 minutes or until brown. Yield: 3 dozen.

Grace Trumbly, United Rescue 450

VERNA'S PUDDING COOKIES

1/2 c. shortening
1/2 c. sugar
1 pkg. instant pudding mix
1 egg
1/2 tsp. each soda, cream of tartar
1 c. sifted flour
1 c. quick-cooking oats
1/2 c. finely chopped nuts
1/2 c. raisins (opt.)

Cream shortening with sugar and pudding mix in mixer bowl until light and fluffy. Beat in egg. Add remaining ingredients 1 at a time, mixing well after each addition. Roll into 1-inch balls. Place on cookie sheet. Press with fork to flatten. Bake at 350 degrees for 10 to 12 minutes or until brown. Yield: 2-3 dozen.

Verna A. Radcliff, San Marcos 633

RUM BALLS

1 6-oz. package chocolate chips
1/3 c. rum
3 tbsp. corn syrup
44 vanilla wafers, crushed
1/2 c. chopped nuts
Confectioners' sugar

Melt chocolate chips in saucepan over low heat. Add rum, corn syrup, cookie crumbs and nuts; mix well. Shape into 1-inch balls. Roll in confectioners' sugar to coat well. Store in refrigerator in airtight container for 4 weeks or less. Note: May substitute Bourbon for rum.

Charles Crile, Humboldt 501

SIMPLE SESAMES

2 c. butter, softened
1 1/2 c. sugar
3 c. flour
1 c. sesame seed
2 c. coconut
1/2 c. finely chopped almonds

Cream butter and sugar in bowl until light and fluffy. Add flour; mix just until combined. Stir in sesame seed, coconut and almonds. Divide dough into 3 portions. Shape each portion into long 2-inch thick roll. Wrap with plastic wrap. Chill for about 1 hour or until firm. Cut into 1/4-inch slices. Place on cookie sheets. Bake at 300 degrees for 30 minutes. Cool on wire racks.

Janis Duncan-Vaughn, Miranda 690

SCOTTISH SHORTBREAD

1 lb. butter, softened
1 c. confectioners' sugar
3 c. sifted flour
1 c. rice flour

Cream butter in mixer bowl until fluffy. Add confectioners' sugar gradually, mixing only until well blended. Add remaining ingredients gradually, mixing well after each addition. Sprinkle work surface lightly with mixture of additional flour and confectioners' sugar. Pat dough into 3/4-inch thick circles. Flute edges; prick with fork. Place on cookie sheet. Chill for 30 minutes. Bake at 375 degrees for 5 minutes. Reduce temperature to 300 degrees. Bake for 45 to 60 minutes or until light brown.

Ellen T. Johnson, Little Lake 670

FRUITY SUGAR COOKIES

1 c. sugar
1 3-oz. package favorite flavor gelatin
3/4 c. shortening
2 eggs
3 c. flour
1 tsp. each baking powder, salt

Combine sugar and gelatin in bowl. Add shortening and eggs; mix well. Add sifted dry ingredients; mix well. Roll out 1/4 inch thick on floured surface. Cut with 3-inch cookie cutter. Place on ungreased cookie sheet. Bake at 375 degrees for 5 to 8 minutes or until brown.

Rose Baley, Tulelake 468

OLD-TIME SUGAR COOKIES

1 3/4 c. butter, softened
2 1/4 c. sugar
3 eggs
4 1/2 c. flour
1 1/2 tsp. baking powder
2 tsp. cream of tartar
1/2 tsp. salt
1 1/2 tsp. vanilla extract
1 tsp. lemon flavoring

Cream butter and sugar in mixer bowl until light and fluffy. Add eggs 1 at a time, mixing well after each addition. Add dry ingredients and flavorings; mix well. Chill, wrapped in plastic wrap, for several hours. Roll out 1/8 inch thick on floured surface. Cut as desired. Sprinkle with additional sugar. Place on cookie sheet. Bake at 350 degrees for 10 to 12 minutes or until lightly browned.

Anna F. Serve, Wyandotte 495

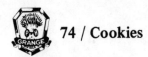

MOLASSES SUGAR COOKIES

1/4 c. melted shortening, cooled
1 c. sugar
1/4 c. molasses
1 egg
2 c. sifted flour
2 tsp. soda
1/2 tsp. each cloves, ginger, cinnamon
    and salt

Beat shortening, sugar, molasses and egg in bowl until smooth. Add sifted dry ingredients; mix well. Chill in refrigerator. Shape into balls. Roll in additional sugar. Place 2 inches apart on greased cookie sheet. Bake at 375 degrees for 8 to 10 minutes or until brown.

Zella Bennett, Elbow Creek 733
Leatha McMains, Ojai Valley 659

PAT'S CONFECTIONERS' SUGAR COOKIES

1/2 c. shortening
1/2 c. butter, softened
1 c. confectioners' sugar
1 egg
2 c. flour
1/2 tsp. each soda, cream of tartar
Pinch of salt
1 tsp. vanilla extract

Cream shortening and butter in mixer bowl until fluffy. Add confectioners' sugar and egg; mix well. Stir in remaining ingredients to form a soft dough. Shape into 1-inch balls. Place on cookie sheet. Press with bottom of glass dipped in sugar to flatten. Bake at 375 degrees for 12 to 14 minutes or until lightly browned.

Pat Saude, San Jose 10

OLD-FASHIONED SUGAR COOKIES

1 c. butter, softened
1 1/2 c. sugar
2 eggs
2 tsp. vanilla extract
4 3/4 c. sifted flour
1 tsp. salt
1 tsp. soda
1 tsp. baking powder
1/2 tsp. nutmeg
1 c. sour cream
Sugar

Cream butter in bowl until light and fluffy. Add sugar gradually; beat well. Add eggs 1 at a time, beating well after each addition. Stir in vanilla. Add sifted dry ingredients alternately with sour cream, mixing well after each addition. Chill, covered, for several hours to overnight. Roll 1/4 inch thick on lightly floured surface. Cut with floured 3-inch cookie cutter; place on ungreased baking sheet. Sprinkle with sugar. Bake at 375 degrees for 10 to 12 minutes or until lightly browned. Yield: 4 dozen.

Photograph for this recipe on opposite page.

ZUCCHINI COOKIES

1/2 c. butter, softened
1 c. sugar
1 egg, beaten
2 c. flour
1 tsp. each soda, cinnamon
1/2 tsp. each salt, cloves
1 c. grated zucchini
1 c. raisins
1 c. chopped nuts

Cream butter and sugar in mixer bowl until light and fluffy. Beat in egg. Add sifted dry ingredients with zucchini; mix well. Stir in raisins and nuts. Drop by teaspoonfuls onto greased cookie sheet. Bake at 375 degrees for 12 to 15 minutes or until light brown. Do not overbake. Yield: 3 dozen.

Georgia Schultz, Apple Valley 593

DANISH APPLE BARS

2 1/2 c. flour
1 tsp. salt
1 c. lard
Milk
1 egg, separated
1 c. cornflake crumbs
Apple slices
1 c. sugar
1 tsp. cinnamon
1 c. confectioners' sugar
1 tsp. vanilla extract

Mix flour and salt in bowl. Cut in lard until crumbly. Add enough milk to beaten egg yolk to measure 2/3 cup. Stir into flour mixture to form dough. Roll out half the dough on floured surface to fit bottom and sides of baking sheet. Layer cornflake crumbs, apples, sugar and cinnamon over dough. Top with remaining pastry; seal edges. Brush with beaten egg whites. Bake at 400 degrees for 1 hour. Combine confectioners' sugar and vanilla with 3 to 4 teaspoons water. Pour over hot pastry. Cut into bars.

Faye Von Hoorebeke, Rohner 509

HELLO DOLLIES

2 c. each vanilla wafer crumbs, graham
    cracker crumbs
1 c. melted margarine
1/2 c. flaked coconut
1 6-oz. package chocolate chips
1/2 to 1 c. chopped walnuts
1 can sweetened condensed milk

Combine crumbs and margarine in 9 x 13-inch
baking pan. Press over bottom of pan. Layer
coconut, chocolate chips and walnuts over
crumb layer. Drizzle with condensed milk. Bake
at 350 degrees for 15 to 20 minutes or until
brown. Cut into bars.

Linda Thruston, Wyandotte 495

GHIRADELLI BROWNIES

4 eggs, at room temperature
2 c. sugar
1/2 c. melted butter
2/3 c. Ghiradelli chocolate
1 c. flour
1/2 tsp. baking powder
1 tsp. vanilla extract
1 c. finely chopped walnuts

Beat eggs in bowl until thick. Add next 6 ingredients in order listed, mixing well after each
addition. Pour into buttered 8 x 8-inch baking
pan. Sprinkle with walnuts. Bake at 375 degrees
for 30 minutes; cool. Cut into squares.

Angela Espinola, Waterford 553

BROOKSIE'S BROWNIES

1/2 stick margarine
2 tbsp. cocoa
1/4 c. oil
1 c. sugar
1 c. flour
1 egg
1/4 c. milk
1/2 tsp. each soda, salt
1/2 tsp. vanilla extract
Nuts (opt.)
1/4 c. milk
1/2 stick margarine
2 tbsp. cocoa
1/2 pkg. (or more) confectioners' sugar
1/2 tsp. vanilla extract

Combine 1/2 stick margarine, 2 tablespoons
cocoa, oil and 1/2 cup water in saucepan. Bring
to a boil, stirring to blend well. Add to mixture
of sugar and flour in bowl; mix well. Add egg,
1/4 cup milk, soda, salt and 1/2 teaspoon vanilla; beat well. Stir in nuts. Pour into greased 9
x 13-inch baking dish. Bake at 375 degrees for
18 to 20 minutes or until brownies test done.
Combine 1/4 cup milk, 1/2 stick margarine and
2 tablespoons cocoa in saucepan. Bring to a
boil, stirring to blend well. Add enough confectioners' sugar to make frosting of desired consistency. Stir in 1/2 teaspoon vanilla. Spread
over hot brownies. Cut into squares when cool.

Brooksie Freeman, Manton 732

CHEWY GRANOLA BROWNIES

1/2 c. melted butter
1 3/4 c. packed brown sugar
2 eggs
1 tsp. vanilla extract
3/4 c. all-purpose flour
3/4 c. whole wheat flour
2 tsp. baking powder
1 tsp. salt
1 1/2 c. granola
1 c. chopped nuts

Melt butter in saucepan over low heat. Remove
from heat; stir in brown sugar. Add eggs and
vanilla; set aside. Combine all-purpose flour,
whole wheat flour, baking powder and salt; stir
to mix well. Add sugar mixture; mix well. Stir
in granola and nuts. Spread in greased 9 x 13-
inch baking pan. Bake at 350 degrees for 25
minutes. Cool in pan on wire rack. Cut into
bars. Yield: 2 dozen.

Viola E. Eddy, Los Alamos Valley 647

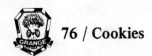

IRISH CREAM BROWNIES

3 oz. unsweetened baking chocolate
1/2 c. butter
1 c. sugar
2 eggs, at room temperature, well beaten
1 tbsp. Irish whiskey
2/3 c. flour
1/4 tsp. salt
2/3 c. semisweet chocolate chips (opt.)
3 tbsp. Irish cream liqueur
1 c. confectioners' sugar
3 tbsp. butter, softened
1/4 c. Irish cream liqueur
Chopped nuts (opt.)

Melt chocolate with 1/2 cup butter in double boiler, stirring to blend well; cool. Beat sugar with eggs in bowl. Add whiskey and cooled chocolate mixture; mix well. Stir in flour, salt and chocolate chips. Pour into buttered and foil-lined 8 x 8-inch baking pan. Bake at 325 degrees for 20 to 25 minutes or until brownies test done. Cool for 2 hours or longer. Pierce with toothpick. Drizzle 3 tablespoons liqueur over brownies. Combine confectioners' sugar, 3 tablespoons butter and 1/4 cup liqueur in bowl; mix well. Spread over brownies. Sprinkle with nuts. Cut into squares. Yield: 10-12 servings.

Shirley L. Warnock, Julian 643

COCONUT CREME BARS

1 sm. package French vanilla pudding
    and pie filling mix
1 3/4 c. milk
1   2-layer pkg. yellow cake mix
1/2 c. melted butter
1/3 c. evaporated milk
1/2 tsp. almond extract
1 c. coconut
1/2 c. sliced almonds
1 c. sifted confectioners' sugar
2 tbsp. butter, softened
1/4 tsp. almond extract
3 to 4 tsp. milk

Combine pudding and pie filling mix with 1 3/4 cups milk in saucepan. Bring to a boil over medium heat, stirring constantly; cool. Combine cake mix, 1/2 cup butter, evaporated milk and 1/2 teaspoon almond flavoring in bowl; mix well. Reserve 1 cup batter. Pour remaining batter in greased and floured 9 x 13-inch baking pan. Bake at 350 degrees for 8 minutes. Spread pudding mixture over baked layer. Stir coconut into reserved batter. Spoon by teaspoonfuls over pudding mixture. Sprinkle with almonds.

Bake at 350 degrees for 20 to 30 minutes longer or until brown. Blend confectioners' sugar, 2 tablespoons butter and 1/4 teaspoon almond flavoring in bowl. Add enough milk to make glaze of desired consistency. Drizzle over warm layers. Cool completely. Cut into bars.

Barbara Marx, Anderson 418

EASY BROWNIES

1 stick butter, softened
1 c. sugar
4 eggs
1 c. flour
1   16-oz. can chocolate syrup
1 c. walnuts
1 1/3 c. sugar
6 tbsp. butter
6 tbsp. milk
1/2 c. chocolate chips
4 marshmallows

Cream 1 stick butter and 1 cup sugar in bowl until fluffy. Add eggs 1 at a time, beating well after each addition. Beat in flour. Stir in chocolate syrup and walnuts. Pour into greased 9 x 13-inch baking dish. Bake at 350 degrees for 30 to 35 minutes or until brownies test done. Combine 1 1/3 cups sugar, 6 tablespoons butter and milk in saucepan. Bring to a boil. Cook for 1 minute, stirring constantly; remove from heat. Add chocolate chips and marshmallows; beat until smooth. Pour over brownies. Cut cooled brownies into squares. Store, tightly covered, in cool place. Yield: 2 dozen.

Sharon Blasingame, Rainbow Valley 689

PEANUT BUTTER FINGERS

1/2 c. butter, softened
1/2 c. sugar
1/2 c. packed brown sugar
1 egg
1/3 c. peanut butter
1/2 tsp. soda
1/4 tsp. salt
1/2 tsp. vanilla extract
1 c. twice-sifted flour
1 c. quick-cooking oats
1 c. semisweet chocolate chips
1/2 c. peanut butter
1/2 c. sifted confectioners' sugar
2 to 4 tbsp. evaporated milk

Cream butter with sugar and brown sugar in mixer bowl until light and fluffy. Blend in egg, 1/3 cup peanut butter, soda, salt and vanilla.

Stir in flour and oats. Spread in greased 9 x 13-inch baking pan. Bake at 350 degrees for 20 to 25 minutes or until cake tests done. Sprinkle chocolate chips over top. Spread evenly when melted. Mix 1/2 cup peanut butter and confectioners' sugar in bowl. Add enough evaporated milk to make glaze of desired consistency. Drizzle over chocolate layer; cool. Cut into bars.

Opal Quigley, Tulelake 468

VERA'S LEMON-COCONUT BARS

1 1/2 c. flour
1/2 c. sugar
1/2 c. margarine
1 c. sugar
2 eggs, beaten
2 tbsp. flour
1/2 tsp. baking powder
1/4 tsp. salt
1 tsp. vanilla extract
1 1/2 c. coconut
1 c. chopped walnuts
1 c. confectioners' sugar
2 tbsp. butter, softened
2 to 4 tbsp. lemon juice

Combine 1 1/2 cups flour and 1/2 cup sugar in bowl. Cut in margarine until crumbly. Press over bottom of greased 9 x 13-inch baking dish. Bake at 350 degrees for 10 minutes. Combine 1 cup sugar, eggs, 2 tablespoons flour, baking powder, salt and vanilla in bowl; mix well. Stir in coconut and walnuts. Spread over baked layer. Bake at 350 degrees for 20 minutes longer; cool. Mix confectioners' sugar and butter in bowl. Add enough lemon juice to make glaze of desired consistency. Spread over top. Cut into bars.

Linda Shaw, Humboldt 501

ITALIAN FIG BARS (CUCCIDATTI)

3 lb. white Calimyrna figs
3 lb. raisins
1 sm. jar orange marmalade
2 c. honey
1 lb. each toasted almonds, walnuts
1 tbsp. each cinnamon, allspice
1 1/2 tsp. nutmeg
1 c. sweet wine
9 c. flour
1/4 c. baking powder
4 c. sugar
1 tsp. salt
2 c. shortening
6 eggs, beaten
1 tbsp. vanilla extract
1 13-oz. can evaporated milk
1 1-lb. package confectioners' sugar
1/2 stick butter, melted
3 tbsp. milk
2 tsp. vanilla extract

Combine figs, raisins, marmalade, honey, nuts, spices and wine in bowl; mix well. Put through food grinder. Sift next 4 dry ingredients into bowl. Cut in shortening until crumbly. Add eggs, 1 tablespoon vanilla and evaporated milk; mix well. Roll out into strips on floured surface. Spread filling down 1 side of each strip. Fold dough in half to enclose filling; seal edges. Place on baking sheet. Bake at 350 degrees for 10 minutes or until brown; cool. Combine remaining ingredients in bowl. Beat until smooth. Spread on cooled strips. Cut into bars.

Connie Zoria, Berryessa 780

LEMON-GLAZED PERSIMMON BARS

1 egg
1 c. sugar
1/2 c. oil
1 8-oz. package dates, finely chopped
1 1/2 tsp. lemon juice
1 tsp. soda
1 c. persimmon pulp
1 3/4 c. flour
1/2 tsp. salt
1 tsp. each cinnamon, nutmeg
1/4 tsp. cloves
1 c. chopped walnuts
1 c. confectioners' sugar
2 tbsp. lemon juice

Combine egg, sugar, oil and dates in bowl; mix well. Stir 1 1/2 teaspoons lemon juice and soda into persimmon pulp. Combine flour, salt and spices. Add to date mixture alternately with persimmon, mixing well after each addition. Stir in walnuts. Spread in greased and floured 10 x 15-inch baking pan. Bake at 350 degrees for 25 minutes or until lightly browned. Cool for 5 minutes. Mix confectioners' sugar and 2 tablespoons lemon juice in bowl. Spread over baked layer. Cool completely; cut into bars. Note: Omit 1 1/2 teaspoons lemon juice from batter if frozen persimmon is used.

Clara Sampson, Berryessa 780
Myrtle Soucie, Oakdale 435

CARROT BARS

2 eggs
1 c. sugar
3/4 c. oil
1 c. flour
1 tsp. each soda, cinnamon
1/4 tsp. salt
1   7 1/2-oz. jar junior baby food carrots
1 c. nuts (opt.)
1 3/4 c. confectioners' sugar
1/4 c. butter, softened
4 oz. cream cheese, softened
1/2 tsp. vanilla extract

Combine eggs, sugar and oil in bowl; beat well. Add next 4 sifted dry ingredients; mix well. Stir in carrots and nuts. Pour into greased and floured 9 x 13-inch baking pan. Bake at 350 degrees for 25 minutes. Combine remaining ingredients in bowl; mix well. Spread on cooled carrot layer. Cut into bars.

Mildred Painter, San Marcos 633

NUT CHEWS

1 egg
1 c. packed brown sugar
5 tbsp. flour
Pinch of soda
1 c. finely chopped nuts

Beat egg with brown sugar in mixer bowl until well mixed. Add sifted flour and soda; mix well. Stir in nuts. Pour into greased 8 x 8-inch baking pan. Bake at 350 degrees for 20 to 30 minutes or until cake tests done. Cut into bars while warm. Yield: 1 dozen.

Frances Baldwin, Kingsburg 679

FRENCH WAFFLE COOKIES

6 eggs
3 sticks butter, softened
1 1/2 c. plus 2 tbsp. packed brown sugar
1/4 c. apricot Brandy
1/2 c. finely chopped pecans
4 c. sifted flour

Combine eggs, butter and brown sugar in mixer bowl. Mix at medium speed until smooth. Stir in Brandy and pecans. Add flour; mix well. Drop by heaping teaspoonfuls into center of each section of waffle iron. Bake for several minutes or until brown; cool. Store in airtight container. Yield: 4 1/2 dozen.

Margaret Butler, Ukiah 419

SPICED DREAM BARS

1 c. flour
1/2 c. packed brown sugar
1/2 c. margarine, softened
2 eggs, well beaten
3/4 c. packed brown sugar
1 tbsp. flour
1 c. coconut
1 c. chopped nuts
1/2 tsp. salt
1 tsp. each baking powder, allspice

Combine 1 cup flour, 1/2 cup brown sugar and margarine in bowl; mix until dough forms ball. Press into greased 9 x 9-inch baking dish. Bake at 350 degrees for 30 minutes or until golden brown. Combine remaining ingredients in bowl; mix well. Spread over baked layer. Bake for 25 minutes longer; cool. Cut into bars.

Mabel Quick, Waterford 553

BLUE RIBBON TOFFEE BARS

1 3/4 c. flour
1 c. sugar
1 c. butter, softened
1 tsp. vanilla extract
1 egg, separated
1/2 c. finely chopped walnuts

Combine first 4 ingredients and egg yolk in mixer bowl. Beat at low speed until blended, scraping bowl occasionally. Beat at medium speed until well mixed. Press into greased 10 x 15-inch baking pan. Beat egg white lightly in small bowl. Brush over top of dough. Sprinkle with walnuts. Bake at 275 degrees for 1 hour and 10 minutes or until golden brown. Cut into bars immediately. Remove to wire racks to cool. Yield: 4 dozen.

Velma Butler, DeSabla 762

WALNUT SQUARES

1 c. flour
2 c. packed brown sugar
1/4 tsp. each soda, salt
2 c. ground walnuts
2 eggs, well beaten
1 tsp. vanilla extract

Combine dry ingredients in bowl. Add walnuts, eggs and vanilla; mix well. Spread thin in well-greased 10 x 15-inch baking pan. Bake at 325 degrees for 25 minutes or until brown. Cut into squares while warm.

Esther Davidson, Kingsburg 679

CASSEROLES

Donaldson's Improved Patent Self-Feeding, Discharging and Separating
HOMINY MILL.

HULLS 30 TO 50 BUSHELS PER DAY! COSTS ONLY $160!

It separates and cleans the hominy ready for market. It works the corn dry, yet hulls it perfectly. Can be run by horse or steam power; can be set from one to four-horse power; one-horse power being sufficient to hull ten pushels per day.

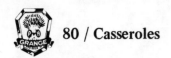

ALMOND-CHICKEN CASSEROLE

1 c. chopped cooked chicken
1 c. chopped celery
2 c. cooked rice
2 green onions, chopped
Salt and pepper to taste
1/2 c. sliced almonds
1 can cream of chicken soup
1 tbsp. lemon juice
3/4 c. mayonnaise
1 3-oz. can sliced water chestnuts
Potato chips, crushed

Combine all ingredients except potato chips in bowl; mix well. Pour into greased 9 x 13-inch baking dish. Top with potato chips. Bake at 350 degrees for 30 minutes. Yield: 12 servings.

Gladys Montgomery, Orangevale 354

NELLIE'S CHICKEN CASSEROLE

2 c. sliced celery
3/4 c. chopped onion
1 chicken, cooked, chopped
2 cans cream of mushroom soup
1 c. broth
2 cans chow mein noodles
1/2 pkg. slivered almonds
1 sm. can pimentos

Saute celery and onion in skillet. Combine with chicken, soup and broth in bowl. Reserve a portion of the noodles. Stir remaining noodles into chicken mixture. Spoon into greased baking dish. Top with almonds, pimentos and reserved noodles. Bake at 350 degrees for 1 hour.
Yield 10 servings.

Nellie Keidel, Fonbloom 602

CHICKEN-CHEESE PUFF

12 slices bread, buttered
2 c. chopped cooked chicken
2 stalks celery, chopped
1 sm. onion, chopped
3 tbsp. mayonnaise
Salt and pepper to taste
3 c. milk
1 can cream of mushroom soup
5 eggs, beaten
Cheddar cheese

Arrange 6 slices bread, buttered side up, in 9 x 13-inch baking pan. Combine chicken, celery, onion and mayonnaise in bowl; toss lightly.

Spoon over bread. Sprinkle with salt and pepper. Top with remaining bread. Combine milk, soup and eggs in bowl; mix well. Pour over bread. Chill overnight. Top with a generous amount of cheese. Bake at 325 degrees for 45 minutes.

Winnie Clark, Quartz Hill 697

CHICKEN AND DRESSING CASSEROLE

1 8-oz. package stuffing mix
3 c. chopped cooked chicken
1/2 c. melted butter
1/2 c. flour
1/4 tsp. salt
Dash of pepper
4 c. chicken broth
6 eggs, slightly beaten
1 can cream of mushroom soup
1 c. sour cream
1/2 c. milk
1/4 c. chopped pimento

Prepare stuffing mix according to package directions. Layer prepared stuffing and chicken in greased 9 x 13-inch baking dish. Blend butter, flour and seasonings in saucepan. Stir in broth gradually. Cook until thickened, stirring constantly. Stir a small amount of hot mixture into beaten eggs; stir eggs into hot mixture. Pour over chicken. Bake at 325 degrees for 45 minutes. Let stand for 5 minutes before serving. Combine remaining ingredients in saucepan; mix well. Heat to serving temperature. Serve over chicken.

Florence Taneyhill, Hessel 750

CHICKEN FLORENTINE

6 chicken breast halves, boned, cut
    into pieces
Salt and pepper to taste
1/4 c. butter
2 tbsp. oil
2 10-oz. packages frozen chopped
    spinach, cooked
1/2 c. mayonnaise
1/4 q. sour cream
1 can cream of chicken soup
1 tbsp. lemon juice
1 tsp. curry powder
1/2 c. grated sharp cheese
1/2 c. cornflake crumbs

Season chicken lightly with salt and pepper. Saute in butter and oil in skillet for 10 minutes. Drain spinach; squeeze dry. Spread spinach in 2-quart casserole. Top with chicken breasts. Mix mayonnaise, sour cream, soup, lemon juice and curry powder in bowl. Pour over chicken. Sprinkle with cheese. Top with cornflake crumbs. Bake at 350 degrees for 25 minutes. Yield: 6 servings.

Clem V. Mulholand, Ripon 511

CHICKEN LASAGNA CASSEROLE

1 1/2 c. chopped onions
1/2 c. chopped green pepper
3 tbsp. butter
1 can cream of chicken soup
1/3 c. milk
1   6-oz. can mushrooms
1/4 c. chopped pimento
1/2 tsp. basil
4 oz. lasagna noodles, cooked
1 1/2 c. cream-style cottage cheese
3 c. chopped cooked chicken
2 c. shredded Cheddar cheese
1/2 c. Parmesan cheese

Saute onions and green pepper in butter in skillet. Add soup, milk, mushrooms, pimento and basil; mix well. Layer half the noodles, sauce, cottage cheese, chicken and Cheddar cheese in 9 x 13-inch baking dish. Repeat layers. Top with Parmesan cheese. Bake at 350 degrees for 45 minutes. Yield: 12-15 servings.

Esther Condray, Kingsburg 679

VIOLA'S CHICKEN CASSEROLE

1 can cream of mushroom soup
1 can cream of chicken soup
1/2 c. chicken broth
2 c. grated cheese
3 c. macaroni, cooked
4 c. chopped cooked chicken

Blend soups and broth in bowl. Stir in cheese, macaroni and chicken. Turn into greased 9 x 13-inch baking pan. Sprinkle with additional cheese. Bake at 350 degrees for 35 minutes or until bubbly. Yield: 10-12 servings.

Viola Hoehlke, Hesperia 682

CHICKEN-MACARONI CASSEROLE

1 1/2 c. uncooked elbow macaroni
1 c. shredded Cheddar cheese
1 1/2 c. chopped cooked chicken
1 can mushrooms, drained
1/4 c. chopped pimentos
1 can cream of chicken soup
1 c. milk
1/2 tsp. salt
1/2 tsp. curry powder

Combine all ingredients in bowl; mix well. Pour into 1 1/2-quart casserole. Bake, covered, at 350 degrees for 1 hour or until macaroni is tender.

Bernice M. Matthews, Ripon 511

CHICKEN-SPAGHETTI CASSEROLE

3 stalks celery, chopped
1 med. onion, chopped
1 green pepper, chopped
1 sm. can sliced mushrooms
4 chicken breast halves, cooked, chopped
1 pkg. thin spaghetti, cooked
2 cans cream of chicken soup

Saute celery, onion and green pepper in skillet. Combine with remaining ingredients in bowl; mix well. Pour into 9 x 13-inch baking dish. Bake at 350 degrees for 20 minutes or until bubbly.

Thelma Worden, Ranchito 654

EASY CHICKEN MIX

1 pkg. croutons
1 stick margarine, melted
3 chicken breasts, cooked, chopped
1/2 c. chopped onion
1/2 c. chopped celery
1/2 c. salad dressing
3/4 tsp. salt (opt.)
1/2 soup can milk
1 can mushroom soup
1 c. grated Cheddar cheese

Mix croutons, margarine and 1 cup water in bowl. Add chicken, onion, celery, salad dressing and salt; mix well. Pour into 9 x 13-inch baking pan. Drizzle milk over mixture. Spread soup over top. Refrigerate overnight if desired. Top with cheese. Bake at 350 degrees for 1 hour. Yield: 12 servings.

Martha M. Tennant, Grover City 746

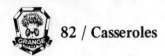

ALICE'S CHICKEN CASSEROLE

1 can cream of mushroom soup
1 13-oz. can evaporated milk
1 sm. can chopped green chilies
1 c. chopped celery
1 c. chopped onion
12 corn tortillas, cut into strips
1 chicken, cooked, chopped
Cheddar cheese, grated

Mix soup, milk, green chilies, celery and onion in bowl. Layer tortillas, chicken, soup mixture and cheese alternately in greased 9 x 13-inch baking dish until all ingredients are used. Refrigerate for 24 hours. Bake at 350 degrees for 45 minutes or until heated through. Yield: 12 servings.

Alice Mason, Morgan Hill 408

CHICKEN-IN-A-WINK

1 can cream of chicken soup
1 can cream of mushroom soup
1 c. milk
1 can chile salsa
1 sm. onion, finely chopped
2 to 3 tbsp. chicken broth
12 corn tortillas, cut into 1-in. squares
4 whole chicken breasts, chopped
1 lb. grated mild Cheddar cheese

Mix soups, milk, salsa and onion in bowl. Sprinkle broth in buttered shallow 9 x 13-inch baking dish. Layer half the tortillas, chicken and soup mixture in prepared dish. Top with cheese. Refrigerate, covered with foil, for 24 hours. Bake, uncovered, at 300 degrees for 1 1/2 hours. Do not overcook. Yield: 6 servings.

Orean Dexter, Greenhorn 384

LILLIAN'S CHICKEN ENCHILADA CASSEROLE

2 c. chopped cooked chicken
1 c. chicken broth
1 can cream of mushroom soup
1/2 c. chopped green chilies
1/2 c. chopped onion
1 clove of garlic, minced
8 corn tortillas, cut into strips
1 c. shredded Monterey Jack cheese
1 c. shredded Cheddar cheese

Combine chicken, broth, soup, green chilies, onion and garlic in bowl; mix well. Layer half the tortillas, chicken mixture and cheeses in buttered 9 x 10-inch baking dish. Repeat layers. Bake at 350 degrees for 50 minutes or until bubbly. Yield: 12-15 servings.

Lillian Reed, Wyandotte 495

BONNIE'S CHICKEN ENCHILADA CASSEROLE

4 chicken breasts
Salt and pepper to taste
2 cans cream of chicken soup
1/2 tsp. oregano
1/4 tsp. each cumin, sage and chili powder
2 cloves of garlic, pressed
12 corn tortillas
2 lg. onions, coarsely chopped
2 4-oz. cans green chilies
1 lb. longhorn cheese, grated
1/4 lb. Monterey Jack cheese

Wrap chicken breasts seasoned with salt and pepper tightly in foil. Bake at 350 degrees until very tender; cool. Bone and coarsely chop chicken; reserve juices. Combine reserved juices with soup and seasonings in saucepan. Heat until well blended, stirring frequently. Dip each tortilla in a small amount of hot oil to soften; drain on paper towels. Arrange 3 whole tortillas in bottom of 2 1/2-quart casserole greased on bottom only. Cut remaining tortillas into fourths. Layer 1/4 of the chicken, tortillas, onions, chilies, mixture of cheeses and soup mixture in prepared casserole. Repeat until all ingredients are used, ending with onions and cheeses. Bake at 375 degrees for 35 minutes or until bubbly. Serve with red beans and crisp green salad. Yield: 8 servings.

Bonnie Manges, Brownsville 708

MARIE'S CHICKEN ENCHILADA CASSEROLE

1 med. onion, chopped
3 tbsp. butter
1 can cream of chicken soup
1 can cream of mushroom soup
1 c. chicken broth
1 4-oz. can chopped green chilies
12 corn tortillas
2 to 2 1/2 c. coarsely chopped cooked chicken
1 lb. longhorn cheese, grated

Saute onion in butter in skillet. Add soups, broth and green chilies; mix well. Fry tortillas in 1/2 inch hot oil in skillet, turning once. Layer half the tortillas, chicken, sauce and cheese in shallow baking dish. Repeat layers. Bake at 350 degrees for 30 minutes. Yield: 6 servings.

Marie M. LaRue, Chico 486

MYRTLE'S CHICKEN ENCHILADA CASSEROLE

2 c. chopped cooked chicken
1 c. chicken broth
1 can cream of chicken soup
1/2 c. chopped green chilies
1/2 c. chopped onion
1 clove of garlic, minced
8 corn tortillas, quartered
1 c. shredded Monterey Jack cheese
1 c. shredded Cheddar cheese
1 avocado, sliced
Cherry tomatoes

Combine chicken, broth, soup, chilies, onion and garlic in bowl; mix well. Layer half the tortillas, chicken mixture and 1/2 of each cheese in buttered 2-quart casserole. Repeat layers except cheese. Bake at 350 degrees for about 50 minutes. Sprinkle remaining cheese over top. Let stand, covered, for 10 minutes. Garnish with avocado slices and tomatoes just before serving.

Myrtle Wolf, Lake Francis 745

CHICKEN MEXICANO

1 can cream of mushroom soup
1 can cream of chicken soup
1 sm. onion, grated
1 soup can milk
1 sm. can chopped chilies
Salt and pepper to taste
12 tortillas, cut into strips
3 or 4 lg. chicken breasts, cooked, chopped
1 c. grated Cheddar cheese

Combine soups, onion, milk, chilies, salt and pepper in bowl; mix well. Layer half the tortillas, chicken, soup mixture and cheese in greased 9 x 13-inch baking dish. Repeat layers. Bake at 350 degrees for 1 hour.

Alice M. McCoy, Davis 393

MEXICAN CHICKEN

1 can cream of mushroom soup
1 can cream of chicken soup
3/4 c. milk
1 sm. onion, grated
Salt and pepper to taste
12 corn tortillas, cut into strips
4 or 5 chicken breasts, cooked, cut into strips
1 4-oz. can whole green chilies, seeded, cut into strips
1 lb. Tillamook cheese, grated

Combine first 4 ingredients, salt and pepper in bowl; mix well. Layer half the tortillas, chicken, chilies, cheese and soup mixture in 9 x 13-inch baking dish. Add layers of remaining tortillas, chicken, chilies, cheese and soup mixture. Chill, covered, for 24 hours. Bake at 350 degrees for 1 hour. Yield: 6-8 servings.

Caroline Smith, Welcome 791

POLLO MEXICANO

1 can cream of chicken soup
2 cans hot chili with beans
1 sm. can chopped green chilies
4 flour tortillas, quartered
4 chicken breasts, cooked, cut into bite-sized pieces
2 c. shredded Cheddar cheese

Combine first 3 ingredients in bowl; mix well. Alternate layers of tortillas, chicken, sauce and cheese in 2 1/2-quart casserole until all ingredients are used, ending with cheese. Bake at 350 degrees for 1 hour. Yield: 4 servings.

Lori Sala, Escalon 447

VIVA LA CHICKEN

12 corn tortillas
1 can cream of chicken soup
1 can cream of mushroom soup
1 c. milk
1 onion, chopped
1 7-oz. can green chili sauce
5 c. chopped cooked chicken
4 c. shredded Cheddar cheese

Cut tortillas into 1-inch strips. Mix soups, milk, onion and chili sauce in large bowl. Layer tortillas, soup mixture, chicken and cheese alternately in greased 9 x 13-inch baking dish until all ingredients are used, ending with thick layer of cheese. Chill for 24 hours to develop maximum flavor. Bake at 350 degrees for 1 hour.

Helen Martin, Escalon 447

TORTILLA CHIP CASSEROLE

1 c. chopped onion
2 tbsp. butter
3 8-oz. cans tomato sauce
1 4-oz. can chopped green chilies
1 tsp. hot chili powder
1 tsp. dried cilantro
1 tsp. salt
1 8-oz. package taco-flavored
    tortilla chips, crushed
1 1/2 c. shredded Monterey Jack cheese
2 c. chopped cooked chicken
1 c. sour cream
1/2 c. shredded Cheddar cheese

Saute onion in butter in skillet until lightly browned. Add tomato sauce, chilies, chili powder, cilantro and salt. Simmer for 5 minutes. Alternate layers of tortilla chips, Monterey Jack cheese, chicken and sauce in buttered 1 1/2-quart casserole until all ingredients are used. Bake at 350 degrees for 25 minutes. Spread sour cream over top; sprinkle with Cheddar cheese. Bake for 5 minutes longer. Garnish with fresh cilantro or parsley.

Photograph for this recipe above.

CHICKEN SALAD CASSEROLE

2 cans cream of chicken soup
2 tbsp. instant onion flakes
3/4 c. mayonnaise
1 tbsp. lemon juice
4 c. cubed cooked chicken
1/2 c. slivered almonds
2 c. cooked rice
1 1/2 c. chopped celery
4 hard-boiled eggs, chopped
Buttered crumbs

Combine first 4 ingredients in bowl; mix well. Combine chicken, almonds, rice, celery and eggs in bowl. Add soup mixture; toss lightly. Spoon into 9 x 13-inch baking dish. Top with crumbs. Bake at 350 degrees for 40 minutes. Yield: 15 servings.

Dorothy Gardner, Ojai Valley 659

MARY'S HOT CHICKEN SALAD

4 c. chopped chicken
2 c. chopped celery
4 hard-boiled eggs, chopped
2 tbsp. lemon juice
2/3 c. slivered almonds
1 2-oz. jar chopped pimento
1 1/2 c. mayonnaise
1 tsp. salt
1/2 tsp. MSG
1 tbsp. minced onion
1 c. shredded sharp Cheddar cheese
1 1/2 c. crushed potato chips

Combine first 10 ingredients in bowl; mix well. Pour into shallow baking dish. Chill overnight. Let stand at room temperature for 2 hours. Top with cheese and potato chips. Bake at 400 degrees for 30 minutes or until heated through. Yield: 12 servings.

Mary Click, DeSabla 762

HOT CHICKEN SALAD

2 c. chopped cooked chicken
2 c. thinly sliced celery
1/2 c. chopped peanuts
1 c. mayonnaise
1/2 tsp. salt
2 tsp. grated onion
2 tsp. lemon juice
1/2 c. grated cheese
1 c. crushed potato chips

Combine all ingredients except cheese and potato chips in bowl; mix well. Spoon lightly into 6 x 8-inch baking dish. Top with cheese and potato chips. Bake at 450 degrees for 10 to 15 minutes. Yield: 8 servings.

Amy Stubbs, Lompoc 646
Marie Streyle, Lompoc 646

CHICKEN CONTINENTAL

1 3-lb. chicken, cut up
Flour
1/3 c. butter

1 can cream of chicken soup
2 1/2 tbsp. grated onion
1 tsp. salt
Dash of pepper
1 tbsp. chopped parsley
1/2 tbsp. celery flakes
1/8 tsp. thyme
1 1/3 c. minute rice

Coat chicken with flour. Brown in butter in skillet; remove chicken. Add soup, 1 1/3 cups water and remaining ingredients except rice to pan drippings; mix well. Bring to a boil, stirring constantly. Sprinkle rice in shallow 1 1/2-quart baking dish. Reserve 1/3 cup soup mixture. Mix remaining soup mixture into rice. Top with chicken. Spoon reserved soup mixture over chicken. Bake, covered, at 375 degrees for 30 minutes. Yield: 4 servings.

Vivian M. Simons, Ripon 511

FAVORITE CHICKEN-RICE CASSEROLE

1 chicken, cut up
Salt and pepper to taste
Garlic salt and paprika to taste
Lemon juice to taste
1 can cream of chicken soup
1 can mushroom soup
1 can cream of celery soup
1 c. long grain rice
1/2 c. chicken broth

Season chicken with salt, pepper, garlic salt, paprika and lemon juice. Mix soups and rice in bowl. Pour into 9 x 13-inch baking pan. Arrange chicken over mixture. Drizzle broth over top. Bake at 325 degrees for 2 hours, adding additional broth if necessary. Yield: 6 servings.

Alice Clark, Kingsburg 679

ALBERTA'S NO-PEEK CHICKEN

1 c. rice
1 can mushroom soup
1 can chicken soup
1 soup can milk
1 chicken, cut up
1/2 pkg. dry onion soup mix

Mix first 4 ingredients in bowl. Pour into greased 9 x 13-inch baking pan. Arrange chicken over mixture. Sprinkle soup mix over top. Bake, covered with foil, at 300 degrees for 2 1/2 hours. Do not peek. Yield: 4-6 servings.

Alberta Ashton, San Marcos 633

RUTH ANN'S NO-PEEK CHICKEN

1 1/2 c. rice
1 can cream of mushroom soup
1 can cream of celery soup
Salt and pepper to taste
1 chicken, cut up
1 pkg. dry onion soup mix

Combine rice, cream soups, 1 soup can water, salt and pepper in bowl; mix well. Pour into 9 x 13-inch baking dish. Arrange chicken pieces over rice mixture. Sprinkle dry soup mix over top. Bake, tightly covered with foil, at 350 degrees for 2 to 2 1/2 hours or until chicken is tender. Yield: 6-8 servings.

Ruth Ann Rowan, El Camino 462

SCALLOPED TURKEY

2 tbsp. butter
1 1/2 c. herb-seasoned stuffing mix
1/4 c. finely chopped parsley
1 can cream of chicken soup
1 c. turkey gravy
2 c. cubed cooked turkey

Heat butter with 1/2 cup water in saucepan until butter is melted; remove from heat. Add stuffing mix and parsley; toss lightly. Blend soup and gravy in saucepan. Bring to a boil, stirring constantly. Layer half the turkey, soup mixture and stuffing in greased 1 1/2-quart casserole. Repeat layers. Bake at 350 degrees for 30 minutes. Yield: 6 servings.

Alanna Hopkins, Morgan Hill 408

CHINESE HAMBURGER

1 lb. ground beef
1 can cream of chicken soup
1 can cream of mushroom soup
1 c. chopped celery
1 4-oz. can sliced mushrooms
1 c. rice
1 can chow mein noodles

Brown ground beef in skillet, stirring until crumbly; drain. Stir in soups, celery, mushrooms, rice and 1 soup can water. Pour into casserole. Bake, covered, at 350 degrees for 30 minutes. Bake, uncovered, for 30 minutes. Sprinkle noodles on top. Bake for 15 minutes longer.

Thelma Worden, Ranchito 654

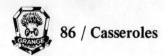

HAMBURGER-MACARONI CASSEROLE

1 1/2 lb. ground beef
1 onion, chopped
1 green pepper, chopped
1 can tomato sauce
1 can whole kernel corn, drained
1 can tomato soup
1 tsp. chili powder
Salt and pepper to taste
2 c. cooked elbow macaroni

Brown ground beef with onion and green pepper in a small amount of oil in skillet, stirring frequently; drain. Add remaining ingredients; mix well. Pour into greased 9 x 13-inch baking pan. Bake at 350 degrees for 30 minutes. Yield: 6 servings.

Mary Krogh, New Era 540

MARY'S LASAGNA

3 lb. ground beef
1 lg. onion, chopped
1 clove of garlic, chopped
1/4 c. olive oil
2 lg. cans tomato sauce
1 lg. can tomato paste
1 sm. can mushrooms
1/2 green pepper, chopped
2 tbsp. wine vinegar
1 tbsp. sugar
3 tbsp. Worcestershire sauce
Dash of Tabasco sauce
1 tbsp. each thyme, oregano,
    rosemary and basil
1 8-oz. box lasagna noodles, cooked
1 lb. mozzarella cheese, grated
1 lb. provolone cheese, grated
1 lg. ricotta cheese

Brown ground beef with onion and garlic in olive oil in skillet, stirring frequently. Add tomato sauce, tomato paste, mushrooms, green pepper, vinegar, sugar and seasonings; mix well. Simmer for 1 hour. Layer noodles, sauce and cheeses alternately in 15-inch baking dish until all ingredients are used, ending with cheese. Bake at 325 degrees until golden brown and bubbly. Yield: 8-12 servings.

Mary Fairbanks, Lompoc 646

EASY SPINACH LASAGNA

1/2 lb. ground beef
1 med. onion, chopped
1 32-oz. jar spaghetti sauce
Salt to taste
1 10-oz. package frozen chopped
    spinach, thawed
1 c. ricotta cheese
1/2 c. Parmesan cheese
2 eggs
1/2 tsp. salt
1/4 tsp. pepper
1/8 tsp. nutmeg
1 8-oz. package lasagna noodles
12 oz. mozzarella cheese, sliced
Parmesan cheese

Brown ground beef with onion in skillet, stirring frequently; drain. Add spaghetti sauce, 1 cup water and salt to taste. Bring to a boil; set aside. Squeeze excess moisture from spinach. Combine spinach, ricotta, 1/2 cup Parmesan cheese, eggs, 1/2 teaspoon salt, pepper and nutmeg in blender container. Process until smooth. Reserve a small amount of ground beef sauce. Pour remaining sauce in 9 x 13-inch baking dish. Arrange uncooked lasagna noodles in sauce. Place half the mozzarella cheese slices over noodles. Spread spinach mixture over cheese. Spoon reserved ground beef sauce over layers. Arrange remaining mozzarella cheese slices over sauce. Sprinkle Parmesan cheese over all. Bake at 375 degrees for 1 hour. Yield: 6-8 servings.

Betty Lee Myers, Ceres 520

WALT'S LASAGNA

4 lb. ground beef
1 lb. sweet Italian sausage
4 med. onions, chopped
4 16-oz. cans tomato puree
4 tsp. garlic powder
4 tsp. oregano
1 tsp. Italian seasoning
1 tsp. pepper
4 15-oz. cartons ricotta cheese
1 c. grated Romano cheese
4 eggs
2 1-lb. packages lasagna
    noodles, cooked
1/2 c. flour
1 lb. mozzarella cheese, grated
1 c. grated Romano cheese

Brown ground beef, sausage and onions in skillet, stirring frequently; drain. Stir in tomato puree and seasonings. Combine ricotta, 1 cup Romano cheese and eggs in bowl; mix well. Place half the lasagna in one 10 x 18-inch casserole. Sprinkle with 1/4 cup flour. Layer half the ricotta mixture, half the meat sauce and half the mozzarella cheese on top. Sprinkle 1/2 cup Romano cheese on top. Repeat process in second casserole. Bake at 350 degrees for 30 minutes or until bubbly. Yield: 40 servings.

Walter Kimbrough, Airport 820

MORE

1 lb. ground beef
1 onion, chopped
1 green pepper, chopped
1 8-oz. package uncooked noodles
1 16-oz. can corn
1 4-oz. can mushrooms
1 8-oz. can tomato sauce
Grated cheese

Saute ground beef with onion and green pepper in skillet, stirring frequently. Alternate layers of noodles, ground beef and vegetables in greased 9 x 12-inch casserole. Pour sauce over top; mix gently. Bake at 350 degrees for 45 minutes. Top with cheese. Bake for several minutes longer or until cheese melts. Yield: 6-8 servings.

Mildred Meek, French Camp-Lathrop 510

MY FAVORITE GROUND BEEF CASSEROLE

1/2 lb. ground beef
1 sm. onion, chopped
1 green pepper, chopped
1 1/2 c. cooked macaroni
1 sm. can sliced olives
2 cans tomato sauce
1 can Mexicorn
1 c. grated Cheddar cheese
Bread crumbs

Saute ground beef with onion and green pepper in skillet, stirring frequently; drain. Combine with macaroni, olives, tomato sauce and corn in greased casserole. Top with cheese and bread crumbs. Bake at 350 degrees for 30 to 45 minutes or until heated through.

Leonard Jackson, Humboldt 501

ENCHILADA CASSEROLE

1 lb. ground round
1 lg. onion, chopped
Salt, pepper and chili powder to taste
1 sm. can chopped olives
2 8-oz. cans tomato sauce
1 16-oz. can corn, drained
1 16-oz. can pinto beans, drained
6 to 8 tortillas, buttered
1 lb. sharp cheese, grated

Brown ground round with onion in skillet, stirring until crumbly. Add seasonings, olives, tomato sauce, corn and beans; mix well. Layer a portion of the sauce, half the tortillas, meat sauce and half the cheese in 9 x 13-inch baking dish. Repeat layers with remaining ingredients. Pour 2/3 cup water carefully over casserole just before baking. Bake, covered, at 400 degrees for 30 minutes. Yield: 6 servings.
Note: May prepare the day before and refrigerate until baking time.

Charlotte Hyun, Ceres 520

LAYERED ENCHILADA PIE

1 lb. ground beef
1 onion, chopped
2 tsp. salt
1/4 tsp. pepper
1 tbsp. chili powder
1 lg. can Las Palmas enchilada sauce
6 buttered tortillas
1 4 1/2-oz. can chopped ripe olives
Green onions, sliced
1 1/2 c. grated sharp Cheddar cheese

Brown ground beef and onion in skillet. Add seasonings and sauce. Alternate layers of tortillas, meat sauce, olives, green onions and cheese in 9 x 13-inch casserole. Add 1 cup water. Bake, covered, at 400 degrees for 20 minutes. Yield: 6 servings.

Vivian M. Simons, Ripon 511

DALZIRE'S TAMALE PIE

1 lb. ground beef
1 onion, chopped
1 jar ripe olives
2 16-oz. cans tomatoes
1 20-oz. can cream-style corn
1/2 c. yellow cornmeal
1 tsp. Grandma's seasoning
Salt and pepper to taste

Brown ground beef in skillet, stirring until crumbly; drain. Add remaining ingredients; mix well. Pour into greased casserole. Bake at 350 degrees for 30 minutes.

Dalzire Bock, Fair Valley 752

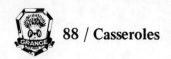

IRENE'S TAMALE CASSEROLE

1 can tamales
1 lg. can hominy, drained
1 can mushroom soup
Grated cheese

Break tamales into small pieces. Combine with hominy and soup in casserole; mix well. Sprinkle cheese on top. Bake at 350 degrees for 45 minutes. Yield: 6 servings.

Irene Beyer, Wyandotte 495

CALIFORNIA TAMALE PIE

1 lb. ground beef
1 onion, chopped
1 or 2 green peppers, chopped
1 can whole kernel corn
1 can pitted olives
1 can tomato sauce
2 c. milk
1 tsp. Spanish seasoning
Salt and pepper to taste
2 c. cornmeal

Brown ground beef with onion and green pepper in skillet, stirring frequently. Add corn, olives, tomato sauce, milk and seasonings; mix well. Bring to a boil. Stir in cornmeal gradually. Pour into greased 9 x 13-inch baking dish. Bake at 350 degrees for 1 1/2 hours or until browned. Yield: 6 servings.

Eva Christensen, Van Duzen River 517

CECILIA'S TAMALE PIE

1 1/4 c. cornmeal
1 tsp. each salt, chili powder
1 lb. ground beef
1/2 c. chopped onion
1/2 c. grated Cheddar cheese
1/2 c. whole kernel corn
2 c. canned tomatoes
1/2 c. olives
1 to 2 tbsp. chili powder
1/2 to 1 tsp. garlic salt
1/2 tsp. salt
1/2 c. grated Cheddar cheese

Combine cornmeal with 1 teaspoon salt, 1 teaspoon chili powder and 2 1/2 cups water in saucepan. Cook for 15 minutes or until thickened, stirring constantly. Line 6 x 10-inch casserole with half the mixture. Brown ground beef with onion in skillet, stirring until crumbly; drain. Stir in next 7 ingredients; mix

well. Simmer for 20 minutes. Pour into prepared casserole. Spoon remaining cornmeal mixture over top. Sprinkle with 1/2 cup cheese. Bake at 350 degrees for 45 minutes.

Cecilia E. Like, Loma Rica 802

QUICK CRESCENT TACO PIE

1 to 1 1/4 lb. ground beef
1 pkg. taco seasoning mix
1/3 c. sliced olives
1 can refrigerator crescent dinner rolls
1 c. crushed corn chips
1 c. sour cream
1 c. shredded cheese
1/2 to 1 c. crushed corn chips
Shredded lettuce
Avocado slices

Brown ground beef in skillet, stirring frequently; drain. Stir in seasoning mix, 1/2 cup water and olives. Simmer for 5 minutes. Press crescent rolls into pie plate to form pie shell; seal perforations. Sprinkle 1 cup corn chips in prepared pie plate. Spoon ground beef mixture over chips. Spread with sour cream. Top with cheese and 1/2 to 1 cup corn chips. Bake at 375 degrees for 20 minutes or until crust is browned. Cut into wedges. Top servings with lettuce and avocado. Yield: 4-6 servings.

Alberta Ashton, San Marcos 633

BEEF AND BISCUIT CASSEROLE

1 lb. ground beef
1/2 onion, chopped
1/4 green pepper, chopped
2 tsp. chili powder
1/2 tsp. garlic powder
1 8-oz. can tomato sauce
3/4 c. grated Cheddar cheese
3/4 c. grated Monterey Jack cheese
1/2 c. sour cream
1 egg, beaten
1 10-count can flaky
*   refrigerator biscuits*

Brown ground beef with onion and green pepper in skillet, stirring until crumbly; drain. Add chili powder, garlic powder and tomato sauce; mix well. Simmer for several minutes. Mix cheeses. Combine sour cream, egg and 3/4 cup mixed cheese in bowl. Stir into ground beef mixture; mix well. Split biscuits. Arrange half in 8 x 8-inch baking dish. Pour sauce over biscuits. Top with remaining biscuits. Sprinkle with remaining mixed cheese. Bake at 350 degrees for 30 minutes. Yield: 8 servings.

Anna L. Hansen, Gold Hill 326

CALICO BEANS

1/2 lb. bacon finely chopped
1 lb. ground beef
1 med. onion, grated
1 lg. can pork and beans
1 can red kidney beans
1 can butter beans
1/2 c. catsup
1/2 c. packed brown sugar
2 tbsp. vinegar
1/2 tsp. salt

Brown bacon, ground beef and onion in skillet, stirring frequently; drain. Drain beans, reserving liquid. Combine beans and ground beef mixture in 3-quart casserole. Pour mixture of catsup, sugar, vinegar and salt over top. Bake at 350 degrees for 1 hour, adding reserved bean liquid if necessary. Yield: 6-8 servings.

Ruth Christensen, Tulelake 468

CHUCK WAGON BAKE

1 lb. ground beef
1/2 c. each chopped celery, green
    pepper and onion
1 6-oz. can tomato paste
1 21-oz. can pork and beans
1 15-oz. can kidney beans
2 tsp. chili powder
10 sm. cubes cheese
1 10-count pkg. refrigerator biscuits
Milk
Crushed corn chips

Brown ground beef in skillet, stirring until crumbly. Add celery, green pepper and onion. Cook until vegetables are tender, stirring constantly; drain. Stir in tomato paste, beans, chili powder and 1/2 cup water. Simmer for several minutes. Place 1 cube cheese in center of each biscuit. Fold to enclose cheese, sealing edges. Dip in milk and corn chips. Pour ground beef mixture into 9 x 13-inch baking dish. Arrange cheese biscuits on top. Bake at 400 degrees for 15 to 18 minutes or until biscuits are golden brown. Yield: 8-10 servings.

Beryl Lawson, Anderson 418

PIZZA BEANS

1 lb. ground beef
1/4 c. chopped green pepper
1/2 c. chopped onion
1 c. chopped celery
1 6-oz. can tomato sauce
2 tbsp. vinegar
1 clove of garlic, crushed
1 tsp. brown sugar
1 tsp. dry mustard
1 28-oz. can baked beans

Brown ground beef in skillet, stirring frequently; drain. Add remaining ingredients except beans; mix well. Simmer for 5 minutes. Add beans. Pour into 2-quart casserole. Bake at 350 degrees for 45 minutes. Yield: 6 servings.

Karen E. Miller, Tulelake 468

WESTERN MEAL-IN-ONE

1 lb. ground beef
1 tbsp. oil
1 lg. onion, chopped
1 tsp. salt
1 tsp. chili powder
1 can tomatoes, chopped
1 c. kidney beans
3/4 c. rice
1/4 c. sliced ripe olives
3/4 c. shredded Cheddar cheese

Brown ground beef in oil in skillet. Add onion, salt and chili powder. Saute for 5 minutes. Add tomatoes, beans and rice. Pour into casserole. Bake, covered, at 350 degrees for 45 minutes. Sprinkle with olives and cheese. Bake, uncovered, for 15 minutes. Yield: 8 servings.

Annetta Griffith, Berry Creek 694

CABBAGE CASSEROLE

1 lg. onion, chopped
1 lb. ground beef
3 tbsp. margarine
6 c. cabbage
1 tsp. salt
1 tsp. pepper
1 can tomato soup

Saute onion and ground beef in margarine in skillet until browned. Spread 3 cups cabbage in 2-quart casserole. Spoon ground beef mixture over cabbage. Sprinkle with seasonings. Layer remaining cabbage and soup over top. Bake at 350 degrees for 1 hour. Yield: 6 servings.

Carl Christensen, Van Duzen-River 517

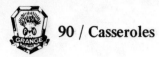

COTTAGE NOODLES

1 lb. ground beef
2 tbsp. butter
1   8-oz. can tomato sauce
1 1/4 tsp. garlic salt
1/8 tsp. pepper
1   8-oz. package egg noodles, cooked
1 1/2 c. sour cream
1 1/2 c. cottage cheese
6 green onions, sliced
3/4 c. grated Monterey Jack cheese

Brown ground beef in butter in skillet, stirring until crumbly. Add tomato sauce and seasonings. Combine noodles, sour cream, cottage cheese and green onions in bowl; mix well. Alternate layers of noodle mixture and sauce in 2-quart casserole until all ingredients are used, ending with sauce. Top with cheese. Bake at 350 degrees for 30 minutes. Yield: 4-6 servings.

Anna Warner, Ripon 511

HOT DISH DELISH

4 oz. noodles
1 tsp. salt
1 sm. onion, chopped
1/2 c. chopped celery
1/4 c. chopped green pepper
1/4 c. butter
1 lb. ground beef
1/2 c. milk
1 can cream of mushroom soup
1 can cream of chicken soup
1/4 c. mayonnaise

Cook noodles with salt in 2 quarts boiling water in saucepan using package directions. Saute onion, celery and green pepper in butter in skillet until browned. Brown ground beef in skillet, stirring until crumbly; drain. Add sauteed vegetables, milk, soups and mayonnaise; mix well. Stir in noodles. Pour into greased 2-quart casserole. Bake at 350 degrees for 1 hour. Yield: 6 servings.

Margaret R. Scott, San Jose 10

JUNK FOOD CASSEROLE

1 lb. ground beef
1 med. onion, finely chopped
1   6-oz. can tomato sauce
1 sm. can corn
1 sm. can sliced olives
1 1/2 c. shredded Cheddar cheese
Corn chips

Brown ground beef with onion in skillet, stirring frequently; drain. Add tomato sauce, corn and olives. Cook until heated through, stirring constantly. Pour into casserole. Top with cheese and chips. Bake at 350 degrees until cheese melts.

Helena Griffith, Humboldt 501

POTATO PUFF CASSEROLE

1 lb. ground beef
1/3 c. chopped onion
1/3 c. chopped green pepper
1 tbsp. catsup
1 can cream of mushroom soup
1   10-oz. package frozen potato puffs

Brown ground beef with onion and green pepper in skillet, stirring frequently. Add catsup, soup and 1/4 cup water; mix well. Pour into 1 1/2-quart casserole. Top with potato puffs. Bake at 375 degrees for 35 minutes or until potatoes are golden brown. Yield: 4 servings.

Elizabeth Poncia, Orland 432

TATER TOT CASSEROLE

1 lb. ground beef
1 can cream of chicken soup
1/4 c. milk
1 sm. package Tater Tots

Press ground beef evenly over bottom of 8-inch baking pan. Pour mixture of soup and milk over ground beef. Place enough Tater Tots on top to cover. Bake at 350 degrees for 45 minutes. Yield: 6 servings.

Clara M. Peterson, Golden Empire 806

ZUCCHINI-GROUND BEEF BAKE

2/3 lb. ground beef
1 sm. clove of garlic, chopped
2 tbsp. oil
1 sm. onion, chopped
1/2 c. rice
2 tbsp. chopped green pepper
1 c. tomato sauce
1 c. mixed vegetable juice
1/2 tsp. salt
4 zucchini, thinly sliced
Parmesan cheese

Brown ground beef with garlic in oil in skillet, stirring until crumbly. Add onion, rice, green pepper, tomato sauce, vegetable juice, salt and 1/4 cup water; mix well. Cook for 5 minutes.

Arrange 1/3 of the zucchini slices in 9 x 13-inch baking dish. Add alternate layers of sauce and zucchini. Top with cheese. Bake at 275 degrees for 1 1/2 hours. Yield: 5 servings.

Mary Krogh, New Era 540

BEEF AND BEAN BAKE

1 c. dried navy beans
2 lb. cubed stew beef
2 tbsp. flour
2 tsp. salt
2 tbsp. bacon drippings
1 8-oz. can tomato sauce
3 sm. onions, cut into halves
2 tbsp. mustard
1 tsp. chili powder

Combine beans and 6 cups water in saucepan. Bring to a boil. Simmer for 2 to 3 minutes; remove from heat. Let stand for 1 hour. Coat beef cubes with mixture of flour and salt. Brown in bacon drippings in skillet; drain. Drain beans, reserving 2 cups liquid. Combine beef, beans, reserved liquid, tomato sauce, onions, mustard and chili powder in casserole; mix well. Bake, covered, at 325 degrees for 2 to 2 1/2 hours or until beans and beef are tender. Yield: 6-8 servings.

Photograph for this recipe below.

VEGERONI-HOT DOG CASSEROLE

1 lb. vegeroni
1 med. onion, chopped

1 lb. frankfurters, cut into
1-in. pieces
2 tbsp. margarine
1/2 c. Parmesan cheese
2 8-oz. cans tomato sauce

Cook vegeroni in boiling water in saucepan until tender; drain. Saute onion and frankfurters in skillet until browned. Layer vegeroni, onion, frankfurters, margarine and cheese in 2 1/2-quart casserole. Pour tomato sauce over layers. Sprinkle with additional Parmesan cheese. Bake at 350 degrees for 35 minutes.

June McMillan, Whitesboro 766

BAKED PORK CHOPS
AND VEGETABLES

4 pork chops
Salt, pepper and paprika to taste
2 tbsp. oil
1 can cream of mushroom soup
1/2 c. sour cream
1 tsp. parsley flakes
4 c. frozen country-style dinner fries
1 8-oz. can cut green beans, drained

Season pork chops with salt, pepper and paprika. Brown in oil in skillet over medium-high heat. Remove pork chops; drain drippings. Add soup, sour cream and parsley to skillet. Cook over low heat until heated through. Do not boil. Layer potatoes, green beans, sour cream mixture and pork chops in shallow 2-quart casserole. Bake at 400 degrees for 45 minutes or until pork chops are tender. Yield: 4 servings.

Eulalia Archer, Bellevue 374

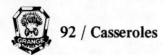

EASY SAUSAGE CASSEROLE

4 c. sliced cooked potatoes
1 4-oz. can mushrooms, drained
1/3 c. sliced celery
1 can cream of mushroom soup
1/2 c. shredded Cheddar cheese
1 8-oz. package brown and serve
  link sausage
1/2 c. shredded Cheddar cheese

Combine potatoes, mushrooms, celery, soup and 1/2 cup cheese in bowl; mix well. Pour into buttered 1 1/2-quart casserole. Arrange sausage over potatoes. Sprinkle with 1/2 cup cheese. Bake at 350 degrees for 35 minutes.

Virginia M. Loftin, Los Banos 79

SAUSAGE AND RICE

2 lb. pork sausage
1 bunch celery, chopped
1 green pepper, chopped
2 sm. onions, chopped
2 c. uncooked rice
3 pkg. dry chicken noodle soup mix
1 c. blanched almonds

Brown sausage in skillet, stirring until crumbly; drain. Add remaining ingredients; mix well. Pour into 15 x 15-inch baking dish. Add 7 cups water; mix well. Bake at 350 degrees for 1 1/4 hours, stirring occasionally. Cover casserole if top becomes too brown. Yield: 16 servings.

Bertha Kellogg, Bear Creek 530

MARTHA'S SAUSAGE CASSEROLE

1 lb. hot sausage
1 c. chopped onion
1 c. uncooked rice
1 c. chopped celery
1 4-oz. can mushrooms
2 cans chicken soup

Brown sausage with onion in skillet, stirring until crumbly; drain. Add remaining ingredients and 3 cups water; mix well. Pour into casserole. Bake at 325 degrees for 1 1/2 hours. Yield: 10 servings.

Martha M. Tennant, Grover City 746

BONNIE'S TAMALE PIE

2 lg. onions, chopped
1/2 c. oil
2 tbsp. butter
2 cloves of garlic, chopped
2 c. chopped cooked ham
1 lg. can tomatoes
1 c. cream-style corn
3 tbsp. chili powder
Salt and pepper to taste
3 eggs, beaten
2 c. milk
2 to 3 c. cornmeal
1 can pitted olives, drained
Grated cheese (opt.)

Saute onions in oil and butter in skillet until tender. Add garlic and ham. Cook for several minutes, stirring constantly. Stir in tomatoes, corn, seasonings and mixture of eggs and milk. Sprinkle enough cornmeal to make of desired consistency over top; mix well. Cook for 15 minutes, stirring constantly. Stir in olives. Pour into greased 9 x 13-inch baking pan. Sprinkle with cheese. Bake at 350 degrees for 30 minutes. Yield: 8-10 servings.
Note: May substitute 1 pound ground beef browned with onions for ham.

Bonnie Peppers, Napa 307

BAKED TONGUE AND NOODLES

3/4 lb. sliced cooked tongue
3 1/2 c. cooked noodles
2 c. cooked tomatoes
1/4 c. cracker crumbs
1 tbsp. butter

Alternate layers of tongue and noodles in 7 x 11-inch casserole. Add tomatoes. Sprinkle crumbs over top; dot with butter. Bake at 350 degrees for 30 minutes. Yield: 6 servings.

Agnes Shideler, Hessel 750

TUNA CASSEROLE

1 7-oz. can tuna
2 c. small green peas
1 c. mushroom soup
3 hard-boiled eggs, sliced
1/2 c. chopped pimento
1 green pepper, chopped
1 8-oz. package macaroni, cooked
1 1/2 c. thick white sauce
Salt and pepper to taste

Layer ingredients in order listed in greased 1 1/2-quart casserole. Bake at 325 degrees for 45 minutes. Yield: 6-8 servings.

Elizabeth Collins, Wood Colony 522

DESSERTS

Avery's High Lift Sulky Plow
(Patent applied for.)

The operator is not obliged to lift the plow plus its load of dirt. A slight pressure upon the foot-lift inclines the point of the plow upward, and it then leaves the ground of its own accord.

The frame is substantial and strongly braced, adequate to resist any strain which may be brought to bear upon it. The lifting devices are so well balanced that a boy can lift the plow from the bottom of the furrow to its transport position. The lift is the highest, and the consequent convenience and ease of transportation are much appreciated by users. All sizes and styles.

Uncle Sam Middle Burster Sulky
(PATENTED)

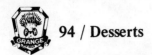

HARRIET'S BOSTON CREAM PIES

1 2-layer pkg. yellow cake mix
1 pkg. vanilla instant pudding mix
1 8-oz. carton whipped topping
1/4 c. cocoa
1/4 c. hot coffee
2 tbsp. light corn syrup
2 tbsp. butter
2 c. confectioners' sugar
Pinch of salt
1/2 tsp. vanilla extract

Prepare and bake cake mix according to package directions for 2 layer cake pans. Cool; split each layer in half. Combine pudding mix and whipped topping in bowl. Place one split layer on serving plate. Spread half the pudding mixture over top. Place second layer on top. Repeat with remaining layers on second serving plate. Combine cocoa, hot coffee, corn syrup and butter in bowl. Stir until butter melts. Beat in remaining ingredients until well blended. Spread glaze over top of each pie. Yield: 16 servings.

Harriet Wilson, Van Duzen River 517

MICROWAVE BOSTON CREAM PIE

1 2-layer pkg. yellow cake mix
1/3 c. sugar
1 tbsp. cornstarch
1/4 tsp. salt
1 c. milk
1 egg, beaten
1/4 tsp. vanilla extract
1 sq. unsweetened chocolate
2 tbsp. butter
1 c. confectioners' sugar

Prepare cake mix using package directions. Grease sides of 2 waxed paper-lined 8-inch glass baking dishes. Spoon cake mix into dishes. Microwave, 1 at a time, on High for 3 1/2 to 4 1/2 minutes or until cake tests done. Cool in dishes for 5 minutes. Remove from dishes to racks; cool completely. Combine next 4 ingredients in glass measure. Microwave on High for 3 to 4 minutes or until boiling, stirring twice in last half of cooking time. Stir a small amount of hot mixture into egg; stir egg into hot mixture. Microwave for 1/2 to 1 minute or until mixture bubbles. Stir in vanilla. Cool until thickened. Microwave chocolate and butter in glass bowl on High for 1 1/2 to 2 minutes or until melted. Add confectioners' sugar and 1 1/2 to 2 1/2 tablespoons hot water to make

of spreading consistency. Place 1 cake layer top side down on serving plate. Spread custard filling over layer. Top with second layer bottom side up. Spoon chocolate glaze over top. Chill until serving time. Yield: 8-10 servings.

Mildred Lovelette, Fair Valley 752

RUSSIAN CREAM

4 tbsp. unflavored gelatin
3 c. sugar
4 c. light cream, chilled
6 c. sour cream
4 tsp. vanilla extract
1 pkg. frozen unsweetened raspberries
3 tbsp. rum
1/2 c. sugar

Soften gelatin in 2 cups water in saucepan. Stir in sugar. Bring to a boil; mix well. Let stand for 4 to 5 minutes. Add cream, sour cream and vanilla, blending with wire whisk after each addition. Pour into bundt pan. Chill until firm. Unmold on serving plate. Combine remaining ingredients in blender container. Puree until smooth. Pour over Russian Cream just before serving. Yield: 20 servings.

Edith Piper, Orland 432

LADY GODIVA PIE

1 pkg. ladyfingers
1 recipe vanilla pudding
1/2 pt. whipping cream, whipped

Line side of 9-inch round casserole with ladyfingers. Fill with vanilla pudding. Spread whipped cream on top. Decorate with shaved sweet chocolate.

Glenn Griffith, Humboldt 501

FRESH ORANGE CUSTARD BRULEE

1 env. unflavored gelatin
2 tbsp. fresh orange juice
2 c. light cream
1 c. milk
5 egg yolks, lightly beaten
1/4 c. sugar
1 tsp. vanilla extract
Candied Orange Slices
1/2 c. packed light brown sugar

Soften gelatin in orange juice. Scald cream and milk in double boiler. Beat egg yolks and sugar in bowl until sugar is dissolved. Stir a small amount of hot mixture into egg yolk mixture; stir egg yolks into hot mixture. Cook over hot water until thickened, stirring constantly. Stir in vanilla and gelatin mixture; mix until gelatin is dissolved. Pour into shallow 1 1/2-quart dish. Chill until firm. Arrange Candied Orange Slices on top. Sprinkle brown sugar over slices and custard. Broil for 1 minute or until brown sugar is melted. Serve immediately or chill until serving time.

CANDIED ORANGE SLICES

3/4 c. sugar
2 med. oranges

Combine sugar and 1/2 cup water in small saucepan. Cook to 240 degrees on candy thermometer. Cut each orange in half lengthwise; cut each half into thin slices. Cook orange slices several at a time in boiling syrup for 5 minutes. Remove from syrup with slotted spoon. Pour remaining syrup over oranges. Cool thoroughly.

Photograph for this recipe below.

OLD-FASHIONED CUSTARD

7 or 8 eggs
1/2 c. sugar

1 tsp. each cinnamon, nutmeg
1 tbsp. vanilla extract
1 qt. milk, scalded, cooled

Beat eggs in bowl until thick. Add sugar, cinnamon, nutmeg and vanilla; mix well. Stir in milk. Pour into 2-quart baking dish. Place in pan of water. Bake at 325 degrees for 1 hour. Yield: 5-6 servings.

Pauline Alleman, Ripon 511

FREDA'S PETITE CHEESECAKES

20 to 24 vanilla wafers
2 8-oz. packages cream cheese, softened
3/4 c. sugar
1 tbsp. lemon juice
2 eggs
1 tsp. vanilla extract
Canned blueberry pie filling
Whipped cream

Place 1 vanilla wafer in bottom of paper-lined muffin cups. Combine cream cheese, sugar, lemon juice, eggs and vanilla in bowl; mix well. Fill each muffin cup 2/3 full. Bake at 350 degrees for 15 minutes; cool. Spoon pie filling onto cheesecakes. Top with dollop of whipped cream. Garnish with blueberries. Yield: 20-24 servings.

Margaret Bell, Keyes 524

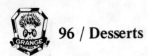

CATHERINE'S CHEESECAKE

2 c. graham cracker crumbs
2 tbsp. sugar
6 tbsp. margarine, softened
3 8-oz. packages cream cheese, softened
4 eggs, separated
1 tsp. vanilla extract
2 tsp. lemon juice
1 c. sugar
1 8-oz. carton sour cream
2 tbsp. sugar

Combine crumbs, 2 tablespoons sugar and margarine in bowl; mix well. Press over bottom of 8 or 9-inch springform pan. Combine cream cheese, egg yolks, vanilla and lemon juice in bowl; mix well. Beat egg whites in bowl until soft peaks form. Add 1 cup sugar gradually, beating until stiff peaks form. Fold gently into cream cheese mixture. Spoon into prepared pan. Bake at 350 degrees for 40 minutes. Mix sour cream with 2 tablespoons sugar in bowl. Spread on cheesecake. Bake at 450 degrees for 5 minutes. Cool before cutting.
Yield: 12 servings.

Catherine Dexter, Apple Valley 593

APPLE PUDDING

1/2 c. margarine, softened
1/2 c. sugar
1/2 c. light corn syrup
1 egg
1 c. flour
1 tsp. each soda, nutmeg
1/4 tsp. salt
2 c. chopped apples
1 c. chopped nuts
1 c. butter, softened
1 c. sifted confectioners' sugar
1 tbsp. cornstarch
1 tsp. vinegar
1 1/2 tsp. vanilla extract

Blend margarine, sugar and corn syrup in bowl. Beat in egg. Stir in next 4 sifted dry ingredients. Add mixture of apples and nuts; mix well. Pour into greased 9 x 9-inch baking pan. Bake at 350 degrees for 45 minutes. Cream 1 cup butter in bowl. Add confectioners' sugar gradually; cream well. Combine cornstarch and 1 cup cold water in saucepan. Cook until mixture is thickened and clear, stirring constantly. Stir into creamed mixture; mix well. Add vinegar and vanilla. Serve warm over hot or cold pudding.

Erol Vickery, San Dimas 658

BREAD PUDDING

4 c. stale bread crumbs
1 c. raisins
3 eggs, slightly beaten
1 c. light cream
1 c. milk
1 c. sugar
1/2 tsp. cloves
1/4 tsp. nutmeg

Pour 1 cup hot water over bread crumbs and raisins in bowl. Let stand for 10 minutes. Mix eggs, cream, milk, sugar and spices in small bowl. Add to bread crumbs; mix gently. Pour into greased 5 x 10-inch baking dish. Bake at 350 degrees for 35 to 40 minutes or until pudding tests done. Yield: 8 servings.

Maud Ray, Mt. Lassen 417

DATE PUDDING

4 egg whites
1/4 c. (heaping) sugar
3 tbsp. flour
Pinch of salt
1 tsp. baking powder
2 c. chopped dates
1 c. chopped nuts
1 tsp. vanilla extract

Beat egg whites in bowl until stiff peaks form. Add sugar gradually, beating until very stiff. Sift flour, salt and baking powder together into bowl. Fold gently into egg whites. Fold in dates, nuts and vanilla. Pour into greased 9 x 11-inch baking pan. Bake at 325 degrees for 1 hour or until set. Serve warm or cold. Garnish with whipped cream. Yield: 6-8 servings.

Hazel Shellberg, Hangtown 464

FRUIT SALAD PUDDING

1 20-oz. can pineapple chunks
1 29-oz. can peaches
1 lg. package vanilla instant pudding mix
3 tbsp. (heaping) powdered orange
    breakfast drink mix
1 sm. can mandarin oranges, drained
5 med. bananas, sliced

Drain pineapple and peaches, reserving juices. Combine pudding mix and breakfast drink mix in bowl. Add reserved juices; mix well. Chop peaches. Stir peaches and remaining fruit into pudding. Chill in refrigerator. Yield: 8 servings.

Emma Mansfield, Hesperia 682

GRANDMA'S LEMON PUDDING

3 tbsp. butter, softened
1 c. sugar
5 tbsp. flour
Dash of salt
3 eggs, separated
Juice of 2 lemons
1 c. milk

Cream butter in bowl. Mix in sugar, flour and salt. Beat egg yolks with lemon juice and milk. Add to creamed mixture; mix well. Fold in stiffly beaten egg whites gently. Spoon into buttered deep baking dish. Place in pan of water. Bake at 350 degrees for 45 minutes. Yield: 6 servings.

Lenora Sprock, Whitesboro 766

GRAPE-GLAZED STEAMED PUDDING

1/2 c. butter, softened
1 1/2 c. Smucker's grape jelly
2 eggs
1 c. whole wheat flour
3/4 c. all-purpose flour
1/4 c. wheat germ
2 1/2 tsp. baking powder
1 tsp. pumpkin pie spice
1/2 tsp. salt
1/2 c. milk
1/2 c. chopped walnuts
1/2 c. seedless raisins
1/2 c. Smucker's grape jelly, melted

Cream butter in large mixer bowl until fluffy. Beat in 1 1/2 cups grape jelly. Add eggs; beat until well blended. Add flours, wheat germ, baking powder, pie spice, salt and milk. Beat at low speed until mixed. Beat at medium speed until fluffy. Fold in walnuts and raisins. Spoon into greased and lightly floured steamed pudding mold. Cover tightly with greased foil. Place on rack in large saucepan. Pour in enough boiling water to come half way up side of mold. Simmer, covered, for 1 1/2 hours or until pudding tests done. Let stand in pan on rack for 5 minutes. Loosen edge; invert on serving plate. Brush melted jelly over pudding. Garnish with walnut halves.

Photograph for this recipe on page 70.

MARSHMALLOW PUDDING

1/2 pt. whipping cream, whipped
30 marshmallows, chopped
1/2 c. chopped nuts
1/2 c. sugar
Pinch of salt
6 bananas, mashed
1 tbsp. lemon juice

Combine whipped cream, marshmallows, nuts, sugar and salt in bowl; mix well. Chill until serving time. Stir in mashed bananas and lemon juice. Garnish with whole marshmallows and maraschino cherries. Yield: 9 servings.

Byron Kearne, Yucaipa Valley 582

PANHANDLER'S PUDDING

20 slices stale bread
1 c. sugar
1/2 tsp. salt
1 tsp. ginger
1/2 tsp. nutmeg
1/2 c. (or more) raisins
Butter
1 pt. whipping cream, whipped
Candied cherries

Pour enough hot water over bread in bowl to moisten. Let stand for several minutes. Press excess water from bread; mash. Add sugar, salt, spices and raisins; mix well. Spoon into buttered 3-quart casserole. Dot with butter. Bake at 325 degrees for 30 minutes or until set. Serve hot or cold topped with whipped cream and cherry. Yield: 10-12 servings.

Phyllis B. Helms, Encinitas 634

PERSIMMON PUDDING

1 c. persimmon pulp
1/2 c. milk
1 tbsp. melted butter
1 tsp. vanilla extract
1 c. flour
3/4 c. sugar
1/2 tsp. each baking powder, soda
*   and cinnamon*
1/4 tsp. each nutmeg, salt

Combine persimmon, milk, butter and vanilla in bowl; mix well. Add sifted dry ingredients; mix well. Pour into buttered 6 x 8-inch baking dish. Place in pan of hot water. Bake at 350 degrees for 1 hour. Serve with lemon sauce or Brandy sauce. Yield: 10 servings.

Edith A. McCoy, Rough and Ready 795

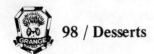

RICE-RAISIN PUDDING

1 c. cooked rice
2 c. milk
2 eggs, separated
1/2 c. sugar
1/4 tsp. salt
Raisins to taste
1/2 tsp. vanilla extract
1/4 c. sugar

Combine rice and milk in double boiler. Heat just to a simmer. Beat egg yolks with 1/2 cup sugar and salt in bowl. Stir a small amount of hot mixture into egg yolks; stir egg yolks into hot mixture. Cook until mixture thickens, stirring constantly. Stir in raisins and vanilla. Pour into buttered baking dish. Beat egg whites in bowl until stiff peaks form. Add 1/4 cup sugar gradually, beating until sugar dissolves. Spread over pudding, sealing to side of dish. Bake at 350 degrees for several minutes or until lightly browned. Yield: 4-5 servings.

Mary C. Bey, Encinitas 634

STOVE-TOP RICE PUDDING

1 c. rice
4 c. milk
3 eggs
3/4 c. sugar
1/2 tsp. salt
1 1/2 tsp. vanilla extract
Cinnamon

Stir rice into 3 cups boiling water in saucepan. Simmer, covered, for 25 minutes. Stir in milk. Simmer for 15 to 20 minutes longer or until very tender. Beat eggs, sugar, salt and vanilla in bowl until well mixed. Stir a small amount of hot mixture into eggs; stir eggs into hot mixture. Simmer for 15 minutes. Pour into serving dish; sprinkle with cinnamon. Serve warm or cold.

Tillie Lima, French Camp-Lathrop 510

DONNA'S EASY SPICE PUDDING

1 1/2 c. packed brown sugar
1 c. sugar
1 c. flour
1 c. milk
2 tsp. baking powder
1/2 tsp. each salt, cloves
2 tsp. cinnamon

1 tsp. nutmeg
1 c. raisins
1 c. chopped nuts

Combine brown sugar and 2 cups water in saucepan. Bring to a boil. Cook for 3 minutes. Pour into 9 x 13-inch baking dish. Combine remaining ingredients in bowl; mix well. Pour into syrup in baking dish. Do not stir. Bake at 350 degrees until knife inserted in center comes out clean. Serve warm or cold with cream. Yield: 12-15 servings.

Donna Corsaut, Goat Mountain 818

NO-BAKE CAKE

1 16-oz. package cinnamon
graham crackers
1 29-oz. can applesauce
1 8-oz. carton whipped topping

Layer graham crackers and applesauce alternately on large serving plate to make cake of desired size. Spread remaining applesauce over top and sides. Chill overnight. Frost with whipped topping. Yield: 25 servings.

Dorothy Hankes, Whitesboro 766

TROPICAL BAKED APPLES A LA MODE

4 lg. baking apples
3/4 c. light corn syrup
Red food coloring
1/4 c. sugar
1 8-oz. package pitted dates, chopped
Pinch of salt
1/2 c. light corn syrup
1/2 c. chopped pecans
1 pt. coffee ice cream

Core apples; peel 1/3 of the way down from stem end. Combine 3/4 cup corn syrup, 1 cup water and enough food coloring to tint deep pink in bowl; mix well. Pour into baking pan. Place apples cut side down in baking pan. Bake at 350 degrees for 35 to 45 minutes or until tender. Turn cut side up in pan; spoon cooking syrup over apples. Sprinkle with sugar. Chill in refrigerator. Combine dates, salt and 1/2 cup water in saucepan. Bring to boiling point. Stir in 1/2 cup corn syrup and pecans. Chill in refrigerator. Top apples with date sauce and ice cream to serve. Yield: 4 servings

Myrtle Gutierrez, Morgan Hill 408

DUTCH APPLE PANCAKE

4 Washington State apples
3/4 c. sugar
3 tbsp. lemon juice
4 whole cloves
Dash of salt
2 tbsp. butter
1/2 c. sifted flour
1/2 c. milk
3 eggs
1/2 tsp. salt
2 tbsp. butter

Peel, core and cut apples into eighths. Combine sugar, 3/4 cup water, lemon juice, cloves and dash of salt in skillet. Bring to a boil. Add apples. Simmer, covered, for 5 minutes. Cook, uncovered, for 3 to 5 minutes longer or until tender, turning and basting constantly to glaze. Discard cloves. Melt 2 tablespoons butter in 9-inch ovenproof skillet. Tilt to coat side. Combine flour, milk, eggs and 1/2 teaspoon salt in bowl. Pour butter from skillet into batter; beat well. Pour into prepared skillet. Bake at 425 degrees for 20 minutes. Reduce temperature to 350 degrees. Bake for 15 minutes longer. Spoon apple slices into pancake. Blend 2 tablespoons butter into apple juices in skillet. Pour over top. Serve hot.

Photograph for this recipe below.

MISSISSIPPI PIE

1 stick margarine, melted
1 c. chopped nuts
1 c. flour
1 c. confectioners' sugar
1 8-oz. package cream cheese, softened
1 c. whipped topping

1 lg. package chocolate instant
  pudding mix, prepared
1 c. whipped topping
1 c. grated milk chocolate bar

Combine first 3 ingredients in bowl; mix well. Spread over bottom of 9 x 13-inch baking pan. Bake at 350 degrees for 25 minutes. Mix confectioners' sugar, cream cheese and whipped topping in bowl. Spread over cooled baked layer. Spoon prepared pudding over top. Spread whipped topping over pudding. Sprinkle with grated chocolate. Chill in refrigerator.

Lola B. Jones, Hemet San Jacinto 693

BANANA SPLIT CAKE

2 sticks margarine
1/2 c. sugar
1 pkg. graham cracker crumbs
1/2 c. melted margarine, cooled
1 egg
1 8-oz. package cream cheese, softened
2 c. confectioners' sugar
1 21-oz. can crushed pineapple
4 or 5 bananas, sliced
1 lg. carton whipped topping

Melt 2 sticks margarine in 9 x 13-inch glass baking dish. Add sugar and graham cracker crumbs; mix well. Press evenly and firmly over bottom of dish. Combine 1/2 cup margarine and egg in mixer bowl; beat well. Add cream cheese; beat well. Add confectioners' sugar; beat well. Spread over crumb layer. Drain pineapple, reserving juice. Dip banana slices in reserved pineapple juice. Arrange over pudding layer. Spread pineapple over bananas. Spread whipped topping over layers. Garnish with nuts and cherries.

Evelyn Dean, Humboldt 501

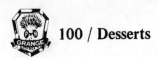

BANANA FRITTERS

3 lb. bananas
1 c. buttermilk baking mix
1/2 c. milk
1 egg
1/2 c. oil
Confectioners' sugar

Cut bananas into halves or thirds; split length-wise. Combine baking mix, milk and egg in bowl; mix well. Dip each banana piece in batter. Place bananas close together in hot oil in skillet. Fry until brown; separate and turn. Brown on remaining side. Remove from skillet; drain. Sprinkle with confectioners' sugar. Repeat with remaining bananas.

Inez Erickson, Humboldt 501

BLUEBERRY DESSERT

Pineapple juice
Blueberry juice
1 pkg. raspberry gelatin
1 c. drained crushed pineapple
1 c. drained blueberries
1/2 c. whipped cream

Combine juices with enough water to measure 1 1/2 cups in saucepan. Bring to a boil. Add gelatin; stir until dissolved. Cool. Fold in fruits and whipped cream. Pour into serving dish. Chill until firm. Garnish with additional whipped cream.

Ruby Lungren, Kingsburg 679

COCONUT FRUIT BOWL

1   20-oz. can pineapple
1   11-oz. can mandarin oranges
1 c. Thompson seedless grapes
1 c. miniature marshmallows
1   3 1/2-oz. can coconut
2 c. sour cream

Combine all ingredients in bowl; mix well. Chill overnight. Yield: 8 servings.

V. F. McKenzie, Greenhorn 384

CHERRY-CREAM DESSERT

6 egg whites
1/4 tsp. cream of tartar
2 c. sugar

2 tsp. vanilla extract
2 c. coarsely crumbled soda crackers
3/4 c. chopped nuts
1/2 pt. sweetened whipping cream, whipped
1   20-oz. can cherry pie filling

Beat egg whites with cream of tartar until soft peaks form. Add sugar and vanilla gradually, beating until stiff peaks form. Fold in crackers and nuts gently. Spread in greased 7 x 11-inch baking pan. Bake at 350 degrees for 20 minutes. Cool. Layer whipped cream and pie filling over top. Chill for 5 hours or longer.

Inez Fullerton, Orangevale 354

FRUIT COMPOTE

3/4 c. Karo light corn syrup
1/2 c. orange juice
2 tbsp. very thin strips lemon rind
1/4 c. lemon juice
8 c. mixed fresh fruit

Blend corn syrup, orange juice, lemon rind and juice in large bowl. Add fruit; toss to coat well. Chill, covered, for several hours.

Photograph for this recipe on page 104.

MICROWAVE CRANBERRY CRISP

2 c. fresh cranberries
2/3 c. sugar
1/2 c. quick-cooking oats
1/4 c. flour
1/2 c. packed brown sugar
1/4 c. butter

Combine cranberries, sugar and 1/3 cup water in 9-inch glass pie plate. Microwave, covered with waxed paper, on High for 2 1/2 to 3 1/2 minutes or until tender. Mix oats, flour and brown sugar in bowl. Cut in butter until crumbly. Sprinkle over cranberries. Microwave on Medium for 5 minutes. Microwave on High for 1 to 2 minutes or until bubbly. Let stand for several minutes. Serve with whipped cream or vanilla ice cream. Yield: 5-6 servings.

Betty Davis, Lucerne Valley 673

SCHAUM TORTE

3 egg whites
1/4 tsp. cream of tartar
Pinch of salt
1/2 tsp. vinegar

1 c. sugar
3 tbsp. cornstarch
1 c. sugar
3 egg yolks, beaten
1 tbsp. lemon juice
2 tsp. grated lemon rind
5 tbsp. lemon juice
1/2 pt. whipping cream, whipped

Beat egg whites, cream of tartar, salt and vinegar in mixer bowl until soft peaks form. Add 1 cup sugar 1 tablespoon at a time, beating until sugar is dissolved after each addition. Beat until very stiff and glossy. Spread in pie plate, shaping into shell. Bake at 325 degrees for 50 minutes. Cool. Combine cornstarch and 1 cup sugar in saucepan. Add mixture of beaten egg yolks and 1 tablespoon lemon juice; mix well. Add 1 cup water; mix well. Bring to a boil, stirring constantly. Add lemon rind and 5 tablespoons lemon juice. Cook for 5 minutes or until thick. Cool. Spread half the whipped cream, all the lemon filling and remaining whipped cream in meringue shell. Chill overnight.

Rosalind Popkey, Van Duzen 517

FRUIT COCKTAIL TORTE

1 1/2 c. flour
1 tsp. baking powder
1 tsp. soda
1 c. sugar
1 tsp. salt
1 egg, slightly beaten
1 16-oz. can fruit cocktail, undrained
1 c. packed brown sugar
1/2 c. chopped nuts

Sift flour, baking powder, soda, sugar and salt together. Combine egg and fruit cocktail in bowl. Fold in dry ingredients. Spread on lightly greased 11 x 16-inch baking sheet. Sprinkle mixture of brown sugar and nuts over top. Bake at 350 degrees for 30 minutes. Serve warm or cold with whipped cream or ice cream. Yield: 12-15 servings.

Gladys Schweder, Manton 732

FRIENDSHIP FRUIT

2 1/2 c. sugar
4 c. peaches and juice
2 1/2 c. sugar
1 20-oz. can crushed pineapple

2 1/2 c. sugar
1 1/4 lb. pitted Bing cherries

Combine first 2 ingredients in 1-gallon glass jar. Let stand, uncovered, for 10 days; stir daily. On 10th day, add 2 1/2 cups sugar and pineapple. Let stand for 10 days; stir daily. On 20th day, add remaining ingredients. Let stand for 10 days; stir daily. Use fruit as sauce for applesauce bundt cake. Give 1 1/2 cups starter juice and instructions to 4 friends.

Marian Bremel, Feather River 440

TEN-DOLLAR FRUIT PIE

4 c. fruit
Sugar to taste
1/2 c. butter
1 c. flour
1 c. sugar
1 tbsp. baking powder
1 c. milk

Combine fruit with sugar to taste in saucepan. Let stand for several minutes. Melt butter in 9 x 13-inch baking dish. Combine remaining ingredients in bowl; mix well. Pour over butter in baking dish. Do not stir. Heat fruit to boiling point; drain. Spread over batter. Bake at 375 degrees for 25 minutes.

Inez Leib, Empire 521

QUICK AND GOOD FRUIT COBBLER

4 to 6 c. fruit
1/4 c. sugar
1/2 c. butter
1 c. sugar
1 c. flour
2 tsp. baking powder
2/3 c. milk
2 tsp. vanilla extract
2 tbsp. cinnamon
2 tbsp. sugar

Combine fruit with 1/4 cup sugar in saucepan. Bring to a boil; keep hot. Melt butter in 9 x 13-inch baking dish. Combine 1 cup sugar, flour, baking powder and milk in bowl; mix well. Stir in vanilla. Pour over hot butter in baking dish. Top with hot fruit. Sprinkle with cinnamon and 2 tablespoons sugar. Bake at 400 degrees for 30 minutes or until brown. Yield: 10 servings.
Note: Batter will rise to top.

Thelma Meyer, Millville 443

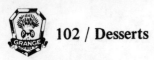 **102 / Desserts**

LEMON BISQUE

1 3-oz. package lemon gelatin
1/8 tsp. salt
1/3 c. sugar
1/4 c. lemon juice
Grated rind of 1 lemon
1 13-oz. can evaporated milk,
*   partially frozen, whipped*
1 1/2 c. graham cracker crumbs
1 tsp. cinnamon
1/4 c. melted butter
1/4 c. sugar

Dissolve gelatin, salt and 1/3 cup sugar in 1 1/4 cups boiling water in bowl. Add lemon juice and rind. Chill in refrigerator. Fold whipped evaporated milk into cooled gelatin mixture. Combine remaining ingredients in bowl; mix well. Reserve a small amount of crumbs. Press remaining crumbs over bottom of 9 x 13-inch dish. Pour lemon mixture into prepared dish. Sprinkle reserved crumbs over top. Chill until firm.

Mae Miller, Empire 521

LEMON DELIGHT

1 stick margarine, melted
1 c. flour
1 c. chopped nuts (opt.)
1 c. confectioners' sugar
1 8-oz. package cream cheese, softened
1 16-oz. carton whipped topping
2 sm. packages lemon instant pudding mix
2 1/2 c. milk

Combine first 3 ingredients in bowl; mix well. Press into bottom of 9 x 13-inch baking pan. Bake at 350 degrees for 20 minutes or until lightly browned. Cool. Cream confectioners' sugar, cream cheese and half the whipped topping in bowl until light and fluffy. Spread over baked layer. Blend pudding mix and milk in bowl. Beat until thickened. Spread over cream cheese layer. Top with remaining whipped topping. Yield: 12 servings.

Christine Kearne, Yucaipa Valley 582

MANDARIN ORANGE AND SHERBET DESSERT

1 3-oz. package orange gelatin
1 pt. orange sherbet
1 can mandarin oranges, drained

Dissolve gelatin in 1 scant cup hot water in bowl. Add sherbet, stirring to dissolve. Stir in oranges. Pour into individual molds. Chill until firm. Unmold on serving plates. Serve with whipped topping. Yield: 6 servings.

Camilla R. Sweatt, Airport 820

LIME MOUSSE

1 env. unflavored gelatin
3 eggs, separated
3/4 c. Karo light corn syrup
1 tsp. grated lime rind
1/2 c. lime juice
2 drops of green food coloring (opt.)
1/4 c. sugar
1 c. whipping cream, whipped

Soften gelatin in 1/4 cup cold water in 2-quart saucepan. Stir in egg yolks, corn syrup, lime rind and juice. Cook over low heat for 5 minutes or until gelatin is dissolved, stirring constantly. Stir in food coloring. Pour into large bowl. Chill for 1 hour or until thick, stirring occasionally. Beat egg whites in small mixer bowl until soft peaks form. Add sugar gradually. Beat until stiff peaks form. Fold into lime mixture. Fold in whipped cream. Spoon into 2-quart serving dish. Chill until firm. Garnish with additional whipped cream and lime slices. Yield: 8 servings.

Photograph for this recipe on page 104.

ORANGE CREME DESSERT

1 8-oz. can juice-pack
*   crushed pineapple*
1 3-oz. package orange gelatin
3/4 c. evaporated milk
1 8-oz. package cream cheese, softened
2 tbsp. orange juice
2 tsp. grated orange rind
1 11-oz. can mandarin oranges, drained

Drain pineapple, reserving juice. Combine reserved juice with 1 cup water in saucepan. Bring to a boil. Add gelatin; stir to dissolve. Cool. Cream evaporated milk and cream cheese in bowl. Stir into gelatin gradually. Add orange juice and rind, pineapple and oranges; mix well. Pour into lightly oiled 6-cup mold. Chill until firm. Unmold on serving plate. Garnish with strawberries or seedless green grapes. Yield: 8 servings.

Edna Paxman, Ripon 511

*ORIENTAL CHICKEN SALAD, recipe on page 147. FRENCH AMERICAN VEGETABLE SALAD, recipe
n page 150. GERMAN POTATO SALAD, recipe on page 151.*

FRUIT COMPOTE, recipe on page 100. LIME MOUSSE, recipe on page 102. STRAWBERRY TART, recipe on page 106.

PEACH CRISP

2 cans sliced peaches, drained
1 c. flour
1 c. sugar
1 tsp. each baking powder, cinnamon
1 egg
1/2 c. melted butter
1/2 tsp. nutmeg

Arrange peaches in 9 x 12-inch baking dish. Combine flour, sugar, baking powder, cinnamon and egg in bowl. Mix with fingers until crumbly. Sprinkle over peaches. Drizzle with butter. Top with nutmeg. Bake at 350 degrees for 35 minutes or until browned and bubbly. Yield: 8-10 servings.

Lillian Harris, Feather River 440

PISTACHIO PUDDING DESSERT

3/4 c. margarine, softened
1/2 c. packed brown sugar
1 1/2 c. flour
1/2 c. chopped nuts
1 sm. package pistachio instant
  pudding mix
2 c. milk
1 8-oz. package cream cheese, softened
1 c. coconut
1 c. chopped nuts
1 15-oz. can crushed pineapple

Combine first 4 ingredients in bowl; mix well. Press into 9 x 13-inch baking pan. Bake at 350 degrees for 12 minutes. Cool. Combine remaining ingredients in bowl; mix well. Pour over crust. Chill for several hours. Yield: 12-15 servings.

Fern Konkel, Kerman 484

PUMPKIN DESSERT

4 eggs, lightly beaten
1 28-oz. can pumpkin
1 1/2 c. sugar
1 tsp. salt
1 tsp. each cinnamon, ginger
1/2 tsp. cloves
1 13-oz. can evaporated milk
1 2-layer pkg. yellow cake mix
2 c. chopped walnuts
1 c. melted butter

Combine first 8 ingredients in bowl; mix well. Pour into buttered 9 x 13-inch baking pan. Sprinkle dry cake mix over top. Top with chopped walnuts. Drizzle butter over all. Bake at 350 degrees for 1 1/2 hours. Cool slightly. Cut into squares. Serve with whipped cream or ice cream. Yield: 24 servings.

Violet Miller, Western Yolo 423

JANIS' REFRIGERATOR DESSERT

1/2 c. butter, softened
1 1/2 c. confectioners' sugar
2 eggs
1 8-oz. can crushed pineapple,
  well drained
1 tsp. lemon juice
1/2 pt. whipping cream, whipped
8 oz. vanilla wafers, finely crushed

Cream butter and confectioners' sugar in bowl. Add eggs; beat well. Fold pineapple and lemon juice into whipped cream. Layer 1/3 of the wafer crumbs, all the butter mixture, half the remaining crumbs, pineapple mixture and remaining crumbs in 8-inch square dish. Chill for 24 hours.

Janis Showalter, Fair Valley 752

FRIED ICE CREAM

1 qt. vanilla ice cream
6 egg whites
1 8-oz. package coconut
  macaroons, crushed
6 whole graham crackers, crushed
6 peach halves
Oil for deep frying

Scoop out six 4-ounce balls of ice cream. Freeze until very firm. Beat egg whites in bowl until foamy. Place macaroon crumbs and graham cracker crumbs in separate bowls. Dip ice cream balls in egg whites. Roll in macaroon crumbs, coating well. Dip again in egg whites. Roll in graham cracker crumbs, coating lightly. Freeze until firm. Place peach halves in serving bowls. Deep-fry ice cream balls in 350-degree oil for 1 minute or until brown on all sides. Place in peach halves. Serve immediately. Yield: 6 servings.

Charlene Alves, Orland 432

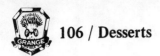

TOSS-AND-BAKE DESSERTS

2 c. flour
1 c. sugar
1 1/2 tsp. soda
2/3 c. oil
2 eggs
1 tsp. vanilla extract
1 21-oz. can pie filling

Combine all ingredients in 9 x 13-inch baking pan; mix well. Spread evenly. Bake at 350 degrees for 35 minutes. Serve with whipped cream or ice cream. Yield: 15-18 servings.

Lorene Miller, Kingsburg 679

STRAWBERRY TART

3/4 c. flour
1/4 c. cornstarch
1/4 c. sugar
1/3 c. margarine
1 egg yolk, slightly beaten
1 pt. (about) strawberries
1/4 c. Karo light corn syrup
1 tsp. lemon juice

Combine flour, cornstarch and sugar in bowl. Cut in margarine until crumbly. Stir in egg yolk. Roll on waxed paper-lined baking sheet to slightly larger than 6 x 12-inch rectangle. Trim to 6 x 12-inch rectangle; reserve excess dough. Trim to 4 x 10-inch rectangle. Cut trimmed strips into four 1/2 x 10-inch strips and four 1/2 x 3-inch strips. Stack two 10-inch strips on long side of rectangle. Stack two 3-inch strips on short ends. Decorate with cutouts from trimmings. Pierce rectangle with fork. Bake at 400 degrees for 8 to 10 minutes or until lightly browned. Cool on baking sheet on wire rack for 5 minutes. Remove from baking sheet; cool slightly. Remove waxed paper. Arrange strawberries stem end down in cooled tart shell. Mix corn syrup and lemon juice in saucepan. Cook over low heat for 1 minute, stirring constantly; remove from heat. Brush over strawberries. Chill for 3 hours.

Photograph for this recipe on page 104.

STRAWBERRY ICE CREAM

1 lg. package strawberry gelatin
2 10-oz. packages frozen strawberries
4 eggs, beaten
1 2/3 c. sugar
3 c. milk
1 pt. whipping cream
1 13-oz. can evaporated milk
Salt to taste
Vanilla extract to taste
Milk

Dissolve gelatin in 2 cups hot water in saucepan. Stir in strawberries until thawed. Beat eggs with sugar in saucepan until thick. Add 3 cups milk. Bring just to a simmer over low heat. Do not boil. Add cream, evaporated milk, salt, vanilla and strawberry mixture; mix well. Pour into freezer container. Add more milk if needed to reach fill line. Freeze according to manufacturer's instructions.

Thelma Steadman, Riverbank 719

ICE CREAM IN-A-CAN

1 egg, beaten
1 c. milk
1 c. whipping cream
1/2 c. sugar
1 tsp. vanilla extract

Combine all ingredients in bowl; mix until sugar dissolves. Pour into 16-ounce can with an airtight lid; tape lid securely. Place in 3-pound can. Fill space between cans with crushed ice and rock salt. Cover larger can securely. Roll can back and forth for 15 minutes or until soft ice cream forms. Yield: 4 servings.

Margaret Hanevik, Apple Valley 593

CIRCLE-B RANCH DESSERT

1 16-oz. can crushed pineapple
1 16-oz. can pitted red sour cherries
1/2 c. sugar
1/3 c. Minute tapioca
1 c. quick-cooking oats
1 c. bran flakes
2 c. flour
1 c. packed brown sugar
1 tsp. soda
1/4 tsp. salt
3/4 c. melted butter
1 1/2 tsp. vanilla extract

Combine first 4 ingredients in double boiler. Cook until thickened and clear, stirring constantly. Mix oats, bran flakes, flour, brown sugar, soda, salt, butter and vanilla in bowl until crumbly. Press half the mixture in 9 x 13-inch dish. Spread cooked filling over crumbs. Sprinkle with remaining crumbs. Bake at 350 degrees for 30 to 35 minutes. Cut into squares. Serve warm or cold with whipped cream.

Wilma Greer, Wood Colony 522

MAIN DISHES

Duvall's Patent Hand Cultivator,

OR

GARDEN HAND PLOW.

PRICE, $2 50.

The *Southern Cultivator*, Athens, Ga., says: "We have tried Duvall's Patent Garden Plow, and found it to do excellent work. It is a small steel turning plow, attached by a curved bar to a handle like that of a hoe, with a second handle projecting from the first, to be grasped by one hand, whilst the other holds the main staff. The point of the plow is turned towards the operator, and is forced through the ground by a stroke like that made in hoeing. It can be worked in very narrow rows, throwing dirt either to or from plants, according as the share or bar is run next to them, whilst it pulverizes the soil much more thoroughly than a hoe would do."

The workmanship is unexceptionable. The wing or share is made of solid cast-steel polished. The *cost* is but little more than that of the ordinary hoe. For *Garden Work* it can't be surpassed. It will do all the work of a hoe, last much longer and do ten times the service. *Worked as a Plow*, it opens the furrow and throws the dirt either to or from the plants. *Worked as a Hoe*, it will open and pulverize the soil instead of leaving it in cakes. IT WILL EXTERMINATE GRASS OR WEEDS, by turning up and exposing the roots to the sun, instead of cutting off the stems and leaving the roots in the ground to appear again in a few days with increased strength and vigor.

T. H. JONES & CO.,
Exclusive Agents, Nashville, Tenn,

Beef

· RETAIL CUTS ·
WHERE THEY COME FROM
HOW TO COOK THEM

ROUND
SIRLOIN
SHORT LOIN
RIB
CHUCK
FLANK
SHORT PLATE
BRISKET
FORE SHANK

Round Steak
Braise, Panfry

Top Round Roast
Roast

Top Round Steak
Broil, Panbroil, Panfry

Boneless Rump Roast
Roast, Braise

Bottom Round Roast
Braise, Roast

Tip Roast, Cap Off
Roast, Braise

Eye Round Roast
Braise, Roast

Tip Steak
Broil, Panbroil, Panfry

ROUND

Sirloin Steak, Flat Bone
Broil, Panbroil, Panfry

Sirloin Steak, Round Bone
Broil, Panbroil, Panfry

Top Sirloin Steak
Broil, Panbroil Panfry

SIRLOIN

Shank Cross Cut
Braise, Cook in Liquid

Brisket, Whole
Braise, Cook in Liquid

Corned Brisket, Point Half
Braise, Cook in Liquid

Brisket, Flat Half
Braise

FORE SHANK
& BRISKET

Chuck Eye Roast
Braise, Roast

Boneless Top Blade Steak
Braise, Panfry

Arm Pot Roast
Braise

Boneless Shoulder Pot Roast
Braise

Mock Tender
Braise

Cross Rib Pot Roast
Braise

Under Blade Pot Roast
Braise, Roast

Blade Roast
Braise

Short Ribs
Braise, Cook in Liquid

7-Bone Pot Roast
Braise

Flanken-Style Ribs
Braise, Cook in Liquid

CHUCK

THIS CHART APPROVED BY
NATIONAL LIVE STOCK & MEAT BOARD

T-Bone Steak
Broil, Panbroil, Panfry

Boneless Top Loin Steak
Broil, Panbroil, Panfry

Tenderloin Roast
Roast, Broil

Porterhouse Steak
Broil, Panbroil, Panfry

Tenderloin Steak
Broil, Panbroil, Panfry

SHORT LOIN

Rib Roast, Large End
Roast

Rib Roast, Small End
Roast

Rib Steak, Small End
Broil, Panbroil, Panfry

Rib Eye Roast
Roast

Rib Eye Steak
Broil, Panbroil, Panfry

Back Ribs
Braise, Cook in Liquid, Roast

RIB

Flank Steak
Broil, Braise, Panfry

Flank Steak Rolls
Braise, Broil, Panbroil, Panfry

Skirt Steak
Braise, Broil, Panbroil, Panfry

FLANK &
SHORT PLATE

Ground Beef
Broil, Panfry, Panbroil, Roast (Bake)

Cubed Steak
Panfry, Braise

Beef for Stew
Braise, Cook in Liquid

Cubes for Kabobs
Broil, Braise

OTHER CUTS

This page is in special recognition to the CALIFORNIA BEEF COUNCIL for providing a monetary donation along with an illustration depicting their commodity. Their generous donation has assisted in the success of this new California State Grange Cookbook.

SWEET AND SOUR BRISKET

2 onions, sliced
1 clove of garlic, minced
1 5 to 6-lb. brisket
3/4 c. packed brown sugar
1 c. catsup
1/2 c. vinegar
1 tbsp. salt
Pepper to taste

Place onions and garlic in roasting pan. Place brisket on onions. Mix remaining ingredients with 1 cup water in bowl. Pour over brisket. Bake, covered, at 350 degrees for 4 hours or until tender. Yield: 10-12 servings.

Lavada Jones, French Camp-Lathrop 510

ITALIAN BEEF

1 4 to 5-lb. rump roast
1 lg. onion, thinly sliced
1 c. steak sauce
1/4 c. Worcestershire sauce
1 12-oz. jar pepperincinis, cut into
*   1/2-in. slices*

Braise roast as desired; slice. Combine with pan juices and remaining ingredients in Crock-Pot. Cook on Low for 5 to 6 hours. Yield: 8-10 servings.

Patricia Meece, Sacramento 12

TEXAS-BARBECUED POT ROAST

1/2 c. catsup
1/2 c. apricot preserves
1/4 c. white vinegar
1/4 c. packed brown sugar
1/2 c. soy sauce
1/4 tsp. pepper
1 tsp. red pepper flakes
1 tsp. dry mustard
1 5-lb. beef roast
1 onion, sliced

Combine catsup, preserves, vinegar, brown sugar, soy sauce, pepper, red pepper flakes and dry mustard in plastic bag; mix well. Add roast; seal. Marinate in refrigerator overnight. Drain, reserving marinade. Place roast, onion and 2 cups water in pressure cooker. Process according to manufacturer's instructions at 15 pounds pressure for 1 hour and 15 minutes. Pour reserved marinade into saucepan. Bring to a boil; reduce heat. Simmer for 15 minutes, stirring frequently. Place roast on warm serving platter. Drain pressure cooker, reserving onion. Place onion in blender container. Process until smooth. Stir into marinade sauce. Serve with roast. Yield: 8 servings.

Janet Treat, Merced Colony 527

ORANGE POT ROAST

1 4 to 5-lb. chuck roast
1 tbsp. bacon drippings
1/2 c. chopped onion
1 clove of garlic, minced
1 8-oz. can tomato sauce
2 c. orange sections and juice
1 tbsp. grated orange rind
2 tbsp. sugar
1/2 tsp. each cinnamon, nutmeg and cloves
1 1/2 tsp. salt
Dash of pepper

Brown roast slowly on both sides in bacon drippings in Dutch oven. Add onion and garlic. Cook, covered, for 20 minutes. Add remaining ingredients. Bake, covered, at 350 degrees for 2 hours or until tender. Yield: 6-8 servings.

Ruby E. Latynski, Del Rosa 711

BEEF IN WHITE WINE

2 c. coarsely chopped fresh tomatoes
1 med. stalk celery, chopped
1/2 c. minced parsley
1 lg. clove of garlic, minced
1 c. dry white wine
3/4 tsp. oregano
1/4 tsp. each pepper, basil
1/2 tsp. thyme
1 1/2 tsp. salt
1 1/2 lb. round steak, cut into
*   1-in. pieces*
1/2 lb. mushrooms, sliced
2 tbsp. flour
1/3 c. dry white wine
8 slices French bread, toasted, buttered

Combine tomatoes, celery, parsley, garlic, 1 cup wine and seasonings in saucepan. Simmer for 30 minutes. Pour into blender container. Process until smooth. Brown steak in a small amount of oil in skillet. Add blended sauce. Simmer, covered, for 1 1/4 hours or until tender. Add mushrooms and flour blended with 1/3 cup wine. Cook until mixture is thickened, stirring constantly. Serve over French bread in bowls.

Larry R. LeVine, Lompoc 646

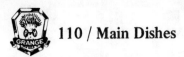

MEXICAN CHILI

1 1/2 lb. stew beef, finely chopped
3 lg. onions, finely chopped
1 can green chilies
1 can chopped pimentos
2 lg. cans tomatoes
Garlic to taste
1 1/2 tsp. chili powder

Brown beef and onions in saucepan, stirring frequently. Add remaining ingredients; mix well. Simmer until chili is of desired consistency. Serve with pinto beans and corn bread. Yield: 5-6 servings.

Florence Taneyhill, Hessel 750

CARNE GUISADA

1 lb. stew beef, cut up
1 16-oz. can stewed tomatoes
1 lg. onion, chopped
1 carrot, thinly sliced
1 stalk celery, thinly sliced
1 env. taco seasoning mix
1 jalapeno pepper, seeded, chopped (opt.)

Brown stew beef in skillet. Add remaining ingredients and 1/3 to 1/2 cup water; mix well. Simmer for 1 hour or until of desired consistency. Serve with refried beans and warmed flour tortillas. Garnish with sliced olives, shredded cheese, chopped onions and hot peppers.

Lori Sala, Escalon 447

STEAK SAN MARCO

2 lb. chuck steak, cut into serving pieces
1 env. dry onion soup mix
1 16-oz. can Italian tomatoes
1 tsp. oregano
Pepper, garlic powder to taste
2 tbsp. each oil, wine vinegar

Place steak in large skillet. Top with soup mix and tomatoes. Sprinkle remaining ingredients over top. Simmer, covered, for 1 1/2 hours or until tender. Serve with rice and pan juices.

Dorothy Buffington, Montgomery 442

GULYAS OF BEEF

1 1/2 to 2 lb. lean beef, cubed
3 or 4 med. onions, finely chopped
Garlic, chopped (opt.)

Marjoram to taste (opt.)
Paprika and salt to taste
3 tbsp. flour
1 c. stock
Potatoes, sliced
1 c. sour cream

Brown beef with onions, garlic and seasonings in a small amount of shortening in skillet, stirring frequently. Sift flour over mixture. Add stock; mix well. Simmer, covered, for 45 minutes. Arrange potatoes over top. Cook until tender. Stir in sour cream. Heat for 10 minutes. Yield: 4-5 servings.
Note: May substitute veal or pork for beef. Flavor improves with long slow cooking.

Alma Taynton, Rio Linda 403

QUICK BEEF STEW

1 sm. onion, chopped
1 sm. green pepper, chopped
1 tbsp. oil
1/2 c. tomato juice
1/2 c. carrot slices
1 clove of garlic, minced
1 tsp. salt
1/2 tsp. each cumin, pepper
1 tbsp. flour
1 c. chopped cooked roast beef
1 c. chopped potato

Saute onion and green pepper in oil over low heat in 2-quart saucepan. Add tomato juice, carrots, garlic and seasonings. Stir in flour mixed with 1 cup water. Simmer for 30 minutes. Add roast beef and potato. Simmer for 15 to 20 minutes or until potato is tender.

Julia Hayes, Fairfax 570

PORTUGUESE SOPAS

1 5 to 6-lb. chuck roast, cut into
    serving pieces
2 med. onions, chopped
2 cloves of garlic, pressed
1 29-oz. can whole tomatoes
2 c. red wine (opt.)
1 lg. bay leaf
2 tsp. each cinnamon, allspice
Salt and pepper to taste
French bread, thinly sliced
3 or 4 sprigs of fresh mint

Combine beef, onions, garlic, tomatoes, wine and seasonings in large saucepan. Add 4 quarts water or enough to cover. Simmer until beef is tender. Remove beef to warmed serving plate. Place French bread slices in large casserole. Top with mint. Strain hot pan juices. Pour over bread. Let stand, covered, for several minutes. Serve with beef.

Ermina C. Wheeler, Thermalito 729

MEAT AND CHILI TACOS

Round steak, trimmed, cut into
*   bite-sized pieces*
2 tbsp. flour
2 cans tomato sauce
1 can chilies
Garlic salt to taste
Chopped potatoes
Flour tortillas

Brown steak in a small amount of shortening in skillet. Remove steak and drain. Blend flour into pan juices. Add 1 1/2 cups water. Cook until thickened, stirring constantly. Stir in tomato sauce, chilies, garlic salt and browned steak. Simmer until steak is tender and sauce is of desired consistency. Brown potatoes in small amount of shortening in skillet. Heat tortillas in oven or microwave until softened. Spoon potatoes and steak mixture onto each tortilla. Fold to enclose filling.

Marie Landry, Humboldt 501

ROULADEN

2 lb. 1/4-in. thick round steak, trimmed
Mustard
Garlic salt and pepper to taste
3 or 4 tomatoes, chopped
2 or 3 dill pickles, chopped
4 slices bacon, chopped
1/2 lb. fresh mushrooms
3/4 c. red wine
1 c. beef broth
Cornstarch

Pound steak to 1/16-inch thickness with meat mallet. Cut into 4 x 6-inch pieces. Spread with mustard; sprinkle with garlic salt and pepper. Combine tomatoes, pickles and bacon in bowl. Spoon onto steak. Roll to enclose filling; secure with toothpicks. Brown rolls in a small amount of hot oil in skillet. Stir in mushrooms, wine and broth. Simmer, covered, for 1 hour, adding water if necessary. Remove rolls to warm serving plate. Stir in paste of cornstarch and a small

amount of water. Cook until pan juices thicken, stirring constantly. Serve with beef rolls. Yield: 6-8 servings.

Alyce Hendricks, Concow 735

SAVORY PEPPER STEAK

1 1/2 lb. round steak, cut into
*   1/2-in. strips*
1/4 c. flour
1/2 tsp. salt
1/8 tsp. pepper
1/4 c. shortening
1 c. canned tomatoes
1/2 c. chopped onion
1 sm. clove of garlic, chopped
1 tbsp. beef-flavored gravy base
1 1/2 tsp. Worcestershire sauce
2 lg. green peppers, chopped

Coat steak with mixture of flour, salt and pepper. Brown in shortening in skillet. Drain and chop tomatoes, reserving juice. Add reserved juice, onion, garlic, gravy base and 1 3/4 cups water to steak. Simmer, covered, for 1 hour and 15 minutes or until steak is tender. Stir in Worcestershire sauce and green peppers. Simmer, covered, for 5 minutes. Add chopped tomatoes. Simmer for 5 minutes longer. Serve over hot rice. Yield: 6 servings.

Carolyn Hill, Empire 521

STUFFED ROUND STEAK

1 lg. round steak
4 slices bacon
Poultry seasoning
4 slices bread, crusts trimmed
1 onion, sliced
3 hard-boiled eggs, sliced
1 jar mushrooms
1 can cream of mushroom soup
3/4 soup can red wine
1 env. dry onion soup mix

Cut round steak into 4 pieces. Pound to flatten slightly. Place 1 slice bacon on each. Sprinkle poultry seasoning on both sides of bread slices. Place 1 slice on each piece of steak. Top with onion, eggs and mushrooms. Roll to enclose filling; tie securely with string. Brown in Dutch oven, turning frequently. Pour mixture of soup, wine, soup mix and 3/4 soup can water over steak rolls. Bake at 325 degrees for 3 to 4 hours or until steak is tender.

Dorothy Graham, Copper Mountain 814

PEPPERED STEAK DIANE

1 2 to 2 1/2-lb. 1-inch thick
    sirloin steak
Salt to taste
1/4 tsp. dry mustard
1/4 c. lemon-pepper butter
3 tbsp. dry white wine
1 tsp. Worcestershire sauce
1 3-oz. can sliced mushrooms, drained
1 6-oz. package saffron rice
    mix, cooked

Cut steak into strips 1/4-inch wide. Sprinkle with salt and dry mustard. Brown in lemon-pepper butter in skillet. Remove steak; drain. Stir in wine and Worcestershire sauce. Bring to a boil. Add mushrooms and browned steak. Cook until heated through, stirring frequently. Serve over hot saffron rice. Yield: 4 servings.

Hazel L. Lynch, Ripon 511

BAKED BEEF AND CRUST DINNER

1 lb. lean ground beef
1/2 c. chopped onion
2 cloves of garlic, chopped
1 8-oz. package cream cheese, softened
2 tbsp. buttermilk
4 hard-boiled eggs, chopped
2 1/2 tbsp. dill
Salt and pepper to taste
1 1/4 c. shortening
3 c. flour
1 egg yolk, beaten

Brown ground beef with onion and garlic in skillet, stirring frequently. Blend cream cheese and buttermilk in bowl. Add to ground beef with hard-boiled eggs and seasonings; mix well. Cut shortening into flour in bowl. Add enough cold water gradually to form dough. Roll out to 16-inch square on floured surface. Spread ground beef mixture on dough, leaving 2-inch margin on 3 sides. Fold margin on 2 opposite sides over filling. Roll as for jelly roll toward third margin; seal edge. Place on greased baking sheet. Brush with beaten egg yolk. Bake at 350 degrees for 1 hour. Slice to serve. Yield: 12 servings.

Lena B. Martin, Chico 486

CHILI-HOMINY SKILLET MEAL

1 lb. lean ground beef
1/2 c. chopped onion
1 15 1/2-oz. can chili with beans
1 29-oz. can yellow hominy, drained
1 2 1/4-oz. can sliced ripe
    olives, drained
1 tsp. (or more) chili powder
1 can cream of chicken soup
1/2 c. shredded sharp Cheddar cheese

Brown ground beef in skillet, stirring until crumbly. Add onion. Cook until tender. Stir in next 5 ingredients. Simmer, covered, for 30 minutes. Remove from heat; sprinkle with cheese. Let stand, covered, until cheese melts. Yield: 6 servings.

Dolly Dightman, Anderson Valley 669

MA BELL'S CHILI

2 lb. lean ground beef
Salt and pepper to taste
2 6-oz. cans tomato paste
3 8-oz. cans tomato sauce
1 lg. spice pkg. from Texas Brand
    chili mix
2 15-oz. cans red kidney beans

Brown ground beef with salt and pepper in skillet, stirring until crumbly. Cook for 15 to 30 minutes or until well done; drain. Add tomato paste, tomato sauce and 2 cups water. Simmer for 15 minutes. Stir in spices. Spoon into Crock·Pot. Add beans. Cook on High for 1 hour, adding water if necessary for desired consistency. Yield: 8-10 servings.

Esther S. Bell, Ramona 632

SMOOTH AND EASY
CHILI BEANS

2 c. dried pinto beans
2 tsp. salt
1 lb. ground beef
1 4-in. chorizo, crumbled
1 10-oz. can enchilada sauce
1/2 tsp. oregano

Combine beans with 4 cups water in 6-quart saucepan. Let stand overnight; drain. Add fresh water to cover and salt. Simmer for 2 to 3 hours or until tender. Brown ground beef and chorizo in skillet, stirring until crumbly. Add enchilada sauce and oregano; mix well. Add ground beef mixture to beans. Simmer for 1 hour or longer. Yield: 4-6 servings.
Note: May bring beans and 4 cups water to a boil in saucepan and let stand for 1 hour instead of soaking overnight.

Eileen Rocksvold, Manton 732

NACHOS

12 snack-sized flour tortillas
Oil for deep frying
1 1/2 lb. ground beef
1/2 c. chopped onion
1 tbsp. cumin
Salt to taste
1/2 c. green chili salsa
4 c. mixed grated Cheddar, Monterey
  Jack cheese
1 lg. can pitted ripe olives, chopped

Cut tortillas in half. Deep-fry in hot oil until golden brown; drain. Arrange on baking sheet. Brown ground beef and onion in skillet, stirring frequently. Add cumin, salt and salsa; mix well. Spoon onto tortillas. Top with cheeses and olives. Bake at 350 degrees for 10 to 15 minutes or until cheese is melted. Garnish with shredded lettuce and chopped tomato.

Katherine Bennett, Rosedale 565

ETHEL'S ENCHILADAS

1 lb. ground beef
1 lg. can enchilada sauce
12 flour tortillas
2 lg. onions, chopped
1 c. grated cheese
Chopped olives

Brown ground beef in skillet, stirring until crumbly. Heat enchilada sauce in saucepan. Dip tortillas in sauce to soften. Layer onions, ground beef, cheese and olives on tortillas. Roll to enclose filling. Place in 10 x 12-inch baking dish. Pour enchilada sauce over top. Sprinkle with additional cheese. Bake at 350 degrees for 30 minutes. Yield: 6-12 servings.
Note: May substitute any chopped leftover meat for ground beef.

Ethel Yokum, Chico 486

FRANCES' ENCHILADAS FOR A CROWD

30 lb. ground chuck
3 cloves of garlic, pressed
1/2 c. oregano leaves
1 tsp. rosemary
20 lb. onions, coarsely ground
3 7-lb. cans enchilada sauce
1 7-lb. can tomato puree
1 46-oz. can tomato juice
18 doz. flour tortillas
20 lb. sharp Cheddar cheese, grated
1 gal. plus 3 sm. cans pitted
  olives, drained

Brown ground chuck with garlic, oregano and rosemary in large pan, stirring until crumbly. Blanch onions in boiling water in saucepan; drain. Add to ground chuck. Season to taste. Cool in pan juices. Combine enchilada sauce and tomato puree in saucepan. Bring to a simmer. Thin to desired consistency with tomato juice; cool slightly. Dip tortillas in warm sauce to soften. Place about 3/4 cup ground beef mixture, 1/3 cup cheese and 2 olives on each tortilla. Roll to enclose filling. Place seam side down in large shallow baking pans. Top with remaining enchilada sauce mixture and cheese. Place olive on each enchilada. Bake at 350 degrees for 30 minutes or until bubbly. Spoon sauce over servings. Yield: 216 servings.

Frances McElhinney, San Luis Obispo 639

BARBECUED MEATBALLS

1 egg, beaten
1 stack crackers, crushed
1 env. dry onion soup mix
1 1/2 lb. ground beef
1/2 bottle of hot barbecue sauce

Mix egg and cracker crumbs in bowl. Add soup mix and ground beef; mix well. Shape into small balls. Brown in a small amount of shortening in skillet. Place in Crock-Pot. Add barbecue sauce. Cook on Medium for 45 minutes. Yield: 6 servings.

Don Landry, Humboldt 501

CRANBERRY MEATBALLS

2 lb. ground chuck
2 eggs
1 c. oats
1 sm. onion, chopped
Salt and garlic salt to taste
Worcestershire sauce to taste
1 16-oz. can cranberry sauce
1 c. chili sauce
2 tbsp. each honey, lemon juice

Combine ground chuck, eggs, oats, onion and seasonings in bowl; mix well. Shape into 2 1/2-inch balls. Place in 2-quart casserole. Combine remaining ingredients in bowl; mix well. Pour over meatballs. Bake at 350 degrees for 30 minutes. Serve with rice. Yield: 6-8 servings.

Marion M. (Pat) Wheeler, Thermalito 729

MEATBALLS WITH SPAGHETTI

    1   46-oz. can tomato juice
    1   6-oz. can tomato paste
    1 c. bread crumbs
    1 lb. ground beef
    1/2 lb. ground pork
    2 eggs, lightly beaten
    1 med. onion, finely chopped
    Chopped parsley to taste
    Salt, pepper and basil to taste
    1   16-oz. package spaghetti, cooked

Combine tomato juice and tomato paste in saucepan. Add 1 to 2 tomato paste cans water or enough to make of desired consistency. Simmer for several minutes. Mix bread crumbs with enough water to moisten in bowl. Add ground meat, eggs, onion, parsley and seasonings; mix well. Shape into 15 to 18 meatballs. Brown in a small amount of oil in skillet. Add to tomato mixture. Simmer for 2 hours. Serve over spaghetti. Yield: 4-6 servings.

Carolina Imbresci, Ripon 511

PARTY MEATBALLS

    2 lb. ground beef
    1/4 c. onion flakes
    Salt and pepper to taste
    1/2 c. catsup
    1/4 c. lemon juice
    2 tsp. vinegar
    1/4 c. packed brown sugar
    2 bay leaves
    Pinch of dry mustard
    3 gingersnaps, crushed

Combine ground beef with onion, salt and pepper in bowl; mix well. Shape into small balls. Place in saucepan with water to cover. Cook for 25 minutes. Drain and discard broth. Combine remaining ingredients with 1/2 cup water in small bowl; mix well. Pour over meatballs in saucepan. Simmer for 30 minutes.

Martha Watkins, Kingsburg 679

SWEDISH MEATBALLS

    1 1/2 c. soft bread crumbs
    1/4 c. milk
    1/2 c. chopped onion
    2 tbsp. butter
    3 lb. ground beef
    1/4 c. finely chopped parsley
    1 c. half and half
    1/4 c. red wine

    1 tsp. each salt, nutmeg
    1/4 tsp. ginger
    1 tsp. MSG (opt.)
    1 tbsp. flour
    3/4 c. half and half
    1 tsp. coffee
    1/2 tsp. concentrated beef extract

Soak bread crumbs in milk in mixer bowl for 5 minutes. Saute onion in butter in skillet until tender but not brown. Add to bread mixture with ground beef, parsley, 1 cup half and half, wine and seasonings. Beat on medium speed until well mixed. Shape into 1-inch balls. Brown in butter in skillet, turning frequently or shaking skillet to maintain round shape. Remove meatballs and drain. Blend flour into pan drippings. Add remaining ingredients. Cook until thickened. Return meatballs to gravy. Simmer for 10 minutes. Yield: 5 dozen.

Note: May substitute 1/2 pound ground veal and 1/4 pound ground pork for portion of beef. May bake meatballs at 400 degrees for 20 to 25 minutes instead of browning in skillet.

June Fredrickson, Freshwater 499

GRANDMA'S MEAT LOAF

    2 lb. ground round
    1 env. onion soup mix
    2 eggs
    1 1/2 c. bread crumbs
    3/4 c. catsup
    1 tsp. seasoned salt
    2 strips bacon
    1   8-oz. can tomato sauce

Combine ground round with next 5 ingredients and 1/2 cup warm water in bowl; mix well. Place in 5 x 7-inch loaf pan. Top with bacon. Pour tomato sauce over top. Bake at 350 degrees for 1 hour. Yield: 6 servings.

Helen Haley, Mt. Lassen 417

SPANISH MEAT LOAF

    1 lb. ground beef
    1/4 lb. ground pork
    1 onion, chopped
    3/4 c. Italian bread crumbs
    3/4 c. tomato soup
    1 egg, beaten
    1 tsp. each salt, pepper and sage
    3 tbsp. brown sugar
    1/4 c. catsup
    1 tsp. prepared mustard
    1 tsp. nutmeg

Combine ground meats, onion, bread crumbs, soup, egg, salt, pepper and sage in bowl; mix well. Shape into loaf. Place in baking pan. Mix remaining ingredients in small bowl. Pour over loaf. Bake at 350 degrees for 1 hour. Yield: 8 servings.

Rose Schuyler, Lompoc 646

COWBOY STEW

6 slices bacon
1/2 c. chopped green pepper
1 c. chopped onion
1 clove of garlic
1 1/2 lb. ground beef
2 cans tomatoes
2 c. diced potatoes
1 can whole kernel corn
1 can red kidney beans
1 tsp. salt
1/4 tsp. pepper

Fry bacon in skillet until crisp. Drain and crumble; reserve drippings. Saute green pepper, onion and garlic in drippings. Add ground beef. Cook until brown, stirring frequently. Add tomatoes and potatoes. Cook, covered, for 30 minutes. Add corn, beans, salt and pepper. Simmer for 15 minutes. Sprinkle with crumbled bacon. Yield: 8 servings.

Beverly Quast, Goat Mountain 818

SALISBURY SAUERBRATEN

1   10 3/4-oz. can Franco-American
   beef gravy
1 lb. ground beef
1/3 c. fine dry bread crumbs
2 tbsp. chopped onion
1/2 tsp. grated lemon rind
1/2 tsp. ginger
1   1-lb. can small whole potatoes
4 gingersnaps, finely crushed
1 tbsp. brown sugar
1 tbsp. wine vinegar

Combine 1/3 cup gravy, ground beef, bread crumbs, onion, lemon rind and ginger in bowl; mix thoroughly. Shape into 4 patties. Place in shallow 6 x 10-inch baking dish. Bake at 350 degrees for 20 minutes; drain. Arrange potatoes around patties. Combine remaining gravy, gingersnaps, brown sugar and vinegar in bowl; mix well. Pour over patties and potatoes. Bake, covered, for 20 minutes longer. Yield: 4 servings.

Photograph for this recipe on this page.

GROUND BEEF MINESTRONE

1 lg. onion, chopped
1/4 c. oil
1/2 lb. ground round
1 can beef bouillon
1 can tomato soup
1 can vegetable soup
1   16-oz. can kidney beans
2 oz. fine noodles
Salt and pepper to taste

Saute onion in oil in skillet until golden brown. Add ground round. Saute until cooked through, stirring frequently. Stir in bouillon, soups, 3 cups water, beans, noodles, salt and pepper. Simmer for 10 to 15 minutes or until noodles are tender. Yield: 8 servings.

Jeannette Deverick, Coalinga 779

HOMEMADE PICNIC SALAMI

4 lb. ground beef
1/4 c. curing salt
2 tbsp. liquid smoke
1 1/2 tsp. each pepper, garlic powder

Combine all ingredients in bowl; mix well. Chill, covered, for 24 hours. Roll into four 8-inch logs. Wrap in nylon netting; tie ends. Place on rack in deep baking pan. Bake at 225 degrees for 4 hours; cool slightly. Remove netting; blot with paper towel. Store in refrigerator for 3 weeks or less or in freezer for 2 months.

Betty Conant, Van Duzen River 517

SPAGHETTI SAUCE

18 lb. ground beef
2 whole garlic buds, peeled, chopped
12 lg. onions, chopped
4 bunches celery, chopped
6 lg. green peppers, chopped
3 lb. fresh mushrooms, sliced
3 7-lb. cans tomatoes
2 7-lb. cans tomato puree
1 7-lb. can catsup
1 1/2 1 3/4-oz. bottles of
Italian seasoning
Salt to taste
2 to 3 tbsp. sugar

Brown ground beef in skillet; drain. Saute garlic, onions, celery, green peppers and mushrooms over low heat. Combine next 4 ingredients with 2 quarts water in 10-gallon stock pot. Bring to a boil, stirring frequently. Simmer for 6 to 8 hours. Add salt and sugar. Add enough additional water to make of desired consistency. Yield: 150 servings.

LeRoy Ratliff, Oakdale 435

ONE-STEP SPAGHETTI
FOR A CROWD

42 lb. ground beef
3 c. onion flakes
6 qt. chopped celery
3 7-lb. cans tomato paste
5 7-lb. cans tomatoes
1/2 c. each salt, sugar and paprika
1 tbsp. each pepper, cayenne pepper
2 tbsp. oregano leaves
3 tbsp. Italian seasoning
20 lb. spaghetti, broken

Brown ground beef in large stock pot. Add 5 gallons water and remaining ingredients except spaghetti; mix well. Simmer for 1 hour or longer, stirring to bottom of pot frequently. Add spaghetti. Cook until spaghetti is tender. Garnish with shredded cheese to serve.
Yield: 150 servings.

Roberta Hilligoss, Stanislaus Mt. View 558

CABBAGE ROLLS

1 head cabbage, cored
1 lb. lean ground beef
1 green pepper, chopped
1 c. chopped onion
2 tbsp. oil
2 c. soft bread crumbs
1/2 c. chili sauce
2 tsp. Worcestershire sauce
1/2 tsp. each salt, marjoram
1 8-oz. can tomato sauce
2 tbsp. butter
1/2 c. sour cream

Cook cabbage in boiling salted water to cover in saucepan for 7 minutes; drain. Remove 12 large outer leaves. Brown ground beef with green pepper and onion in oil in skillet, stirring frequently. Add bread crumbs, chili sauce and seasonings; mix well. Spoon onto cabbage leaves. Roll to enclose filling; secure with toothpicks. Place in 9 x 13-inch baking dish. Top with tomato sauce; dot with butter. Bake at 350 degrees for 1 hour. Remove rolls to serving platter. Stir sour cream into pan juices. Serve with rolls.

Luella Venner, Palermo 493

GOOD CABBAGE ROLLS

4 lg. cabbage leaves
1/2 lb. ground beef
1/2 c. bread crumbs
1/2 onion, chopped
1/4 c. evaporated milk
1 egg
1 tsp. (rounded) prepared mustard
with horseradish
Dash each of Worcestershire, taco,
Tabasco and soy sauce
1/2 tsp. seasoned salt
1 16-oz. can stewed tomatoes

Simmer cabbage leaves in water to cover in saucepan for 10 minutes; drain. Combine ground beef with bread crumbs, onion, evaporated milk, egg and seasonings in bowl; mix well. Spoon onto cabbage leaves. Roll to enclose filling. Place seam side down in 8-inch casserole. Pour tomatoes over top. Bake at 350 degrees for 1 hour. Serve with baked potatoes. Yield: 4 servings.

Frances Kline, Buckeye 489

RUNZAS

2 pkg. dry yeast
1/2 c. sugar
1 1/2 tsp. salt
1 egg

1/4 c. melted margarine, cooled
6 1/2 c. flour
1 1/2 lb. ground beef
1/2 c. chopped onion
3 c. shredded cabbage
1 1/2 tsp. salt
1/2 tsp. pepper

Dissolve yeast with sugar and 1 1/2 teaspoons salt in 2 cups warm water in bowl. Add egg and margarine; mix well. Stir in flour; mix to form dough. Chill for 4 hours. Brown ground beef and onion in skillet, stirring frequently; drain. Add remaining ingredients and 1/2 cup water. Simmer for 15 to 20 minutes or until tender; cool. Roll dough out into rectangle on floured surface. Cut into 16 to 20 squares. Place 1 spoonful beef mixture on each square. Fold corners to enclose filling, sealing edges. Place on greased baking sheet. Bake at 350 degrees for 20 minutes.

Myra Eberspecher, Anderson 418

TED'S STUFFED PEPPERS

8 green peppers
1 lb. ground beef
1 c. quick-cooking rice
1 clove of garlic, chopped
2 to 3 cans tomato soup
1 can tomato sauce
Parmesan cheese

Slice tops from peppers; discard seed. Parboil in water to cover in saucepan; drain. Brown ground beef with rice and garlic in skillet, stirring frequently. Spoon into peppers. Place in 6-quart saucepan. Add soup and tomato sauce. Sprinkle with cheese. Simmer for 1 hour or until tender. Yield: 8 servings.

Lorena Wasley, Banner 627

HAM MEAT LOAF

2 1/2 lb. mixed ground ham, beef
    and pork
2 tbsp. grated onion
1 1/2 c. soft bread crumbs
1/2 c. evaporated milk
1 egg
3 tbsp. minced parsley
1/2 tsp. each salt and pepper
1 1/2 tsp. MSG
1   9-oz. can pineapple slices
1/4 c. packed brown sugar

Combine ground meat, onion, bread crumbs, milk, egg, parsley and seasonings in bowl; mix well. Arrange pineapple slices in bottom of greased loaf pan. Sprinkle with brown sugar. Spoon meat mixture into pan. Bake, covered, at 350 degrees for 30 minutes. Bake, uncovered, for 1 hour longer. Invert on serving platter. Yield: 8 servings.

Pearl Zeck, Humboldt 501

HAM-BEEF LOAVES FOR A CROWD

16 lb. ground ham
8 lb. ground beef
16 c. cracker crumbs
16 eggs, well beaten
8 tsp. dry mustard
3   3-lb. packages brown sugar
1/3 c. prepared mustard
Pineapple juice

Combine ground ham and beef with cracker crumbs, eggs and dry mustard in large bowl; mix well. Shape into loaves. Place in baking pans. Bake at 350 degrees for 45 minutes. Mix brown sugar with prepared mustard in bowl. Stir in enough pineapple juice to make a thin glaze. Pour over loaves. Bake for 30 to 45 minutes longer or until cooked through. Yield: 128 servings.

Mary Kimbrough, Airport 820

SPANISH HAM AND RICE

1 c. chopped cooked ham
1/2 c. chopped onion
1/2 c. green pepper
1 lg. clove of garlic, minced
1 tbsp. paprika
2 tbsp. oil
1 can chicken broth
3/4 c. rice
1/4 c. sliced pimento-stuffed olives
1 c. chopped canned tomatoes
Grated cheese

Saute ham, onion, green pepper, garlic and paprika in oil in skillet. Add broth, rice and olives. Bring to a boil; reduce heat. Simmer, covered, for 25 minutes or until rice is tender, stirring occasionally. Stir in tomatoes. Pour into baking dish. Sprinkle with cheese. Bake at 350 degrees until cheese melts. Yield: 6 servings.

Deloris Matheny, Whitesboro 766

HAM ROLLS

2 c. hot mashed sweet potatoes
1 c. soft bread crumbs
2 tbsp. finely chopped onion
2 tbsp. melted butter
6 thin serving-sized slices ham
1 c. pineapple juice

Combine sweet potatoes, bread crumbs, onion and butter in bowl; mix well. Place mound of stuffing on each ham slice. Roll to enclose filling; secure with toothpicks. Arrange rolls in baking dish. Add pineapple juice. Bake at 350 degrees for 30 to 40 minutes or until heated through. Yield: 6 servings.

Myrtle Stacey, Napa 307

SHEEPHERDER'S DELIGHT

3/4 c. shortening
5 lb. red potatoes, peeled, sliced
2 onions, sliced
1 to 2 tsp. salt
4 to 6 garlic sausages
12 eggs
Pepper to taste

Heat shortening in very large iron skillet over high heat until melted. Add potatoes, onions and salt, stirring to coat with shortening. Reduce heat to medium. Cook until potatoes are tender, stirring frequently. Remove casings from sausages. Cut into 1/4-inch slices. Add to potatoes. Cook until potatoes are golden brown, stirring frequently; drain. Beat eggs and pepper in bowl. Pour over potatoes. Cook until eggs are set, stirring gently. Yield: 8 servings.

Floyd Freeny, Fieldbrook 771

AWARD-WINNING PORK VERDE WITH CHILI

1 5 to 6-lb. pork shoulder, cut
into 1/2-in. cubes
4 lg. green peppers, cut into
1/2-in. pieces
4 med. red onions, cut into
1/2-in. pieces
2 tsp. salt
1 1/2 oz. chili seasoning

Combine first 3 ingredients in heavy saucepan. Brown, covered, over medium-high heat for 20 to 25 minutes, stirring frequently. Place in Crock-Pot. Cook on High for 3 hours. Add seasonings. Cook on Low for 3 to 4 hours longer. Serve on hot tortillas or rice pilaf. Yield: 10-12 servings.

Kenneth Han, Western Yolo 423

BARBECUED SPARERIBS

1/4 c. vinegar
1/4 c. Worcestershire sauce
1 c. catsup
1/4 c. honey
1 tsp. chili powder
1/4 c. packed brown sugar
1 tsp. dry mustard
4 to 5 lb. spareribs, split lengthwise
Garlic salt and pepper to taste
Liquid smoke
5 or 6 onion slices

Mix first 4 ingredients and 2 cups water in saucepan. Stir in chili powder, brown sugar and mustard. Bring to a boil. Place ribs meaty side up in roasting pan. Sprinkle with garlic salt and pepper. Brush with liquid smoke. Let stand for 30 minutes. Bake, uncovered, at 450 degrees for 45 minutes; drain. Place onion slices on top. Reduce temperature to 350 degrees. Bake for 15 minutes; drain. Pour sauce mixture over ribs. Bake for 45 minutes or until sauce thickens, basting every 15 minutes. Yield: 4-6 servings.

Grace Munger, Kelseyville 778

DELUXE RICE

1 pkg. Rice-A-Roni fried rice
2 lg. pork steaks, cut into
bite-sized pieces
1 lg. onion, chopped
3 stalks celery, chopped
1 green pepper, chopped
1 sweet red pepper, chopped
1 can sliced mushrooms, drained
1 med. carrot, shredded
Soy sauce to taste
3 green onions, sliced

Prepare fried rice according to package directions; set aside. Cook pork in skillet until cooked through, stirring frequently; remove. Saute onion, celery, peppers and mushrooms in skillet for 8 to 10 minutes. Add rice, carrot and pork; mix well. Cook for 5 minutes. Stir in soy sauce and green onions.

Doris Murphy, Van Duzen River 517

LORENE'S CHINESE PORK

1 pork shoulder roast
1 c. soy sauce
3/4 c. packed brown sugar
Dry mustard
Flat beer

Slice pork into 2 1/2 to 3-inch strips. Combine soy sauce, brown sugar and 1/2 teaspoon dry mustard in baking dish. Add pork. Marinate for 2 to 3 hours. Place in baking dish. Bake at 250 degrees for 1 1/2 hours, basting every 20 minutes. Combine additional dry mustard with enough beer to make of desired consistency. Serve dishes of mustard sauce and toasted sesame seed with pork for dipping.

Edna Jones, Dow's Prairie 505

PORK CHOPS AND PINEAPPLE

4 to 6 pork chops
1 tbsp. oil
Salt to taste
4 to 6 slices pineapple
1 c. pineapple juice

Brown pork chops on both sides in oil in skillet. Season to taste. Arrange pineapple slices on pork chops. Add pineapple juice and 1/2 cup water. Simmer, covered, for 40 minutes or until tender, adding water if necessary.
Yield: 4-6 servings.
Note: May thicken pan juices in gravy.

Eleanor Elwart, Encinitas 634

ROAST PORK

1 lean pork roast
1 tbsp. flour
1 tbsp. dry mustard
1/2 tsp. paprika
1 tsp. Tabasco sauce
1 green pepper, finely chopped

Place roast in roasting pan; pierce in several places. Rub with mixture of dry ingredients and Tabasco sauce. Let stand for several minutes. Roast at 450 degrees until browned. Combine green pepper and 2 cups water in saucepan. Simmer for several minutes. Pour over roast. Reduce temperature to 350 degrees. Roast to 185 degrees on meat thermometer, basting every 15 minutes.

Agnes M. Mairose, San Jose 10

PEPPER POT STEW

2 lb. lean pork, cut into cubes
2 tbsp. flour
2 tbsp. oil
2 cloves of garlic
1/2 c. chopped onion
1 13-oz. can tomatoes
2 7-oz. cans chopped green chilies
1/2 tsp. oregano
Salt and pepper to taste

Coat pork with flour. Brown in oil in saucepan. Add remaining ingredients and 2 cups water. Simmer for 2 hours or until pork is tender. Serve over rice if desired. Yield: 8 servings.
Note: May substitute beef for pork.

Evelyn Ruckman, Morgan Hill 408

HOMEMADE CHORIZO

1 lb. coarsely ground lean pork
2 tbsp. vinegar
1 clove of garlic, pressed
1 tsp. each salt, oregano
1/2 tsp. pepper
1/8 tsp. cumin

Combine all ingredients in bowl; mix well by hand. Pack into crock or jar. Store in refrigerator for 1 week or less. Yield: 4 servings.
Note: Use 1/3 cup mixture for each commercial sausage link.

Dolores Jimenez, French Camp-Lathrop 510

DEANNA'S SPICY KNACKWURST AND VEGETABLES

1 16-oz. package knackwurst
1 med. onion, chopped
2 tbsp. oil
1 10-oz. package frozen whole green beans, cooked
1 16-oz. can garbanzo beans
1 c. milk
3 tbsp. mustard
1/8 tsp. crushed red pepper

Brown knackwurst with onion in oil in skillet. Add remaining ingredients; mix well. Cook until heated through, stirring occasionally. Arrange on warm serving platter. Yield: 4 servings. Note: May substitute smoked sausage for knackwurst.

Edna L. Wagner, Woodbridge 482

CORN DOGS

2 c. pancake mix
1 c. cornmeal
2 eggs
Milk
Wieners
Oil for deep frying

Combine pancake mix and cornmeal in bowl. Add eggs; mix well. Beat in enough milk to make thick batter. Dip wieners in batter, coating well. Deep-fry in 375-degree oil for 3 minutes or until golden brown.

Renee Swain, Van Duzen River 517

CHORIZO BREAKFAST

1 to 1 1/2 lb. chorizo
6 eggs
1   10 1/2-oz. can whole kernel corn
1/2 to 1 c. minute rice, cooked
12 flour tortillas

Brown chorizo in skillet, stirring frequently. Add eggs 1 at a time, stirring constantly. Stir in corn and rice. Cook until chorizo is done. Serve in folded tortillas or with buttered tortillas in place of toast.

Pat Mendenhall, Muscoy 589

SAUSAGE SOUP

1 lb. sweet Italian sausage
1 tsp. oil
1   16-oz. can stewed tomatoes
2   8-oz. cans tomato sauce
2 tsp. sugar
1/4 c. parsley flakes
2 beef bouillon cubes
1/2 tsp. Italian seasoning
1 c. sliced carrots
1 c. sliced celery
1 c. sliced zucchini
1 c. chopped onion

Brown sausage in oil in large saucepan. Remove sausage; slice and set aside. Add tomatoes, tomato sauce, sugar, parsley, bouillon, seasoning and 1 cup water to saucepan. Simmer for several minutes. Stir in vegetables. Simmer for 1 hour. Stir in sausage. Cook for 10 to 20 minutes longer or until vegetables are tender. Ladle into soup bowls. Garnish with Parmesan cheese. Yield: 6 servings.

Sheila Rae Bassett, San Marcos 633

CROCK•POT GROUND TURKEY GUMBO

3 slices bacon
1 lb. ground turkey
3 stalks celery, sliced
1 med. onion, chopped
1 green pepper, chopped
1   10-oz. package frozen okra
2 c. canned tomatoes
1/2 c. whole kernel corn
2 cloves of garlic, pressed
1 tsp. Tabasco sauce
2 tbsp. parsley flakes
1 tsp. basil
1/2 tsp. thyme
2 bay leaves
1 tsp. salt
1/3 c. oil
1/2 c. flour
4 c. chicken broth
1   6-oz. can shrimp, drained (opt.)

Brown bacon in skillet; remove and crumble. Saute turkey in skillet until lightly browned. Place in Crock·Pot with bacon, vegetables and seasonings. Combine oil and flour in saucepan. Cook over low heat until medium brown, stirring constantly. Add chicken broth. Cook until thickened, stirring constantly. Pour into Crock·Pot. Cook on High for several hours or until vegetables are tender-crisp. Add shrimp. Cook for 10 minutes longer. Serve with rice or corn bread. Yield: 14 servings.

Luella Johnson, Stanislaus Mt. View 558

MICROWAVE GROUND TURKEY DOLMAS

1 lb. ground turkey
2 c. cooked rice
1 lg. onion, chopped
1/4 c. melted butter
1   8-oz. can tomato sauce
1/2 c. chopped parsley
1 tbsp. each mint, dill
1 tsp. salt
Dash of pepper
50 canned grape leaves
1 c. chicken broth

Combine first 10 ingredients in bowl; mix well. Place grape leaves 1 at a time with shiny side down on work surface. Spoon a small amount of filling onto each leaf. Roll to enclose filling, tucking ends in. Line 9 x 13-inch glass baking dish with additional grape leaves. Arrange dolmas in dish. Pour broth over dolmas. Microwave, covered, on Medium for 30 minutes. Let stand for several minutes. Serve hot or cold. Yield: 10 servings.

Note: To use fresh grape leaves, soak in hot water for 5 minutes to soften.

Betty Swanson, Stanislaus Mt. View 558

MACARONI-TURKEY STEW

    2 c. chopped cooked turkey
    1 1/2 c. chopped onions
    1/2 c. chopped parsley
    4 tsp. salt
    1/2 tsp. sage
    10 peppercorns
    1 turkey carcass, broken up
    1 c. chopped carrots
    1 c. sliced celery
    2 c. elbow macaroni

Combine first 7 ingredients and 3 quarts water in large stock pot. Simmer, covered, for 3 hours. Remove and discard bones. Add carrots and celery. Simmer, covered, for 10 minutes or until vegetables are almost tender. Bring to a boil. Add macaroni gradually. Cook, uncovered, for 10 to 15 minutes or until macaroni is just tender, stirring occasionally. Serve immediately. Yield: 6-8 servings.

Photograph for this recipe below.

CHICKEN AND DUMPLINGS

6 slices bacon, chopped
1 onion, chopped
1 4 to 5-lb. chicken, cut up
Salt and pepper
2 10 3/4-oz. cans chicken broth
1 tbsp. angostura bitters
3 white turnips, peeled, chopped
18 sm. white onions
6 med. potatoes, peeled, cut into
    1-in. cubes
1 c. light cream
1/2 c. flour
4 eggs
1 tsp. salt
1/2 c. milk
2 c. flour

Fry bacon and onion in large saucepan. Add chicken seasoned with salt and pepper to taste. Brown on all sides. Add chicken broth and enough water to cover. Simmer, covered, for 1 to 1 1/2 hours or until chicken is tender. Add bitters and vegetables. Simmer, covered, for 20 to 25 minutes or until vegetables are tender. Add mixture of cream and 1/2 cup flour. Cook over low heat until thickened, stirring constantly. Season to taste with salt and pepper. Beat eggs, 1 teaspoon salt and milk in bowl. Stir in enough flour to make of muffin batter consistency. Drop by heaping tablespoonfuls into boiling salted water. Simmer, covered, for 20 minutes. Serve chicken with dumplings. Garnish with finely chopped parsley. Yield: 6 servings.

Photograph for this recipe above.

HAWAIIAN-STYLE CHICKEN

1/4 c. butter
1 chicken, cut up
1 8-oz. can crushed pineapple
1/3 c. catsup
2 tbsp. lemon juice
2 tbsp. chili sauce
1/4 c. packed brown sugar
1 tsp. soy sauce
1/2 tsp. Worcestershire sauce
2 tbsp. cornstarch
1 tsp. salt

Melt butter in 9 x 11-inch baking dish. Coat chicken pieces with butter. Arrange skin side up in prepared dish. Combine remaining ingredients in saucepan. Cook until thickened, stirring constantly. Pour over chicken. Bake, covered, at 350 degrees for 30 minutes. Bake, uncovered, for 30 to 40 minutes longer or until tender. Yield: 6 servings.

Kay Morris, Antelope 161

CHICKEN LEGS FOR A CROWD

6 lb. onions, thinly sliced
150 chicken thighs
150 chicken drumsticks
3 c. flour
1 tbsp. salt
1 tbsp. paprika
1 tsp. pepper
3 lb. butter, melted

Place half the onion slices in large shallow baking pans. Arrange chicken in single layer over onions. Top with remaining onions. Sift mixture of dry ingredients over top. Drizzle with butter. Bake at 350 degrees for 1 hour or until browned and tender. Serve with onions and pan juices. Yield: 100 servings.

Hortense Freeman, Santa Ynez Valley 644

OVEN-FRIED CHICKEN

1 chicken, cut up
1 c. baking mix
1 1/2 tsp. salt
1/4 tsp. pepper
2 tsp. paprika
1 stick butter

Coat chicken with mixture of baking mix, salt, pepper and paprika. Melt butter in shallow baking dish. Roll chicken in butter to coat well. Arrange skin side down in single layer in dish. Bake at 400 degrees for 1 hour, turning chicken over after 30 minutes.

Marie Sanders, Quartz Hill 697

POULET CHAUSSEUR

3 chickens, cut up
1 env. garlic salad dressing mix
2 to 4 tbsp. oil
3 tbsp. butter, melted
1 lb. mushrooms
1 c. chopped onion
2 tbsp. flour
1 16-oz. can tomatoes
2 tsp. oregano
1 1/4 c. Sauterne

Sprinkle chicken with 2 teaspoons salad dressing mix. Brown in oil in skillet. Remove chicken; drain pan drippings. Add butter, mushrooms and onion. Saute until tender. Blend in flour. Add tomatoes, oregano, remaining salad dressing mix and 1 cup wine; mix well. Return chicken to skillet. Simmer, covered, for 35 to 40 minutes or until tender, turning chicken occasionally. Arrange chicken on serving platter. Stir remaining 1/4 cup wine into sauce. Bring to a boil. Pour over chicken.

Nettie Larson, Encinitas 634

CHICKEN TERIYAKI

1 chicken, cut up
1 c. soy sauce
1/2 c. packed brown sugar
6 tbsp. butter
1/4 tsp. dry mustard

Arrange chicken in 9 x 13-inch baking dish. Combine remaining ingredients and 1 cup water in saucepan. Bring to a boil. Pour over chicken. Bake at 350 degrees for 1 1/2 hours.

Virginia Higgins, Waterford 553

OVEN-FRIED CHICKEN MONTEREY

1/4 c. flour
1 1 1/4-oz. envelope taco seasoning mix
16 chicken thighs
1/4 c. butter
1 c. crushed tortilla chips
2 tbsp. finely chopped onion
1 tbsp. oil
2 tbsp. flour
1/4 tsp. salt
1 13-oz. can evaporated milk
1/4 tsp. hot pepper sauce
1 c. shredded Monterey Jack cheese
1/4 c. sliced ripe olives
1 tsp. lemon juice

Combine 1/4 cup flour and taco seasoning mix in bag. Shake 2 or 3 pieces of chicken at a time in bag to coat. Melt butter in 10 x 15-inch baking dish. Coat chicken with butter then crushed chips. Arrange in baking dish. Bake at 375 degrees for 45 to 50 minutes or until tender. Saute onion in oil in skillet. Blend in 2 tablespoons flour and salt. Add evaporated milk and pepper sauce. Cook until mixture thickens, stirring constantly. Add remaining ingredients, stirring until cheese melts. Do not boil. Line serving dish with lettuce. Arrange chicken on lettuce. Spoon half the cheese sauce over chicken. Garnish with additional tortilla chips and ripe olives. Serve with remaining cheese sauce. Yield: 8 servings.

Jo Severance, Apple Valley 593

MEXICAN-STYLE CHICKEN KIEV

8 chicken breasts, boned
1   7-oz. can chopped green
  chilies, drained
1/4 lb. Monterey Jack cheese, cut
  into 8 strips
1/2 c. fine dry bread crumbs
1/4 c. Parmesan cheese
1 tbsp. chili powder
1/2 tsp. salt
1/4 tsp. each pepper, cumin
Butter
1   15-oz. can tomato sauce
1/2 tsp. cumin
1/3 c. sliced green onions
Salt, pepper and hot pepper sauce
  to taste

Pound chicken breasts to 1/4-inch thickness. Place 1 spoonful chilies and 1 piece of cheese on each chicken breast. Roll to enclose filling, tucking edges in. Combine bread crumbs, Parmesan cheese, chili powder, 1/2 teaspoon salt, 1/4 teaspoon pepper and 1/4 teaspoon cumin in bowl. Dip chicken rolls in 6 tablespoons melted butter; coat with bread crumb mixture. Place seam side down in 8 x 12-inch baking dish. Drizzle with additional melted butter. Chill, covered, for 4 hours to overnight. Bake at 400 degrees for 20 minutes or until tender. Combine remaining ingredients in saucepan. Cook until heated through. Serve with chicken rolls.

Esther F. Russell, Rainbow Valley 689

MEXICAN-BARBECUED CHICKEN

1   8-oz. can tomato sauce
1/2 c. corn syrup
1 to 2 tbsp. minced jalapeno pepper
1 clove of garlic, minced
1 tsp. Worcestershire sauce
1/2 tsp. salt
1 chicken, cut up

Combine first 6 ingredients in saucepan; mix well. Bring to a boil over medium heat. Cook for 5 minutes, stirring frequently. Grill chicken 6 inches from heat source for 30 minutes, turning frequently. Brush with sauce. Grill for 15 minutes longer or until tender, turning and basting frequently. Yield: 4 servings.

Thelma Langston, Escalon 447

JAN'S FLORIDA CHICKEN

2 chickens, cut up
1 env. dry onion soup mix

1   10-oz. jar apricot preserves
1 sm. bottle of Russian dressing

Arrange chicken in shallow baking dish. Combine remaining ingredients in bowl; mix well. Pour over chicken. Bake at 375 degrees for 1 1/2 hours. Reduce temperature if necessary to prevent overbrowning. Yield: 4-6 servings.

Janet Johnson, Hangtown 464

HERB-ROASTED CHICKEN BREASTS

3 1/2 tbsp. melted butter
1 tbsp. each finely chopped onion, garlic
1 tsp. thyme
1/2 tsp. each salt, pepper and rosemary
1/4 tsp. sage
1/8 tsp. marjoram
Dash of hot pepper sauce
4 chicken breasts, boned

Combine all ingredients except chicken breasts in bowl; mix well. Coat chicken breasts with herb mixture. Place skin side up in baking dish, tucking ends under. Bake at 425 degrees for 14 minutes or until cooked through, basting occasionally with herb sauce. Broil for several minutes to brown. Arrange on serving plate. Spoon pan juices over top. Garnish with parsley.

Dorris Gibson, Feather River 440

CHICKEN IN-A-BLANKET

1 pkg. frozen unbaked patty shells, thawed
4 chicken breasts, boned
4 thin slices ham
4 thin slices Swiss cheese
1 recipe white sauce
1 tsp. dillseed

Roll out each patty shell into rectangular shape on floured surface. Pound chicken breasts thin. Place on pastry. Top each with 1 slice ham and cheese. Roll pastry to enclose chicken breasts, overlapping ends. Place seam side down in buttered baking dish. Bake at 375 degrees for 40 to 45 minutes or until browned. Combine white sauce and dillseed. Serve over chicken.

Dorothy Graham, Copper Mountain 814

MARINATED CHICKEN BREASTS

4 chicken breasts, skinned, boned
3/4 tsp. salt
1/2 tsp. freshly ground pepper
4 tsp. cornstarch
4 tsp. oil
1 egg white
Lemon juice

Pound chicken breasts to 1/4-inch thickness. Sprinkle with salt and pepper. Let stand for 20 minutes. Sprinkle with cornstarch and oil. Let stand for 20 minutes. Add to egg white in bowl; stir to coat. Let stand for 30 minutes. Cook in generous amount of lemon juice in skillet for 1 1/2 minutes on each side or until tender. Serve with lemon juice. Yield: 2-3 servings.

Edcil Zoller, Greenhorn 384

CHINESE CHICKEN IN FOIL

1 tbsp. each soy sauce,
  Worcestershire sauce
1 tbsp. pale dry Sherry
1 tbsp. Hoisin sauce
3 tbsp. oil
1 tsp. sesame oil
1 1/2 tbsp. cornstarch
1 sm. clove of garlic, minced
2 green onions, chopped
Salt to taste
3 c. 1-inch pieces of uncooked chicken

Combine all ingredients except chicken in bowl; mix well. Add chicken; mix well. Marinate for 30 minutes or longer. Drop by tablespoonfuls on double-thick 6-inch foil squares. Fold in triangles and tuck corners under to enclose filling. Place foil packets on baking sheet. Bake at 450 degrees for 17 minutes. Unwrap packets. Serve chicken with rice and Chinese vegetables. Yield: 4 servings.

Jane V. Trask, Manton 732

CHICKEN A LA CRESCENT

1 3-oz. package cream cheese, softened
2 tbsp. butter, softened
1/2 tsp. lemon-pepper seasoning
1 c. chopped cooked chicken
1 2-oz. can chopped mushrooms, drained
1 8-count can refrigerator crescent
  dinner rolls
3 tbsp. melted butter
1/3 c. Italian-style bread crumbs
1 pkg. chicken gravy mix

Combine cream cheese, 2 tablespoons butter and seasoning in bowl. Add chicken and mushrooms; mix well. Separate crescent rolls. Spread 1/4 cup chicken mixture on each triangle. Roll up from wide end. Turn sides under and pinch to seal well. Dip rolls in melted butter. Coat with bread crumbs. Place on baking sheet. Bake at 375 degrees for 15 to 20 minutes or until golden brown. Prepare gravy mix according to

package directions. Serve over rolls.
Note: May substitute 1 to 2 five-ounce cans boned chicken for chopped cooked chicken.

Julie Jones, Mt. Lassen 417

CRESCENT CHICKEN SQUARES

2 tbsp. melted butter
1 3-oz. package cream cheese, softened
2 tbsp. milk
1/4 tsp. salt
1/8 tsp. pepper
2 c. chopped cooked chicken
1 tbsp. chopped onion
1 8-oz. can refrigerator crescent
  dinner rolls
1 tbsp. melted butter
3/4 c. seasoned croutons, crushed

Blend 2 tablespoons butter and cream cheese in bowl. Add milk, salt and pepper; mix well. Stir in chicken and onion. Separate roll dough into 4 rectangles, pressing to seal perforations. Spoon chicken mixture onto rectangles. Pull corners to center to enclose filling; twist to seal. Brush tops with remaining 1 tablespoon butter. Dip in crumbs. Place on baking sheet. Bake at 350 degrees for 20 to 25 minutes or until golden brown. Yield: 4 servings.

Barbara Staples, Whitehorn 792

SOUR CREAM
CHICKEN ENCHILADAS

2 cans cream of chicken soup
1 16-oz. carton sour cream
2 4-oz. cans chopped green
  chilies, drained
1/2 tsp. salt
2 c. grated Cheddar cheese
2 c. chopped cooked chicken
12 tortillas
1 c. oil
Grated Cheddar cheese

Combine soup, sour cream, chilies and salt in saucepan. Heat until smooth and well blended, stirring frequently. Mix 2 cups cheese and chicken in bowl. Dip tortillas in hot oil in skillet for several seconds to soften. Place 1/3 cup chicken mixture and 1 tablespoon sour cream sauce on each tortilla. Roll to enclose filling. Arrange in 9 x 12-inch baking dish. Pour remaining sauce over enchiladas. Top with additional cheese. Bake at 350 degrees for 20 to 30 minutes or until bubbly. Yield: 6-8 servings.

Betty Creason, Three Forks 449

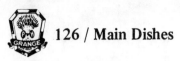

CHICKEN-FILLED BISCUIT DUMPLINGS

1 can cream of chicken soup
1 can golden mushroom soup
1/2 c. chopped green pepper
2 tbsp. chopped onion
3 5-oz. cans boned chicken
1/4 c. chopped celery
2 tbsp. chopped onion
1 tsp. parsley flakes
1/8 to 1/4 tsp. pepper
1 10-count can buttermilk
* refrigerator biscuits*

Combine soups, green pepper, 2 tablespoons onion and 1 1/4 cups water in large saucepan. Simmer for several minutes, stirring occasionally. Combine next 5 ingredients in bowl; mix well. Roll biscuits into 4-inch circles on floured surface. Place 1/4 cup chicken mixture on each biscuit. Fold biscuits to enclose filling, pinching to seal edges. Drop in simmering soup mixture, spooning sauce over dumplings. Simmer, tightly covered, for 15 to 20 minutes or until dumplings test done. Serve with cooking sauce. Yield: 4-5 servings.

Yvonne Hart, Waterford 553

CREAM OF CHICKEN-CHEESE SOUP

1/3 c. each finely chopped carrot,
* onion and celery*
1 c. chicken stock
2 cans cream of chicken soup
1/2 c. milk
1 c. chopped Velveeta cheese
1 c. chopped cooked chicken

Cook vegetables in stock in saucepan until tender. Mix soup with milk in bowl. Add soup mixture and remaining ingredients to vegetables. Cook over low heat until cheese melts. Yield: 4-6 servings.

Geraldine Metzger, Vista 609

ALMOND FISH FILLETS

2 lb. frozen fish fillets, thawed
Salt and pepper to taste
1/4 c. butter
2 tbsp. butter
2 tbsp. flour
1/2 c. milk
1/2 c. slivered toasted almonds

Sprinkle fish fillets with salt and pepper. Place in 1/4 cup melted butter in skillet; add 1/2 cup water. Simmer, covered, for 10 minutes or until fish flakes easily. Remove fish to heatproof serving platter. Cook pan juices until reduced by 1/3. Cream 2 tablespoons butter and flour in bowl. Add with milk to pan juices. Simmer until thickened, stirring occasionally. Sprinkle almonds around fish. Pour sauce over fish. Broil until brown. Serve immediately.

Photograph for this recipe on opposite page.

BAKED PARMESAN FISH

1 lb. small fish fillets
1/2 tsp. salt
1/8 tsp. pepper
1/2 c. sour cream
1 tbsp. Parmesan cheese
1/4 tsp. paprika
1/8 tsp. tarragon
3 green onions, sliced
1 tomato, sliced

Roll up fish fillets. Place seam side down in ungreased square baking dish. Sprinkle with salt and pepper. Mix sour cream, cheese, paprika and tarragon in bowl. Spread over fish. Bake at 350 degrees for 20 to 30 minutes or until fish flakes easily. Top with onions and tomato slices. Yield: 6 servings.

Thelma Jackson, Humboldt 501

FISH DELISH

1 tsp. white wine
1 7-in. fish fillet
2 tsp. mayonnaise
Salt, pepper and onion powder to taste
Chopped parsley
1 tsp. white wine

Pour 1 teaspoon wine into saucepan. Place fish fillet in saucepan. Spread with mayonnaise. Sprinkle with seasonings and parsley. Drizzle 1 teaspoon wine over top. Cook, covered, on low heat for 5 to 8 minutes or until fish flakes easily. Yield: 1 serving.

Mary Pelmulder, Sebastopol 306

SALMON DUFF

1 16-oz. can salmon, flaked
3 eggs, slightly beaten
1 7-oz. package potato chips, crushed
1 tbsp. lemon juice
1 tsp. salt
Dash of pepper
1/4 c. melted butter

Combine salmon, eggs, potato chips, lemon juice and seasonings in bowl; mix well. Coat 1-quart baking dish evenly with butter. Spoon salmon mixture into dish. Bake at 450 degrees for 20 minutes. Invert on serving platter. Serve with buttered green beans and carrots.
Yield: 6 servings.

Eulah Childs, Porterville 718

SALMON LOAF

1 16-oz. can salmon, flaked
1 can cream of celery soup
1/2 c. chopped onion
1/4 c. chopped green pepper
1 pimento, chopped
1/3 c. mayonnaise
1 c. cracker crumbs
2 eggs, beaten
1/2 c. milk
1 tbsp. lemon juice

Combine all ingredients in bowl; mix well. Spoon into greased loaf pan. Bake at 350 degrees for 1 hour. Yield: 4-6 servings.

Ermina C. Wheeler, Thermalito 729

CLAUDINE'S SALMON ROLL

1 lg. can salmon
1 8-oz. package cream cheese, softened
1 tbsp. each liquid smoke,
    Worcestershire sauce
1 tbsp. each horseradish, grated onion
1 tbsp. lemon juice
1 tbsp. dry mustard
Salt and pepper to taste
1/4 c. chopped nuts
2 tbsp. parsley flakes

Combine all ingredients except nuts and parsley in bowl; mix well. Shape into roll. Chill for 1 1/2 hours or longer. Roll in mixture of nuts and parsley flakes. Serve with crackers or rye bread.

Claudine Anderson, DeSabla 762

MARGARET'S SALMON ROLL

1 c. flour
2 tsp. baking powder
1/4 tsp. salt
2 tbsp. butter
1 16-oz. can salmon
1 egg, well beaten

Sift dry ingredients together in bowl. Cut in butter until crumbly. Add about 1 cup water or enough to form dough. Roll out into rectangle on floured surface. Mix salmon and egg in bowl. Spread over dough. Roll as for jelly roll to enclose filling. Place on baking sheet. Brush with additional beaten egg. Bake at 400 degrees for 25 to 30 minutes or until browned. Serve with parslied white sauce. Yield: 6 servings.

Margaret Lundgren, Humboldt 501

SMOKED SALMON

2 16-oz. packages brown sugar
1 c. salt
1 tsp. garlic powder
Fresh salmon

Combine first 3 ingredients in bowl; mix well. Cut salmon into pieces for smoking. Coat with brown sugar mixture. Place in dish. Sprinkle remaining brown sugar mixture over top. Let stand overnight. Rinse salmon; pat dry. Place on rack in smoker. Smoke using smoker directions.

Gerald Hiner, Humboldt 501

SALMON SOUFFLE

1/4 c. melted butter
5 tbsp. flour
1/2 tsp. salt
1 c. milk
1 c. flaked salmon
3 eggs, separated

Blend butter, flour and salt in saucepan. Add milk gradually. Cook until thickened, stirring constantly; cool. Add salmon and lightly beaten egg yolks. Fold stiffly beaten egg whites gently into mixture. Pour into buttered 1 1/2-quart casserole. Place in pan with 1 inch hot water. Bake at 325 degrees for 1 hour.
Yield: 4 servings.

Ida Sordello, Mt. Hamilton 469

STUFFED SQUID

1 clove of garlic
1/4 c. oil
1 20-oz. can tomatoes
1 1/2 c. bread crumbs
1 tsp. chopped parsley
1 egg, beaten
Salt, pepper and garlic powder to taste
8 sm. squid, cleaned

Brown garlic in oil in skillet; remove garlic. Stir in tomatoes. Simmer for 30 minutes. Combine bread crumbs, parsley, egg and seasonings in bowl; mix well. Spoon into squid cavities; skewer with toothpicks to enclose stuffing. Place in tomato sauce in skillet. Simmer for 45 minutes or until tender. Serve stuffed squid whole with sauce. Yield: 4-6 servings.

Loraine Squillace, Pine Creek 770

TUNA LOAF

1 lg. can tuna, flaked
1 can mushroom soup
2 1/2 c. soft bread crumbs
1/2 c. milk
2 eggs, beaten
1/4 c. chopped pimento
3 tbsp. chopped parsley
1 tsp. salt
1/8 tsp. pepper

Combine tuna and mushroom soup in bowl. Add bread crumbs soaked in milk and remaining ingredients; mix well. Spoon into greased muffin cups. Bake at 350 degrees for 30 to 40 minutes or until firm. Yield: 6 servings.

Agnes Shideler, Hessel 750

CRAB MOLD

1 env. unflavored gelatin
1/2 can cream of mushroom soup
3/4 c. mayonnaise
1 8-oz. package cream cheese, softened
3 sm. stalks celery, finely chopped
2 sm. green onions, finely chopped
1 6 1/2-oz. can crab meat

Soften gelatin in soup in saucepan. Heat until gelatin dissolves, stirring constantly. Do not boil. Add remaining ingredients; mix well. Spoon into oiled mold. Chill for 6 hours or longer. Unmold on serving plate. Serve with crackers or chips.

Geri Schwartzler, Rincon Valley 710

ONE-POT CLAM CHOWDER

1 c. sliced onion
1 1/2 c. chopped carrots
1 1/2 c. chopped celery
1 med. green pepper, chopped
3 tbsp. bacon drippings
1   28-oz. can tomatoes
1/4 tsp. pepper
1 tsp. salt
1/2 tsp. thyme
1 tsp. oregano
3 beef bouillon cubes
2 c. elbow macaroni
3   6 1/2-oz. cans minced clams
1/2 lb. bacon, crisp-fried, crumbled

Saute onion, carrots, celery and green pepper in bacon drippings in 5-quart saucepan until tender-crisp. Add tomatoes, 6 cups water, seasonings, bouillon cubes and macaroni. Bring to a boil, stirring frequently; reduce heat. Simmer, covered, for 10 minutes or until macaroni is almost tender, stirring occasionally. Add undrained clams. Simmer until macaroni is tender. Sprinkle bacon over top. Yield: 3 1/2 quarts.

Photograph for this recipe above.

CLAM-ENGLISH MUFFIN-CHEESE BREAKFAST

8 oz. canned clams
1 c. skim milk
3 English muffins, split, cut into
    1/2-in. cubes
2 tbsp. margarine
3 eggs, separated
Salt to taste
1/4 c. grated cheese

Drain clams, reserving liquid. Heat milk in double boiler. Add reserved clam liquid, muffin cubes, margarine, well-beaten egg yolks and salt; mix well. Cook until thickened, stirring constantly; remove from heat. Add cheese, stirring until melted. Cool for 10 to 15 minutes. Stir in clams. Fold in stiffly beaten egg whites. Pour into well-greased large pie plate. Place in shallow pan of hot water. Bake at 375 degrees for 1 hour or until knife blade inserted in center comes out clean. Yield: 6 servings.
Note: May substitute salmon or shrimp for clams.

Ora R. Saalma, Sierra Nevada 454

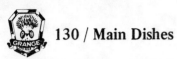

JENNY'S CLAM CHOWDER

1 can minced clams
1 c. chopped potatoes
1 c. chopped onions
1 c. chopped celery
3/4 c. flour
3/4 c. margarine
1 can evaporated milk
1 qt. milk
1 1/2 tsp. salt
1/2 tsp. sugar
1/4 c. chopped parsley

Drain clams, reserving juice. Combine reserved juice with vegetables in saucepan. Add enough water to cover. Cook until vegetables are tender. Stir flour into melted margarine in small saucepan. Cook for 1 minute. Add evaporated milk and milk. Cook until thickened, stirring constantly. Stir into vegetables with clams. Cook until heated through. Add seasonings. Sprinkle with parsley. Yield: 8 servings.

Jenny Briggs, Rough and Ready 795

BATTER-FRIED SHRIMP

1/2 c. flour
1/3 c. cornstarch
1 tsp. soy sauce
Oil for deep frying
2 tsp. baking powder
Shrimp

Mix flour and cornstarch in bowl. Stir in soy sauce and 1/2 cup water gradually, mixing until smooth. Heat oil to 375 degrees. Stir 1 tablespoon hot oil and baking powder into batter. Add more water, 1 tablespoon at a time, until batter is just thick enough to coat shrimp. Dip shrimp in batter. Deep-fry until golden brown.

Ione Poore, Feather River 440

SHRIMP-CHEESE SOUFFLE

8 slices white bread, buttered
1 lb. American cheese, grated
2 c. shrimp, cut into halves
4 eggs, beaten
4 c. milk
Pinch each of salt and pepper
Pinch of dry mustard

Arrange 4 bread slices in buttered 8 x 12-inch baking pan. Sprinkle with half the cheese. Add half the shrimp. Layer remaining 4 bread slices, cheese and shrimp on top. Mix eggs, milk and seasonings in bowl. Pour over bread. Bake at 350 degrees for 20 minutes or until set and browned. Yield: 8 servings.

Byron Kearne, Yucaipa Valley 582

MICROWAVE COQUILLE ST. JACQUES

3 tbsp. butter
2 green onions, sliced
1   4-oz. can mushrooms, drained
1 lb. sea scallops
1/2 c. white wine
1 tbsp. chopped pimento
1/2 tsp. salt
1/8 tsp. pepper
1 bay leaf
3 tbsp. flour
1/4 c. light cream
2 c. cooked rice

Combine butter, onions and mushrooms in 2-quart glass casserole. Microwave on High for 2 to 3 minutes or until tender. Add scallops, wine, pimento and seasonings; mix well. Microwave for 7 minutes. Blend flour and cream in small bowl until smooth. Stir into scallops. Microwave until thickened. Remove bay leaf. Let stand for 5 minutes. Serve over rice. Yield: 4 servings.
Note: May substitute whitefish fillets cut into bite-sized pieces for scallops.

Vicki Landrus, Garden Grove 613

SEAFOOD CIOPPINO

1 c. chopped onion
4 cloves of garlic, minced
2 green peppers, chopped
1/4 c. oil
1 lg. can tomatoes
1 can tomato sauce
2 bay leaves
1 tsp. oregano
Salt and pepper to taste
1/4 c. dry white wine
1 lb. cod fillets, chopped
1 crab, cracked
1/2 lb. shrimp
1 can minced clams

Saute onion, garlic and green peppers in oil in stock pot for 10 minutes. Add tomatoes, tomato sauce, 2 cups water and seasonings. Cook for 45 minutes. Stir in wine and cod. Cook for 10 minutes. Add remaining ingredients. Cook for 10 minutes longer. Ladle into soup bowls. Serve with crusty French bread. Yield: 4-6 servings.

Violet Imoto, Bennett Valley 16

ANN'S FRIDAY CASSEROLE

1/4 c. melted butter
1 c. diced celery
1 c. grated Cheddar cheese
1 onion, minced
1 tsp. each salt and pepper
2 c. grated carrots
1 c. soft bread crumbs
1/2 c. chopped nuts
2 eggs, beaten
1 can cream of mushroom soup

Combine all ingredients except soup in bowl; mix well. Pack into 9-inch square baking dish. Bake at 350 degrees for 30 minutes. Spread soup over top. Bake for 1 or 2 minutes longer. Yield: 8 servings.

Edna Jones, Dow's Prairie 505

CHEESE CHOPS

2 eggs, beaten
3/4 c. grated cheese
2 tsp. prepared mustard
1 tsp. chopped parsley
1 c. finely crushed crackers
1/4 c. melted butter
Salt and pepper to taste
Flour

Combine first 6 ingredients, salt and pepper in bowl; mix well. Shape into chops. Coat with flour. Brown in shortening or butter in skillet. Yield: 4 servings.

Beulah M. Spurlock, LaAvenida 655

PEANUT-CHEESE LOAF

2/3 c. cooked wheat cereal, oatmeal or rice
3 tbsp. minced onion
1/2 c. chopped green pepper
1/3 c. milk

1 tsp. salt
2 tsp. lemon juice
1 c. chopped peanuts
2/3 c. fine bread crumbs
1/4 lb. cheese, grated
1 egg

Combine all ingredients in bowl; mix well. Pour into greased loaf pan. Bake at 350 degrees for 1 hour. Serve with hot mushroom sauce or tomato sauce.

Flossie Barto, Glen Avon 591

DINNER PATTIES

4 eggs, beaten
1 1/2 c. cracker crumbs
1 1/2 c. oats
2/3 c. evaporated milk
1 c. finely chopped nuts
2/3 c. diced celery
1 tbsp. parsley
1 tsp. savory salt
1/2 tsp. salt
1/2 tsp. MSG
2 tbsp. butter
2 cans mushroom soup

Combine first 5 ingredients with 1/3 cup water in bowl; mix well. Saute celery and parsley with seasonings in butter in skillet. Add to oats mixture; mix well. Shape into patties. Brown on both sides in skillet. Place in 9 x 13-inch baking dish. Top with mixture of soup and 1 1/2 soup cans water. Bake at 350 degrees for 45 to 60 minutes.
Note: May freeze before adding soup.

Carole Dunlap, Van Duzen River 517

GRAPE NUTS ROAST

1 1/2 c. Grape Nuts
1 1/2 c. milk
2 tbsp. butter, softened
2 tsp. salt
1 c. crushed walnuts or peanuts
2 eggs
1 onion, chopped
1 c. chopped celery

Mix Grape Nuts and milk in bowl. Let stand for 5 minutes. Add butter, salt, walnuts, eggs, onion and celery; mix well. Place in 9 x 13-inch baking pan. Bake at 350 degrees for 45 minutes or until cooked through. Yield: 6 servings.

Elizabeth Eyler, Berry Creek 694

POACHED EGGS PLUS

1/4 c. vinegar
4 to 6 eggs, at room temperature

Bring 3 cups water and vinegar to a rapid boil in 10-inch skillet. Break eggs 1 at a time into boiling water. Simmer for 3 minutes. Remove eggs to second skillet containing 3 cups hot but not boiling water. Let stand until ready to serve. Season and garnish as desired.

Cam Stevens, Fort Bragg 672

STUFFED BELL PEPPERS

2 green peppers
1 eggplant
1 egg
1/2 c. milk
1/2 c. bread crumbs
1/2 tsp. salt
1/2 c. ground nuts (opt.)
Chopped onion (opt.)

Parboil green peppers until soft. Cut into halves; remove seed. Parboil eggplant until soft. Peel and mash. Combine eggplant with remaining ingredients in bowl; mix well. Spoon into peppers. Sprinkle with additional crumbs. Place in baking dish. Bake at 350 degrees for 30 minutes. Yield: 4 servings.

Mary Burns, Rough and Ready 795

SOYBEAN TACOS

3 c. dried soybeans
1 c. mayonnaise
Catsup
Dash of Worcestershire sauce
2 drops of lemon juice
1 pkg. corn tortillas
1 lg. onion, chopped
1 lb. Cheddar cheese, grated
1 med. head lettuce, shredded
3 tomatoes, chopped

Cook soybeans in water to cover in saucepan until tender. Mash soybeans. Store in refrigerator. Blend mayonnaise, enough catsup to make of desired color, Worcestershire sauce and lemon juice in bowl. Brown soybeans in a small amount of oil in skillet. Brown tortillas on both sides in oil in skillet. Place spoonful of soybeans on each tortilla. Garnish individual portions as desired with onion, cheese, lettuce, tomatoes and mayonnaise mixture.

Mildred Anderson, Kingsburg 679

VEGETARIAN SPAGHETTI

1/3 c. chopped celery
1/3 c. chopped green pepper
1 c. chopped onion
2 tbsp. butter
1 16-oz. can tomatoes
1 8-oz. can tomato paste
1 tbsp. sugar
1 tsp. oregano
1 tsp. basil
2 c. sliced zucchini
1 c. mushrooms
2 tbsp. butter
1/3 c. Parmesan cheese
6 oz. spaghetti, cooked
1 c. cottage cheese
1/2 c. grated mozzarella cheese

Saute celery, green pepper and onion in 2 tablespoons butter in skillet. Add tomatoes, tomato paste, sugar, oregano and basil; mix well. Simmer for 20 to 30 minutes, adding a small amount of water to make of desired consistency. Add zucchini and mushrooms. Simmer for 15 minutes. Add 2 tablespoons butter and Parmesan cheese to hot spaghetti; toss to mix. Layer spaghetti, cottage cheese and sauce in large deep pie plate. Bake at 350 degrees for 20 minutes. Top with mozzarella cheese. Bake for 5 minutes longer. Yield: 4 servings.

Jeanie Barone, San Jose 10

TOFU LASAGNA

1 c. fresh sliced mushrooms
1 green pepper, chopped
1 lg. onion, chopped
2 sm. zucchini, chopped
Margarine
1 c. chopped tofu
1 handful chopped parsley
1/2 c. Parmesan cheese
3 c. spaghetti sauce
1 12-oz. package whole wheat
    lasagna noodles, cooked
1 1/2 c. shredded Monterey Jack cheese

Saute vegetables in margarine in skillet. Mix tofu, parsley and Parmesan cheese in bowl. Layer sauce, sauteed vegetables, noodles, tofu mixture and Monterey Jack cheese alternately in 9 x 13-inch baking pan. Bake at 350 degrees for 45 minutes. Serve with green salad and garlic toast. Yield: 12-15 servings.

Beverly L. Quast, Goat Mountain 818

PIES

Avery's Riding Cotton and Corn Planter

Mr. Bill

(PATENTED)

With Fertilizer Attachment.

This Fertilizer Attachment is simple of adjustment. The delivery is regular, the fertilizer is deposited directly behind the sweep or lister bottom, which protects it from the wind. Hopper has large capacity.

Mr. Bill, by the use of this attachment, sows fertilizer, opens, plants and covers at one "through."

Avery's Corn Planters

Corn Queen

Sled Runners—Open Wheels

PIE & PASTRY TIPS

- *For perfectly round pie crusts,* form a ball with the dough and flatten it by pressing the side of your hand into it three times in a top-to-bottom direction and three times in a side-to-side direction. Then roll as usual.

- *To put the top crust onto your pie easily,* roll it out until it is ready to be put on the pie. Cut the slits you want for air vents, then pick up one edge of the crust on your rolling pin and roll to wrap the entire crust loosely around the pin. "Roll" the top crust over your pie.

- *To fit a crumb crust into a 9-inch plate,* place the crumb dough into the plate and press down with an 8-inch plate. The crust will shape itself between the two plates.

- *For a non-stick crumb crust,* when you're ready to serve your pie, wrap a hot, wet towel around the outside of the pie plate. Hold it there for two or three minutes. Every slice you cut will come out of the pan easily.

- *To save yourself the trouble of thickening juices* for fruit pies, substitute tapioca for the flour. Combine the tapioca with the sugar and seasoning you use then add liquid and fruit according to your recipe, turn the mixture into a pie crust and bake. The tapioca thickens the juices during baking.

- *To prevent a soggy bottom crust if your pie has a juicy filling,* brush the crust with an egg white or melted butter before adding the filling. And do be sure that the filling is very hot.

- *When pie juices spill into your oven,* sprinkle the spill with salt to prevent smoke and smell.

- *To avoid spills* when you're preparing to bake custard pie, place the shell on your oven rack and pour the filling into it. This trick bypasses the precarious balancing of a full custard pie as you carry it to the oven.

- *To prevent ragged edges on your pie meringue* when it is cut, dip the knife you use in warm water. Repeat as often as necessary while you're cutting your slices.

- *To freeze pies and crusts,* remember: fruit, mince, and chiffon pies freeze well, but custard and meringue ones don't; freeze a filled pie without wrapping it until it is almost solid — then wrap it, using moisture-and vapor-proof freezer paper. These pies can be frozen for two to three months.

- *When thawing a frozen pie baked before freezing,* heat at 350 degrees just until warm. The exception to this rule is chiffon pie which must never be heated. Thaw a chiffon pie in the refrigerator for three hours or at room temperature for 45 minutes.

- *When cooking a frozen, unbaked pie,* bake at the temperature specified in your recipe for the given time plus 15 to 20 minutes.

FLAKY PIE CRUSTS

3 c. flour
1 tsp. salt
1 1/4 c. shortening
1 egg
1 tbsp. vinegar

Sift flour and salt together in bowl. Cut in shortening until crumbly. Beat egg with vinegar and 5 tablespoons water in bowl. Stir into flour mixture to form dough.
Yield: Two 1-crust pie pastries.

Eunice Howard, Fairfax 570

HOT WATER PIE CRUSTS

1 c. shortening
3 c. flour
1/2 tsp. salt
1 tsp. baking powder

Melt shortening in 1/2 cup boiling water in bowl. Add remaining ingredients; mix well. Chill for several minutes to overnight.
Yield: Two 2-crust pie pastries.

Lorita Schelling, Mt. Lassen 417

NEVER-FAIL PIE CRUST

2 c. flour
1/4 c. sugar
1 tsp. salt
1 c. shortening
1 egg, lightly beaten

Combine flour, sugar and salt in bowl. Cut in shortening until crumbly. Add enough water to egg to measure 1 cup. Stir into flour mixture to form dough. Yield: One 2-crust pie pastry.

Thelma Sandburg, Waterford 553

SHORT PIE CRUST

1 c. baking mix
1/4 c. butter, softened

Combine baking mix and butter in bowl; mix well. Add 3 tablespoons boiling water, stirring with fork to form soft dough. Press onto bottom and side of 9-inch pie plate, fluting edge.
Yield: One 9-inch pie shell.
Note: This pastry is good for lemon and cream pies.

Edna F. Ohnstad, Banner 627

PIE CRUSTS

1 1/2 lb. cold lard
1 1/2 tbsp. salt
2 1/2 lb. flour
1/4 c. light corn syrup

Cream lard and salt in bowl. Blend in flour just until mixed. Add mixture of corn syrup and 1 1/2 cups cold water. Mix until well blended, scraping side and bottom of bowl. Divide into 10 to 12 portions with floured hands; wrap. Freeze until needed.
Yield: Five to six 2-crust pie pastries.
Note: May mix with electric dough hook.

Gertrude Laughridge, Waterford 553

AVOCADO PIE

2 avocados, chopped
1 8-oz. package cream cheese, softened
1 can sweetened condensed milk
Juice of 2 limes or to taste
1 tbsp. grated lime rind
1 9-in. graham cracker crumb pie shell

Combine first 5 ingredients in blender container. Process on medium speed until smooth. Pour into pie shell. Chill for 4 hours.
Yield: 8 servings.

Yvonne White, Oakdale 435

CRANBERRY-APPLE PIE

3 c. sliced peeled tart apples
2 c. cranberries
1/4 c. flour
1 3/4 c. sugar
1 recipe 2-crust pie pastry
2 tbsp. butter
Evaporated milk (opt.)
Sugar (opt.)

Combine apples and cranberries in bowl. Stir in mixture of flour and sugar. Spoon into pastry-lined 9-inch pie plate. Dot with butter. Top with remaining pastry; seal edge and cut vents. Brush with evaporated milk; sprinkle with sugar. Cover edge with narrow strip of foil to prevent overbrowning. Bake at 425 degrees for 40 to 50 minutes or until crust is golden. Remove foil strip during last 15 minutes baking time. Yield: 6-8 servings.

Vesta Gold, Waterford 553

KIWI-APPLE PIE

1 c. sugar
2 tbsp. flour
Pinch of salt
1/2 to 1 tsp. cinnamon
Pinch of nutmeg (opt.)
1 c. thinly sliced peeled kiwi fruit
6 or 7 tart apples, peeled, thinly sliced
1 recipe 2-crust pie pastry
2 tbsp. butter
Sour cream (opt.)
Sugar (opt.)

Mix sugar, flour, salt and spices in bowl. Add kiwi fruit and apples; mix gently. Spoon into pastry-lined 9-inch pie plate. Dot with butter. Top with remaining pastry; seal edge and cut vents. Brush with sour cream; sprinkle with sugar. Bake at 400 degrees for 50 minutes.

Della McNaught, Clear Lake 680

DIABETIC APPLE PIE

1 1/2 c. flour
1/2 c. oil
2 tbsp. milk
Dash of artificial sweetener
1 pkg. D-Zerta vanilla pudding
*   mix, prepared*
4 sm. apples, peeled, chopped
1 8-oz. can unsweetened
*   crushed pineapple*
2 tbsp. tapioca

Mix first 4 ingredients in bowl. Roll out; fit into pie plate. Pierce with fork generously. Bake at 400 degrees until lightly browned. Pour cooled pudding into pie shell. Combine apples, pineapple and tapioca in saucepan. Cook until apples are tender, stirring frequently. Cool. Pour over pudding. Yield: 6-8 servings.

Maye I. McCoy, Oakdale 335

NO-SUGAR APPLE PIE

1 12-oz. can frozen apple juice
*   concentrate, thawed*
3 tbsp. cornstarch
1 tbsp. butter
1/2 tsp. cinnamon
Pinch of salt
5 lg. golden Delicious apples, peeled,
*   thinly sliced*
3 tbsp. lemon juice
1 recipe 2-crust pie pastry

Mix apple juice concentrate and cornstarch in saucepan. Cook over low heat until thickened.

Stir in butter, cinnamon and salt. Cook apples in a small amount of water in saucepan until tender-crisp. Add lemon juice and cornstarch mixture. Pour into pastry-lined 9-inch pie plate. Top with remaining pastry; seal edge and cut vents. Bake at 350 degrees for 30 to 40 minutes or until golden brown. Yield: 6 servings.

Greta Cornell, Atascadero 563

FUDGE WALNUT PIE

3 tbsp. cocoa
1/2 c. melted butter
2 c. sugar
1/2 c. flour
1/8 tsp. salt
1 tsp. vanilla extract
1 can evaporated milk
1 c. walnut halves
1 unbaked 9-in. pie shell
1 c. whipped topping

Stir cocoa into butter in bowl until dissolved. Add 3/4 cup hot water; mix well. Add sugar, flour, salt, vanilla and evaporated milk; stir with wire whisk until smooth. Fold in walnuts. Pour into pie shell. Bake on preheated cookie sheet at 350 degrees for 50 minutes or until set. Garnish with whipped topping. Yield: 6-8 servings.

Marjorie Lindbeck, Waterford 553

CREAMY APRICOT PIE

1 17-oz. can apricots
1 sm. package vanilla pudding mix
1 can evaporated milk
1 egg yolk, beaten
1 9-in. baked pie shell
2 tsp. cornstarch
2 tbsp. lemon juice
1 tbsp. grated lemon rind
1 sm. can mandarin oranges, drained

Drain and chop apricots, reserving syrup. Combine pudding mix, evaporated milk, 1/2 cup reserved syrup and egg yolk in saucepan. Bring to a boil over medium heat, stirring constantly. Stir in chopped apricots. Pour into pie shell. Chill in refrigerator. Combine 2/3 cup reserved syrup, cornstarch, lemon juice and rind in saucepan. Bring to a boil over medium heat, stirring constantly. Boil for 1 minute, stirring constantly. Arrange orange slices over top of pie. Spoon sauce over pie. Serve with whipped cream. Yield: 8-10 servings.

Evelyn McWalters, Berry Creek 694

SWEDISH PIES

6 tbsp. packed brown sugar
6 tbsp. sugar
1 egg
1 c. flour
Pinch of salt
1 tsp. baking powder
1/2 tsp. cinnamon
1/2 tsp. vanilla extract
1 c. chopped apple
1 c. chopped nuts

Mix first 3 ingredients in bowl. Add sifted dry ingredients and vanilla; mix well. Stir in apple and nuts. Spoon into two 8-inch pie plates. Bake at 350 degrees for 35 minutes.

Mary Cordileone, San Diego Harbor 775

CHOCOLATE CHIFFON PIE

1 env. unflavored gelatin
1/4 c. sugar
1/4 tsp. salt
1/2 c. cocoa
6 eggs, separated
1 c. milk
1 tsp. vanilla extract
1/2 tsp. cream of tartar
3/4 c. sugar
1 baked 9-in. pie shell

Combine first 4 ingredients in double boiler. Beat egg yolks with milk. Stir into gelatin mixture. Cook over 2 inches boiling water for 10 minutes or until thickened and gelatin is dissolved, stirring constantly. Stir in vanilla. Chill until partially set, stirring occasionally. Beat egg whites with cream of tartar until soft peaks form. Add 3/4 cup sugar gradually, beating constantly until stiff peaks form. Fold in chocolate mixture gently. Chill until partially set. Spoon into pie shell. Chill until set. Garnish with whipped cream and chocolate curls.

Photograph for this recipe above.

OLD KENTUCKY BOURBON PIE

4 eggs, beaten
1/2 c. melted butter, cooled
1 c. light corn syrup
1/2 c. sugar
1/2 c. packed brown sugar
1/4 c. Bourbon
1 tsp. vanilla extract
1 c. chopped pecans
1/2 c. semisweet chocolate chips
1 unbaked 9-in. pie shell

Mix eggs, butter and corn syrup in bowl. Add sugars; mix well. Stir in Bourbon, vanilla and pecans. Sprinkle chocolate chips in pie shell. Spoon egg mixture into pie shell carefully. Bake at 350 degrees for 45 to 55 minutes or until golden brown. Serve with whipped cream. Yield: 6-8 servings.

Evelyn H. Litzinger, Lompoc 646

COCONUT MACAROON PIE

2 eggs
1 1/2 c. sugar
1/2 tsp. salt
1/2 c. butter, softened
1/4 c. flour
1/2 c. milk
1 c. coconut
1 unbaked 9-in. pie shell
1/2 c. coconut

Beat eggs with sugar and salt in bowl until light and lemon colored. Blend in butter and flour. Add milk; mix well. Fold in 1 cup coconut. Pour into pie shell. Sprinkle 1/2 cup coconut over top. Bake at 325 degrees for 1 hour or until set. Yield: 5-6 servings.

Jesse Tibbs, Scott Valley 386

LEMON CUSTARD PIE

2 whole eggs
1 egg, separated
2 tsp. grated lemon rind
2/3 c. sugar
1 lg. can evaporated milk
1 tsp. lemon extract
Pinch of salt
2 tbsp. sugar
1 unbaked 9-in. pie shell

Beat 2 whole eggs and 1 egg yolk with lemon rind in medium mixer bowl. Stir in 2/3 cup sugar, evaporated milk and lemon extract gradually. Add salt to egg white; beat until foamy. Add 2 tablespoons sugar gradually, beating until stiff peaks form. Fold in custard mixture gently. Pour into pie shell. Bake at 425 degrees for 10 minutes. Reduce temperature to 300 degrees. Bake for 20 minutes or until knife inserted in center comes out clean. Cool on wire rack.

Photograph for this recipe on opposite page.

CUSTARD PIE

1 c. sugar
3 tbsp. flour
1/4 tsp. salt
3 eggs
1/2 stick butter, melted
1 tsp. lemon flavoring
1 13-oz. can evaporated milk

Combine first 6 ingredients in bowl. Beat until well blended. Add evaporated milk; mix well. Pour into greased and floured pie plate. Bake at 350 degrees for 45 minutes.

Dorothy Hanes, Quartz Hill 697

MAPLE-YAM CUSTARD PIE

2 eggs, lightly beaten
3/4 tsp. salt
1 1/2 c. cream
1 1/2 c. mashed cooked yams
1/2 c. packed brown sugar
2 tbsp. maple syrup
1/2 tsp. cinnamon
1/4 tsp. each nutmeg, allspice
1 unbaked 9-in. pie shell

Blend eggs with salt and cream in mixer bowl. Combine yams, brown sugar, maple syrup and spices in large bowl; mix well. Add egg mixture gradually to yam mixture, beating until smooth. Pour into pie shell. Bake at 425 degrees for 15 minutes. Reduce temperature to 350 degrees. Bake for 30 to 35 minutes longer or until set. Garnish with whipped topping. Yield: 6-8 servings.

Loura Kavanaugh, Ostrom 751

RAISIN CUSTARD PIE

3/4 c. sugar
2 tbsp. flour

2 eggs, separated
1 c. milk
1/4 tsp. salt
2 tbsp. butter
1 c. stewed raisins
1 baked pie shell
1/4 tsp. baking powder
4 tsp. sugar

Combine 3/4 cup sugar, flour, egg yolks, milk and salt in saucepan; mix well. Cook until mixture thickens, stirring constantly. Stir in butter and raisins. Pour into pie shell. Beat egg whites with baking powder and 4 teaspoons sugar in bowl until stiff peaks form. Spread on pie, sealing to edge. Bake at 350 degrees for 10 minutes or until lightly browned. Yield: 6-8 servings.

Bernice Buck, Rough and Ready 795

RHUBARB CUSTARD PIE

3 eggs, lightly beaten
8 tsp. milk
2 c. sugar
1/4 c. flour
3/4 tsp. nutmeg
4 c. chopped rhubarb
1 recipe 2-crust pastry
1 tbsp. butter

Mix eggs and milk in bowl. Stir in mixture of sugar, flour and nutmeg. Add rhubarb; mix well. Pour into pastry-lined pie shell. Dot with butter. Top with lattice crust; seal edge. Bake at 400 degrees for 50 to 60 minutes or until browned.

Gwendolyn Paul, Encinitas 634
Bill Shaw, Humboldt 501

CHRISTMAS EGGNOG PIE

2 c. graham cracker crumbs
1/4 c. sugar
1/2 c. melted butter
1 env. unflavored gelatin
2 eggs
1/3 c. sugar
1/8 tsp. salt
3/4 c. milk
2 tbsp. Brandy
1 tsp. vanilla extract
1 c. whipping cream, whipped
Nutmeg

Combine cracker crumbs, 1/4 cup sugar and butter in bowl; mix well. Press over bottom and side of 9-inch pie plate. Chill in refrigerator. Soften gelatin in 1/4 cup cold water. Beat eggs with 1/3 cup sugar, salt and milk in double boiler. Cook until slightly thickened, stirring constantly. Stir in gelatin; cool. Fold in Brandy, vanilla and whipped cream. Pour into pie shell. Sprinkle with nutmeg. Chill in refrigerator. Yield: 8 servings.

Neola Kreiss, Pescadero 793

2 tbsp. flour
Juice and grated rind of 1 lemon
1 c. milk
1 unbaked 9-in. pie shell

Cream sugar and butter in bowl until fluffy. Stir in beaten egg yolks, flour, lemon juice, lemon rind and milk. Fold in stiffly beaten egg whites gently. Pour into pie shell. Bake at 450 degrees for 10 minutes. Reduce temperature to 325 degrees. Bake for 20 minutes longer. Yield: 6 servings.

Rosie Laman, Feather River 440

LEMON-RAISIN DELIGHT PIE

1 c. seedless raisins
1 c. sugar
5 tbsp. cornstarch
1/4 tsp. salt
3 eggs, separated
1/4 c. lemon juice
1 1/2 tsp. grated lemon rind
1 1/2 tbsp. butter
1 baked 9-in. pie shell
1/4 tsp. cream of tartar
6 tbsp. sugar
1/2 c. shredded coconut

Stir raisins into 1 3/4 cups hot water in double boiler. Add mixture of 1 cup sugar, cornstarch and salt; mix well. Cook over direct heat until clear and thickened, stirring constantly. Place over boiling water. Cook for 20 minutes, stirring occasionally. Stir a small amount of hot mixture into beaten egg yolks; stir egg yolks into hot mixture. Cook for 4 minutes, stirring constantly. Add lemon juice, lemon rind and butter; cool. Pour into pie shell. Beat egg whites with cream of tartar in bowl until frothy. Add 6 tablespoons sugar gradually, beating until stiff and glossy. Spread over pie, sealing to edge. Sprinkle with coconut. Bake at 400 degrees for 8 to 10 minutes or until lightly browned.

Marna Linzy, Capay 461

HARVEST MOON MUSCAT RAISIN PIE

1 1/3 c. seeded Muscat raisins
3 eggs, separated
1 c. sugar
2 tbsp. flour
2 tbsp. vinegar
2 tbsp. butter
1 baked 9-in. pie shell
1/4 tsp. cream of tartar
6 tbsp. sugar

Simmer raisins and 2 cups water in saucepan for 5 minutes. Beat yolks, 1 cup sugar, flour and vinegar in bowl until light and creamy. Add to raisins; mix gently. Cook for 4 minutes or until thickened, stirring constantly. Remove from heat; blend in butter. Cool slightly. Pour into pie shell. Beat egg whites and cream of tartar until foamy. Add 6 tablespoons sugar gradually, beating until stiff peaks form. Spread meringue over pie, sealing to edge. Bake at 425 degrees for 4 minutes or until delicately browned. Cool on wire rack.

Photograph for this recipe above.

LEMON CAKE-TOP PIE

1 c. sugar
1 tbsp. butter, softened
2 eggs, separated

DELUXE PECAN PIE

3 eggs, lightly beaten
1 c. dark corn syrup
1 c. sugar
1 tbsp. melted butter
1 tsp. vanilla extract
1/8 tsp. salt
1 c. pecan halves
1 unbaked 9-in. pie shell

Combine first 6 ingredients in bowl; mix well. Stir in pecans. Pour into pie shell. Bake at 350 degrees for 55 minutes or until knife inserted halfway between center and edge comes out clean. Yield: 8 servings.

John McGraw, Lompoc 646

PEANUT BUTTER PIE

4 oz. cream cheese, softened
1/2 c. peanut butter
1 c. confectioners' sugar
1 baked 9-in. pie shell
2 c. whipped topping

Combine cream cheese, peanut butter and confectioners' sugar in mixer bowl; beat until smooth. Spoon into pie shell. Spread whipped topping over top. Yield: 6-8 servings.

Vada Gardiner, Fairfax 570

POMEGRANATE PIE

4 1/2 tbsp. cornstarch
3 c. pomegranate juice
1 c. sugar
1/8 tsp. salt
1 baked 8-in. pie shell

Blend cornstarch with small amount of pomegranate juice in saucepan. Add remaining juice, sugar and salt; mix well. Bring to a boil, stirring constantly. Cook for 5 minutes, stirring constantly. Cool for 15 minutes, stirring occasionally. Pour into pie shell. Chill for 4 hours or until set. Garnish with whipped cream.

Frances Mattice, Capay 461

RASPBERRY PIE

1 c. sugar
3 tbsp. cornstarch
1 tbsp. lemon juice
1 sm. package raspberry gelatin
1 pt. raspberries
1 baked 8-in. pie shell

Combine sugar, cornstarch, lemon juice and 1 1/2 cups water in saucepan. Cook until mixture is clear and thickened, stirring constantly. Add gelatin, stirring until dissolved. Stir in raspberries. Pour into pie shell. Chill until firm. Serve with whipped cream or ice cream.

Daisy D. Schultz, Pleasant Valley 675

NO-BAKE RHUBARB PIE

2 c. sugar
4 c. finely chopped rhubarb
1 3-oz. package strawberry gelatin
1 c. whipping cream, whipped
1 9-in. graham cracker pie shell

Sprinkle sugar over rhubarb in bowl. Let stand overnight. Pour into saucepan. Simmer until tender. Add gelatin, stirring until dissolved; cool. Fold in whipped cream. Pour into pie shell. Chill until firm. Yield: 6-8 servings.

Cora H. Darling, Bennett Valley 16

LEOTA'S SUPER DUPER PIE

1 env. unflavored gelatin
1/2 c. Rose
2 tbsp. lemon juice
1 10-oz. package frozen sliced
   strawberries, thawed
2 egg whites
1/4 tsp. salt
1/4 c. sugar
1/2 c. whipping cream, whipped
1 baked 9-in. pie shell

Sprinkle gelatin over wine in double boiler. Let stand for several minutes to soften. Heat until gelatin dissolves, stirring constantly. Stir in lemon juice. Chill until partially set. Stir in strawberries. Beat egg whites with salt and sugar in bowl until stiff peaks form. Fold in whipped cream and strawberry mixture. Chill until mixture mounds on spoon. Pour into pie shell. Chill for 2 hours or until firm.

Leota Ness, Humboldt 501

HOOSIER SUGAR CREAM PIE

1/2 c. sugar
1/2 c. packed brown sugar
2 tbsp. flour
1 3/4 c. half and half
1/4 c. whipping cream
1/2 tsp. vanilla extract
1 unbaked 8-in. pie shell, chilled
Nutmeg to taste

Combine sugar, brown sugar and flour in bowl. Add half and half, cream and vanilla. Pour into pie shell. Sprinkle with nutmeg. Bake at 400 degrees for 30 to 40 minutes or until set. Edge of filling will have wrinkled appearance. Garnish with whipped cream and cherries.

Corene Carlson, Kingsburg 679

ANN'S SUGAR CREAM PIE

2 c. milk
1 c. sugar
1 stick margarine
1/4 c. (or more) cornstarch
1/4 c. cold milk
1 tsp. vanilla extract
1 baked 8-in. pie shell
Nutmeg

Combine 2 cups milk, sugar and margarine in saucepan. Heat almost to the simmering point, stirring to blend well. Remove from heat. Add mixture of cornstarch and cold milk; stir until thickened. Stir in vanilla. Pour into pie shell. Sprinkle with nutmeg. Bake at 350 degrees for 10 minutes.

Ann Stowell, Hesperia 682

GREEN TOMATO PIE

2 c. chopped green tomatoes
1 tbsp. flour
1 c. sugar
1 tbsp. lemon juice
1 tbsp. melted butter
1 tsp. cinnamon
1/4 tsp. nutmeg
Pinch of salt
1 recipe 2-crust pie pastry

Combine tomatoes with flour, sugar, lemon juice, butter and seasonings in bowl; mix well. Pour into pastry-lined 9-inch pie plate. Top with remaining pastry. Cut steam vents in top; seal edge. Bake at 350 degrees for 45 minutes.

Lulu Kistle, Banner 627

TROPICAL PIE

1 tbsp. unflavored gelatin
2 bananas
2 tbsp. lemon juice
1 c. milk
3 eggs, separated
1/3 c. sugar
1 tsp. vanilla extract
1 c. crushed pineapple
1/3 c. sugar
1 9-in. graham cracker crumb pie shell

Soften gelatin in 1/4 cup cold water. Mash bananas in small bowl. Sprinkle with lemon juice. Scald milk in double boiler; cool slightly. Add mixture of egg yolks and 1/3 cup sugar. Cook for 5 minutes or until mixture coats spoon, stirring constantly. Add gelatin, stirring to dissolve. Stir in vanilla. Chill until partially set. Stir in bananas and pineapple. Beat egg whites with 1/3 cup sugar in bowl until thick. Fold into fruit mixture. Pour into pie shell. Garnish with additional graham cracker crumbs. Chill until firm. Yield: 6-8 servings.

Barbara Kleespie, Fort Bragg 672

APPLE TART

2 1/2 c. sifted flour
1 tsp. baking powder
1/2 c. sugar
1/2 c. margarine
1 1/2 tsp. cinnamon
4 cooking apples, peeled, sliced
    1/4-in. thick

Sift first 3 ingredients into bowl. Cut in margarine until crumbly. Mix 1 cup mixture with cinnamon; set aside. Press remaining mixture over bottom and side of lightly greased 9-inch cake pan. Combine apple slices and 1/2 cup water in saucepan. Simmer until apples are tender and liquid is reduced. Spoon into prepared pan. Sprinkle cinnamon mixture over top. Bake at 425 degrees for 10 minutes. Reduce temperature to 350 degrees. Bake for 30 minutes longer. Cool. Yield: 8 servings.

Constance Baer, Rough and Ready 795

CHESS TARTS

2 c. flour
2 tsp. sugar
1 tsp. salt
2/3 c. shortening
1 c. sugar
1 stick butter, softened
3 eggs
1 tsp. vanilla extract
1 c. raisins
1 c. chopped walnuts

Sift flour, 2 teaspoons sugar and salt together in bowl. Cut in shortening until crumbly. Add 6 or 7 tablespoons water 1 at a time, mixing with fork to form dough. Divide into 2 portions. Roll out very thin on floured surface. Cut out with 3-inch cutter. Fit into muffin cups. Cream 1 cup sugar and butter in bowl until light and fluffy. Add eggs 1 at a time, beating well after each addition. Stir in remaining ingredients. Spoon into tart shells. Bake at 350 degrees for 15 minutes or until set. Yield: 2 dozen.

Elsie Erwin, Wood Colony 522

sALADs

Avery's Riding Cultivators

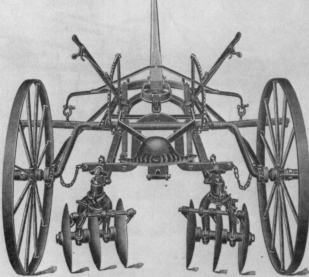

Rear View

Uncle Sam Disc Cultivator.

The Uncle Sam Disc Cultivator is the most modern machine of this style on the market.   It embodies several new features which put it far in the lead when considering lightness of draft, ease of adjustments, simplicity and durability.

Frame.   The frame being constructed entirely of steel and malleables is exceptionally strong; possesses no unnecessary parts, and having an open pole extension at the rear gives full view of the crop.   The axles are readily adjustable for any width of track from 50 to 63 inches, and can be moved forward or backward as desired in order to balance frame according to the weight of the operator. Frame is equipped with spiral lifting and compression springs.

Built in Three Styles.

No. 1.   Rigid Pole.

AMBROSIA

1 c. miniature marshmallows
1 c. drained mandarin oranges
1 c. drained pineapple chunks
1 c. sour cream
1 c. grated coconut

Combine first 4 ingredients in bowl; mix well. Chill for several hours. Sprinkle coconut over top. Yield: 10 servings.

Claudia Vollintine, Concow 735

APPLE-WALNUT SALAD

1/2 c. apple juice
1/2 tsp. cinnamon
1/4 tsp. nutmeg
Pinch of cloves
1/4 c. raisins
1   3-oz. package lemon gelatin
1/2 c. chopped apple
1/2 c. chopped celery
1/2 c. chopped walnuts

Combine apple juice and spices in saucepan. Cook over medium heat for 3 minutes. Add raisins and gelatin. Stir until gelatin is dissolved. Add 1 1/2 cups cold water; mix well. Chill until thickened. Fold in remaining ingredients. Pour into 3-cup mold. Chill for 3 hours or until firm. Unmold on serving plate. Garnish with celery leaves and lemon slices. Yield: 4 servings.

Ruby Fox, San Marcos 633

AVOCADO SALAD

1 pkg. lime gelatin
1/2 c. mayonnaise
1/2 c. whipping cream, whipped
1 c. chopped celery
1 1/2 c. chopped avocado
Pinch of salt
1 tsp. lemon juice
1 tsp. chopped onion

Dissolve gelatin in 1 cup boiling water. Cool until thickened. Beat until light and fluffy. Add mayonnaise, whipped cream, celery, avocado, salt, lemon juice and onion. Pour into molds. Chill until firm. Unmold on serving plates.

Christine Kearne, Yucaipa Valley 582

ALOHA BANANA CREAM SALAD

1   3-oz. package lemon gelatin
2   3-oz. packages cream cheese, softened

2/3 c. evaporated milk
2 tbsp. mayonnaise
1/4 c. chopped maraschino cherries
1/2 c. chopped walnuts
3 med. bananas, chopped
2/3 c. crushed pineapple, drained

Dissolve gelatin in 1 cup boiling water. Cool. Combine cream cheese, evaporated milk and mayonnaise in bowl; mix well. Add cooled gelatin; mix well. Fold in remaining ingredients. Chill, covered, for 1 hour to overnight.

Ann Clark, Santa Cruz-Live Oak 503

BILTMORE SALAD

1 c. crushed pineapple
1 c. shredded cabbage
1 c. salad dressing
1/2 c. chopped nuts
1/4 c. chopped marshmallows
1/4 c. chopped cherries
1/2 c. mayonnaise
1 c. whipping cream, whipped

Combine all ingredients in bowl; mix well. Pour into buttered 8 x 8-inch pan. Freeze for 3 to 4 hours. Yield: 6 servings.

Sylvia Harlan, Estrella 488

CRANBERRY-SOUR CREAM MOLD

1   3-oz. package red gelatin
1   8-oz. can whole cranberry sauce
1 tsp. grated orange rind
1/2 c. sour cream

Dissolve gelatin in 1 cup boiling water in bowl. Mash cranberry sauce with fork. Stir into gelatin with orange rind. Fold in sour cream. Pour into mold. Chill until firm. Unmold on serving plate. Yield: 4 servings.

Betty Tucker, San Bernardo 506

CRANBERRY VELVET

1   3-oz. package raspberry gelatin
1 1/2 tsp. unflavored gelatin
1 c. unflavored yogurt
1   16-oz. can cranberry sauce

Combine raspberry and unflavored gelatins. Dissolve in 3/4 cup boiling water. Chill until slightly thickened. Combine yogurt and cranberry sauce in blender container. Process until almost smooth. Add thickened gelatin. Process until smooth. Pour into mold. Chill until firm. Unmold on serving plate. Yield: 6 servings.

Eve Erickson, San Jose 10

SOUR CREAM FRUIT SALAD

1 c. sour cream
1 c. coconut
1 c. drained pineapple tidbits
1 c. miniature marshmallows
1 c. drained mandarin oranges

Combine all ingredients in bowl; mix well. Chill overnight. Yield: 6-8 servings.

Vera Bryson, Orland 432

FROSTED SALAD

2 pkg. lemon gelatin
2 c. 7-Up
1 c. miniature marshmallows
2 bananas, sliced
1 c. crushed pineapple, drained
1 c. apricots, drained
2 tbsp. flour
2 tbsp. butter, melted
1 c. fruit juice
1 egg, beaten
1/2 c. sugar
1 c. whipped cream
Grated cheese

Dissolve gelatin in 1 1/2 cups boiling water. Add next 5 ingredients; mix well. Pour into 9 x 13-inch dish. Chill until firm. Blend flour and butter in saucepan. Stir in juice. Cook until thickened, stirring constantly. Stir a small amount of hot mixture into egg; stir egg into hot mixture. Add sugar. Cook until thickened, stirring constantly. Cool. Fold in whipped cream. Spread over congealed layer. Sprinkle with cheese.

Lloyd Larson, Humboldt 501

HEAVENLY SALAD

1 3 1/2-oz. package lime gelatin
1 8-oz. package cream cheese, softened
1/2 c. whipping cream, whipped
1 8-oz. can crushed pineapple
2 tbsp. chopped maraschino cherries

Dissolve gelatin in 1 cup boiling water in bowl. Chill until set. Combine cream cheese and whipped cream in mixer bowl. Beat until smooth. Stir gelatin until broken into small pieces. Add pineapple with juice; beat well. Add creamed mixture; beat well. Stir in cherries. Pour into 1-quart mold. Chill for 4 hours or longer. Unmold on lettuce-lined serving plate. Yield: 12 servings.

Wava Moore, Tulare 198

SPECIAL LEMON-LIME CONGEALED SALAD

1 sm. package lemon gelatin
1 sm. package lime gelatin
1 c. mayonnaise
1 c. evaporated milk
1 c. crushed pineapple
2 c. cottage cheese
1/4 tsp. horseradish

Dissolve gelatins in 2 cups boiling water. Add mayonnaise; mix well. Add evaporated milk, pineapple and cottage cheese. Add horseradish; mix well. Pour into 2 serving dishes.
Yield: 8-10 servings.
Note: May be served as luncheon salad with mayonnaise or as dessert with whipped topping.

Helen Johnson, Fieldbrook 771

MINCEMEAT SALAD

1 pkg. mincemeat, broken
1 tbsp. sugar
1 env. unflavored gelatin
1 c. boiling pineapple juice
1/4 tsp. salt
3/4 c. chopped celery
1 c. cottage cheese
1/2 c. evaporated milk, partially frozen, whipped

Combine mincemeat, sugar and 1/2 cup water in saucepan. Cook over low heat until crumbly. Boil for about 3 minutes or until moisture is nearly evaporated; cool. Soften gelatin in 1/4 cup cold water for 5 minutes. Add hot pineapple juice. Stir until gelatin is dissolved. Add salt; mix well. Chill until thickened. Add mincemeat, celery and cottage cheese; mix well. Fold in whipped evaporated milk. Chill until firm. Yield: 8-10 servings.

Audrey Travis, Hemet-San Jacinto 693

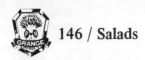

MOM KRIEL'S PINEAPPLE SALAD

2 env. unflavored gelatin
Juice of 2 lemons
1 c. sugar
1 c. cottage cheese
1 8-oz. can crushed pineapple
1 pt. whipping cream, whipped
2 pkg. raspberry gelatin

Soften unflavored gelatin in 1/2 cup cold water for 10 minutes. Add lemon juice; mix well. Combine 1/2 cup water and sugar in saucepan. Bring to a boil. Add gelatin; mix until gelatin is dissolved. Cool. Stir in cottage cheese and pineapple. Chill until thickened. Fold in whipped cream. Pour into 9 x 13-inch dish. Chill overnight. Prepare raspberry gelatin using package directions. Pour over congealed layer. Chill until firm.

Iva Little, Empire 521

PINEAPPLE GELATIN SALAD

3 sm. packages lemon gelatin
1 c. drained crushed pineapple
1 1/2 c. miniature marshmallows
4 bananas, crushed
1 c. sugar
1/4 c. flour
2 c. pineapple juice
2 eggs, beaten
Whipped topping
Walnuts, broken

Dissolve gelatin in 5 cups boiling water. Cool. Add pineapple, marshmallows and bananas; mix well. Pour into serving dish. Chill until firm. Combine sugar, flour, pineapple juice and eggs in saucepan; mix well. Cook over medium heat until thickened, stirring constantly. Chill in refrigerator. Spread over congealed layer. Top with whipped topping and walnuts. Yield: 24 servings.

Marian Nichols, Western Yolo 423

PISTACHIO SALAD

1 sm. package pistachio pudding mix
1 1/2 c. miniature marshmallows
1 12-oz. carton whipped topping
1 20-oz. can crushed pineapple
3/4 c. chopped walnuts

Combine all ingredients in bowl; mix well. Pour into serving dish. Store in refrigerator.

Evelyn Rensted, Ceres 520

RASPBERRY SALAD

1 3-oz. package lemon gelatin
1 16-oz. package miniature marshmallows
1 16-oz. can crushed pineapple
1 c. mayonnaise
1/2 pt. whipping cream, whipped
2 3-oz. packages raspberry gelatin
1 10-oz. package frozen raspberries

Dissolve lemon gelatin in 1 cup boiling water. Add marshmallows; stir until marshmallows are melted; cool. Add pineapple; mix well. Fold in mayonnaise and whipped cream. Pour into 9 x 13-inch dish. Chill until firm. Dissolve raspberry gelatin in 2 3/4 cups boiling water. Add frozen raspberries; mix well. Cool. Pour over congealed layer. Chill until firm. Yield: 12 servings.

Anna Mitchell, Rio Linda 403

STRAWBERRY GELATIN MOLD

1 6-oz. package strawberry gelatin
1 16-oz. package frozen strawberries
1 16-oz. can crushed pineapple
3 bananas, mashed
1/2 c. sour cream

Dissolve gelatin in 2 cups boiling water. Add frozen strawberries; stir until strawberries separate. Add pineapple and bananas. Pour half the mixture into 4-cup mold. Chill until firm. Spread sour cream over congealed layer. Spoon remaining gelatin mixture over sour cream. Chill until firm. Unmold on serving plate.

Peggy Bullaro, Valley Oaks 368

PRETZEL SALAD

2 c. crushed pretzels
1 1/2 sticks margarine
1/4 c. sugar
1 8-oz. package cream cheese, softened
1 c. sugar
1 pkg. whipped topping mix, prepared
2 3-oz. packages strawberry gelatin
2 c. pineapple juice
2 10-oz. packages frozen strawberries

Combine pretzels, margarine and 1/4 cup sugar in 9 x 13-inch baking pan; mix well. Bake at 350 degrees for 10 minutes. Combine cream cheese, 1 cup sugar and whipped topping; mix well. Spread over baked layer. Dissolve gelatin in boiling pineapple juice. Add frozen strawberries; mix well. Chill until thick. Spread over cream cheese mixture. Chill until firm.

Violet McReynolds, Napa 307

WALDORF SALAD

4 med. unpeeled apples, coarsely chopped
1 tbsp. lemon juice
1 c. chopped celery
1 c. California walnuts
1 c. miniature marshmallows
1/2 c. salad dressing
Salt to taste

Sprinkle apples with lemon juice. Combine apples, celery, walnuts and marshmallows in bowl. Fold in salad dressing. Season with salt. Serve in lettuce-lined salad bowl.

Photograph for this recipe above.

MOLDED WALDORF SALAD

1 pkg. lemon gelatin
4 med. apples, chopped
1 tbsp. lemon juice
1 c. chopped celery
1 c. California walnuts
1 c. miniature marshmallows

Prepare gelatin using package directions. Chill until partially set. Fold in remaining ingredients. Pour into mold. Chill until firm. Unmold on lettuce-lined plate. Garnish with slices of jellied cranberry sauce.

Photograph for this recipe above.

CREAMY BLEU CHEESE SALAD

2 3-oz. packages lemon gelatin
1 tsp. salt
2 3-oz. packages cream cheese, softened
1/2 c. crumbled bleu cheese
1/2 tsp. paprika
1 1/2 c. whipped topping

Dissolve gelatin and salt in 2 cups boiling water in bowl. Add 1 1/2 cups cold water. Blend cream cheese, bleu cheese and paprika in bowl. Add gelatin gradually, beating constantly. Fold in whipped topping gently. Pour into 8 x 12-inch dish. Chill, covered, for 5 hours or until firm. Serve on lettuce-lined serving plate. Garnish with fruit. Yield: 12-14 servings.

Marguerite King, Berry Creek 694

OPAL'S CHEESE SALAD

2 env. unflavored gelatin
2 20-oz. cans crushed pineapple
2 c. sugar
Juice of 2 or 3 lemons
1 lb. Cheddar cheese, grated
1 c. chopped walnuts
3 c. whipped cream

Soften gelatin in a small amount of cold water. Combine pineapple and sugar in saucepan. Bring to a boil; remove from heat. Stir in lemon juice. Add gelatin; stir until dissolved. Chill, covered, until thickened. Fold in cheese, walnuts and whipped cream. Store in refrigerator.

Opal Clark, Goat Mountain 818

LUAU CHICKEN SALAD

1 chicken, cooked, chopped
1 red apple, chopped
4 lg. stalks celery, chopped
1 2-oz. package walnuts, chopped
1 8-oz. can pineapple tidbits, drained
3 tbsp. mayonnaise
1 1/2 tsp. curry powder
1 can pitted ripe olives

Combine chicken, apple, celery and walnuts in bowl. Add pineapple, reserving several tidbits for garnish. Add mixture of mayonnaise and curry powder; toss to mix. Pack into bowl. Chill for several hours. Unmold on lettuce-lined serving plate. Garnish with reserved pineapple and olives. Store in refrigerator.

David Shultz, Adelanto 603

ORIENTAL CHICKEN SALAD

3/4 c. Ocean Spray cranberry-orange sauce
1 tbsp. soy sauce
1/2 tsp. ginger
3/4 tsp. red wine vinegar
2 c. chopped cooked chicken
1/2 c. blanched snow peas
1 c. thinly sliced Chinese cabbage
1/4 c. thinly sliced carrots
1/4 c. thinly sliced sweet red pepper
2 tbsp. sliced scallions

Combine first 4 ingredients in bowl; mix well. Chill, covered, in refrigerator. Combine chicken and vegetables in large bowl; toss gently. Serve with dressing. Yield: 6 servings.

Photograph for this recipe on page 103.

TURKEY-TOMATO SALAD

1 c. sour cream
1/4 c. mayonnaise
2 tbsp. lemon juice
1 tsp. sugar
1/2 tsp. curry powder
1/2 tsp. paprika
1/2 tsp. dry mustard
1/2 tsp. salt
2 c. chopped cooked turkey
2 c. sliced celery
2 hard-boiled eggs, chopped
1/2 c. sliced almonds, toasted
6 lg. tomatoes, chilled

Combine sour cream, mayonnaise and seasonings in bowl; mix well. Combine turkey, celery, eggs and almonds in bowl. Add dressing; mix lightly to coat. Chill for several hours. Cut tomatoes into wedges to but not through bottom. Fill with salad mixture.

Photograph for this recipe on opposite page.

CORNED BEEF SALAD

1 6-oz. package lemon gelatin
1 c. chopped celery
1/2 c. chopped green onions
1/2 c. chopped sweet pickles
2 hard-boiled eggs, chopped
1 c. mayonnaise
1 c. cubed corned beef

Dissolve gelatin in 1 1/2 cups boiling water. Let stand until thick. Add remaining ingredients; mix well. Chill until firm.

Gladys Janke, Humboldt 501

HAM SALAD

2 c. cubed cooked ham
2 c. frozen green lima beans, cooked
1 c. chopped celery
1 tbsp. minced onion
4 c. chopped hard-boiled eggs
1/2 c. mayonnaise
1/2 tsp. curry powder
Dill pickle juice
Salt and pepper to taste

Combine all ingredients in bowl; mix well. Turn into serving bowl.

Sharon Grant, Van Duzen River 517

SUPERB CRAB MOLD

1 env. unflavored gelatin
1 can cream of mushroom soup
1 8-oz. package cream cheese, softened
1 c. mayonnaise
3 stalks celery, chopped
1 sm. red onion, chopped
Dash of lemon juice
1 7-oz. can crab meat, drained

Measure 1 soup can water. Pour 3 tablespoons into small bowl; add gelatin. Let stand to soften. Combine remaining water and soup in saucepan. Bring to a boil. Add gelatin. Stir to dissolve gelatin. Blend cream cheese and mayonnaise in bowl. Add celery and onion; mix well. Add to soup with mixture of lemon juice and crab meat; mix well. Pour into medium-sized mold. Chill overnight. Unmold on serving plate. Yield: 10 servings.

Nell Bonham, Thermalito 729

CHINESE NOODLE SALAD

1 can Chinese noodles
1 can bean sprouts, drained
1 can water chestnuts, chopped
1/2 c. chopped green onions
1 can sm. shrimp
1/2 c. chopped celery
1 tbsp. soy sauce
1/2 tsp. MSG
1/2 tsp. ginger
1 tsp. lemon juice
1 c. mayonnaise

Combine all ingredients in bowl; mix well. Turn into serving dish.

Kathryn Moore, Tulelake 468

SHRIMP ASPIC SALAD

1   3-oz. package lemon gelatin
1   8-oz. can tomato sauce
1 1/2 tsp. Worcestershire sauce
1 c. peas
1/2 c. chopped celery
1 c. grated carrots
1/2 tsp. finely chopped onion
1/2 tsp. vinegar
1   6-oz. can shrimp

Dissolve gelatin in 1 cup boiling water in bowl.
Add remaining ingredients; mix well. Pour into
mold. Chill until firm. Unmold on serving plate.
Yield: 6 servings.

Hilda Cooley, Greenhorn 384

SHRIMP GELATIN SALAD

1   6-oz. package lemon gelatin
3 1/2 c. tomato juice
1/4 c. chopped onion
1/4 c. (or less) sugar
3/4 tsp. salt
1/2 tsp. cloves
1/4 c. vinegar
1/2 c. chopped nuts
1 c. chopped celery
1   6-oz. can shrimp

Dissolve gelatin in boiling tomato juice in bowl.
Add onion, sugar, salt, cloves and vinegar. Chill
until partially set. Add nuts, celery and shrimp.
Pour into 9 x 13-inch dish. Chill until firm.
Yield: 10-12 servings.

Vera Jackson, Lake Earl 577

LUCILE'S SHRIMP SALAD

2 c. shredded carrots
2 green onions and tops, finely chopped
3 stalks celery, finely chopped
2   6-oz. cans shrimp
Salt and lemon-pepper to taste
Lemon juice to taste
Mayonnaise
1 can chow mein noodles

Combine vegetables, shrimp and seasonings in
bowl in order listed. Let stand until serving
time. Stir in enough mayonnaise to moisten.
Add noodles just before serving.

Lucile DeLacy, Napa 307

MARINATED AVOCADO AND MUSHROOM SALAD

1 med. avocado, sliced
1 c. sliced fresh mushrooms
2 thin slices onion, separated into rings
1/4 c. dry white wine
2 tbsp. vinegar
1/4 c. oil
1/2 tsp. sugar
1/4 tsp. salt
1/4 tsp. basil

Combine avocado, mushrooms and onion rings
in bowl. Mix remaining ingredients in jar; shake
until blended. Pour over mushroom mixture.
Chill, covered, for 2 to 3 hours, stirring occasionally. Drain. Serve on Bibb lettuce-lined
plates. Yield: 4 servings.

Bonnie Fairbanks, Lompoc 646

DUO BEAN SALAD

1/2 c. sour cream
2 tbsp. wine vinegar
1 tbsp. prepared mustard
1/4 tsp. Tabasco sauce
1/4 tsp. salt
2 tbsp. chopped green pepper
1 onion, thinly sliced
2 c. cooked green beans
1   1-lb. can kidney beans, drained

Blend sour cream, vinegar, mustard, Tabasco
sauce and salt in medium bowl. Stir in green
pepper, onion, green beans and kidney beans.
Chill for 1 hour or longer. Yield: 4-6 servings.

Photograph for this recipe on page 161.

SUPER BEET SALAD

1/4 c. vinegar
1/2 c. beet juice
1/2 c. sugar
1 sm. package raspberry gelatin
1 sm. can julienne beets, well drained
1 c. sour cream

Combine vinegar, beet juice, 1/2 cup water and
sugar in saucepan. Bring to a boil. Add gelatin.
Boil for 2 minutes. Add beets. Pour into mold.
Chill until firm. Unmold on serving plate. Top
with sour cream. Yield: 5-6 servings.

Vivian Barber, Morro Bay 749

BEET SALAD

 1 3-oz. package lemon gelatin
 1 c. beet juice
 2/3 c. orange juice
 1 tsp. scraped onion
 2 tsp. horseradish
 1 tsp. vinegar
 1 tsp. salt
 1 16-oz. can diced beets
 1 c. chopped celery

Dissolve gelatin in boiling beet juice. Add orange juice, onion and seasonings; mix well. Chill until slightly thickened. Stir in beets and celery. Pour into ring mold. Chill until firm. Unmold on serving plate. Fill center with fruit if desired. Yield: 6 servings.

Elaine Wichers, Napa 307

BROCCOLI SALAD

 1 head broccoli, finely chopped
 1 red onion, finely chopped
 1/2 can ripe olives, finely chopped
 4 to 6 stalks celery, finely chopped
 1 8-oz. can water chestnuts,
   finely chopped
 Several dashes of oregano

 1 lg. bottle of Italian salad dressing
 1 box cherry tomatoes
 Bacon bits (opt.)
 Salt and pepper to taste

Combine all ingredients in bowl; toss to mix well. May store for several days.

Marie Mickey, Lompoc 646

PERFECTION SALAD

 1 env. unflavored gelatin
 1/4 c. sugar
 1/4 tsp. salt
 1/4 c. lemon juice
 3/4 c. finely shredded cabbage
 1 c. chopped celery
 1/4 c. chopped green pepper

Mix gelatin, sugar and salt in saucepan. Stir in 1/2 cup cold water. Heat until gelatin and sugar are dissolved, stirring constantly. Remove from heat; stir in 3/4 cup water and lemon juice. Chill until partially set. Fold in cabbage, celery and green pepper. Turn into 6-cup mold. Chill until firm. Unmold on lettuce-lined plate. Serve with mayonnaise. Yield: 6 servings.

Photograph for this recipe above.

ORIENTAL CABBAGE SALAD

1/2 c. oil
1/4 c. vinegar
1 tsp. salt
1/4 tsp. pepper
2 tbsp. sugar
1 pkg. top ramen oriental-flavored
  noodle soup
1/2 head cabbage, very thinly sliced
1/4 c. sunflower seed
1/4 c. slivered almonds
2 tbsp. sesame seed
3/4 c. fresh peas
1 sm. bunch green onions, thinly sliced

Combine first 5 ingredients and noodle seasoning packet in bowl; mix well. Combine cabbage
and remaining ingredients in bowl. Add dressing; toss to mix. Yield: 15-20 servings.

Muriel McGlashan, Gilroy 398

MARINATED CARROTS

1 can tomato soup
1 c. sugar
1 c. oil
1 tsp. dry mustard
3/4 c. vinegar
1 tsp. salt
1/2 tsp. pepper
2 lb. carrots, sliced, cooked
1 lg. green pepper, sliced
1 lg. onion, sliced

Combine first 7 ingredients in bowl; mix well.
Add vegetables; mix well. Marinate in refrigerator overnight.

Marion Guthridge, Bayside 500

MARINATED CARROT SALAD

1/2 c. oil
1/2 c. sugar
1 tsp. salt
1 can tomato soup
1/2 c. vinegar
1 tsp. pepper
1 tsp. dry mustard
3 lb. carrots, sliced, cooked
1 med. onion, sliced
1 can sliced water chestnuts

Combine first 7 ingredients in saucepan. Bring
to a boil. Pour over mixture of carrots, onion
and water chestnuts in bowl. Marinate overnight.
Note: May store, covered, in refrigerator for 3 to
4 weeks.

Juanita Runyon, Hesperia 682

CHINESE SALAD

1 16-oz. package frozen peas, thawed
3/4 c. chopped scallions
1 c. chopped celery
1 c. chopped green pepper
2 tbsp. lemon juice
1/2 c. sour cream
2 tbsp. lemon juice
1 lg. can chow mein noodles

Combine peas, scallions, celery, green pepper
and 2 tablespoons lemon juice in bowl; mix
well. Chill until serving time. Mix sour cream
and 2 tablespoons lemon juice. Add to pea mixture; mix well. Stir in chow mein noodles.
Yield: 20 servings.
Note: May add 1 can tuna if desired.

Lucille McCrea, Rough and Ready 795

COLESLAW SOUFFLE

1 3-oz. package lemon gelatin
2 tbsp. vinegar
1/2 c. mayonnaise
1/4 tsp. salt
1/8 tsp. pepper
2 tbsp. minced onion
2 tbsp. chopped green pepper (opt.)
2 c. finely chopped cabbage
1/4 tsp. celery seed

Dissolve gelatin in 1 cup boiling water in bowl.
Add 1/2 cup cold water, vinegar, mayonnaise,
salt and pepper; mix well. Chill in freezer for 15
to 20 minutes or until frozen 1 inch from edge.
Beat with mixer until fluffy. Fold in onion,
green pepper, cabbage and celery seed. Pour
into 1-quart mold. Chill for 30 minutes. Unmold on serving plate.

Audrey White, Ripon 511

FROZEN COLESLAW

1 med. head cabbage, shredded
1 tsp. salt
3 stalks celery
1 green pepper
1 sm. onion
1 carrot
1 c. vinegar
2 c. sugar
1 tsp. celery seed
1 tsp. mustard seed (opt.)

Sprinkle cabbage with salt. Let stand for 1
hour; drain. Put celery, green pepper, onion and
carrot through food chopper. Combine with

cabbage; mix well. Combine 1/4 cup water, vinegar, sugar and celery and mustard seed in saucepan. Cook for 1 minute; cool. Add to cabbage mixture. Spoon into freezer container. Store in freezer.

Note: Slaw is good before freezing also.

Ethel Bose, San Dimas 658

OVERNIGHT SALAD

1 head lettuce, torn
1 pkg. frozen peas, cooked
Cucumbers, peeled, thinly sliced
1 Spanish onion, sliced into rings
3 c. mayonnaise
6 tsp. (heaping) sugar

Layer lettuce, peas, enough cucumbers to cover layers, onions and mixture of mayonnaise and sugar in 9 x 13-inch glass dish. Chill, tightly covered, for 24 hours. Yield: 20-25 servings.

Florence Kraft, Lompoc 646

PEA AND PEANUT SALAD

1 16-oz. package frozen peas, blanched
3 stalks celery, chopped
3 green onions and tops, chopped
3 hard-boiled eggs, chopped
Salt and pepper to taste
Mayonnaise
1 c. Spanish peanuts

Combine first 4 ingredients with seasonings and enough mayonnaise to bind ingredients in bowl; mix well. Stir in peanuts just before serving. Yield: 8 servings.

Helen Riley, DeSabla 762

CHEESY PEA SALAD

2 17-oz. cans peas, drained
1/2 c. sweet pickle relish
1 c. diced cheese
1/3 c. mayonnaise
2 hard-boiled eggs, chopped (opt.)
2 med. stalks celery, chopped (opt.)

Combine all ingredients in bowl; mix gently. Yield: 6-8 servings.

Stella Dier, Meadow Vista 721

GERMAN POTATO SALAD

2 knackwurst, cut into halves, sliced
2 tbsp. butter

1 med. onion, sliced
3 tbsp. butter, melted
2 tbsp. flour
3/4 c. red wine vinegar
3/4 c. apple juice
1 1/2 tsp. sugar
1/4 tsp. pepper
6 med. potatoes, cooked, peeled, sliced

Saute knackwurst in 2 tablespoons butter in skillet until brown. Add onion. Cook until onion is tender, stirring frequently. Remove from skillet. Blend 3 tablespoons butter and flour in skillet; remove from heat. Beat in vinegar and apple juice. Stir in sugar and pepper. Simmer until thickened, stirring constantly. Stir in knackwurst and onion; remove from heat. Let stand, covered, for several minutes. Add potatoes; stir gently to coat. Heat to serving temperature. Yield: 6 servings.

Photograph for this recipe on page 103.

HOT GERMAN POTATO SALAD

6 slices crisp-fried bacon, crumbled
4 med. potatoes, sliced
1 onion, thinly sliced
2 1/2 tbsp. sugar
1 tsp. salt
1/4 tsp. pepper
1 tsp. prepared mustard
1/3 c. vinegar
2 tbsp. minced parsley

Combine all ingredients and 2 tablespoons water in pressure cooker; mix lightly. Cook at 15 pounds pressure for 5 minutes, using manufacturer's directions. Remove from heat; cool quickly under cold water. Remove lid. Serve immediately.

Evelyn Ray, San Damas 658

KRAUT SALAD

2/3 c. vinegar
1 1/2 c. sugar
1/2 c. oil
1 16-oz. can sauerkraut, drained
1 c. chopped celery
1 green pepper, chopped
1 c. chopped onion
1 can pimento, chopped

Combine vinegar, sugar, oil and 1/3 cup water in bowl; mix well. Pour over mixture of remaining ingredients in bowl. Marinate, covered, in refrigerator overnight.

Norma Canfield, San Dimas 658

SAUERKRAUT SALAD

1 jar sauerkraut, drained
1 c. grated carrots
1 c. chopped celery
1 c. chopped green pepper
1 c. chopped green onions
1 jar chopped pimento
1/4 c. oil
1/4 c. white vinegar
1 c. sugar

Combine first 6 ingredients in bowl. Mix oil, vinegar and sugar in saucepan. Bring to a boil. Pour over vegetables; mix well. Marinate in refrigerator overnight. Yield: 12 servings.

Lucy Hunt, Millville 443

SPINACH SALAD

1 1/2 lb. fresh spinach
8 oz. bean sprouts
1 6-oz. can sliced water
*   chestnuts, drained*
5 slices crisp-fried bacon, crumbled
1/3 c. sugar
1/3 c. catsup
1/3 c. wine vinegar
1/3 c. chopped onion
2/3 c. oil
Salt and pepper to taste
2 tsp. Worcestershire sauce
2 hard-boiled eggs, sliced

Remove stems from spinach. Wash and dry leaves; tear into bite-sized pieces. Place in large salad bowl. Add bean sprouts, water chestnuts and bacon. Combine remaining ingredients except eggs in jar. Shake well until blended; pour over salad. Adjust seasonings. Top with sliced eggs. Yield: 8 servings.

Joan Boyle, Millville 443

TOMATO ASPIC SALAD

2 c. tomato juice
1 bay leaf
1/2 sm. onion, sliced
1/2 tsp. salt
Dash of pepper
1 pkg. lemon gelatin
2 tbsp. vinegar
1 to 2 c. chopped cooked vegetables

Combine tomato juice, bay leaf, onion, salt and pepper in saucepan. Bring to a boil; strain. Dissolve gelatin in hot liquid. Add vinegar. Chill until slightly thickened. Fold in vegetables. Pour into mold. Chill until firm. Unmold on lettuce-lined serving plate. Serve with mayonnaise. Yield: 6 servings.

Alice Cerine, Hessel 750

GAZPACHO SALAD

1 3-oz. package lemon gelatin
1 can Spanish-style crispy vegetable soup

Dissolve gelatin in 1 cup boiling water. Drain soup, reserving liquid. Add enough water to reserved liquid to measure 1 cup. Add to gelatin; mix well. Add drained vegetables. Pour into 2 1/2-cup mold. Chill until partially set. Stir to distribute vegetables. Chill until firm. Unmold on serving plate. Yield: 6-8 servings.

Edith Harbuck, Napa 307

ROSE SALAD

6 firm tomatoes, peeled
Salt and paprika to taste
2 tsp. minced onion
3 tbsp. minced celery
3 tbsp. chopped lettuce
3 tbsp. mayonnaise

Cut each tomato into 6 petals to but not through bottom. Season with salt and paprika. Place on lettuce-lined plates. Spoon mixture of remaining ingredients into centers. Chill in refrigerator. Yield: 6 servings.

Agnes Mairose, San Jose 10

FRENCH-AMERICAN VEGETABLE SALAD

1/2 c. Ocean Spray jellied cranberry sauce
1/2 c. yogurt
1 sm. clove of garlic, crushed
2 tbsp. chopped parsley
1/3 c. chopped celery
1 tbsp. catsup
4 tomatoes, cut into wedges
1 to 1 1/2 lb. asparagus spears,
*   cooked, chilled*
1/2 avocado, cut into wedges
1 8-oz. can artichoke hearts
1/4 to 1/2 head romaine

Beat cranberry sauce in bowl with wire whisk until smooth. Stir in yogurt and next 4 ingredients. Chill, covered, in refrigerator. Arrange tomatoes, asparagus, avocado and artichoke hearts on romaine-lined serving plate. Drizzle with cranberry dressing just before serving.

Photograph for this recipe on page 103.

FRIEDA'S VEGETABLE SALAD

1 c. sugar
3/4 c. vinegar
1/2 c. oil
1 can French-style green beans
1 can Shoe Peg corn
1 can sm. green peas
1 sm. jar chopped pimento
1 tsp. celery salt
1 c. finely chopped celery
4 green onions, finely chopped
Salt and pepper to taste

Combine sugar, vinegar and oil in saucepan. Heat until sugar is dissolved. Combine with remaining ingredients in bowl. Chill overnight or longer. Yield: 10-15 servings.

Frieda Merrigan, Hi Desert 821

CONGEALED VEGETABLE SALAD

2 15-oz. cans mixed vegetables
1 15-oz. can tomatoes
1 6-oz. package lemon gelatin
2 tbsp. vinegar

Drain vegetables and tomatoes, reserving liquid. Add enough water to reserved liquid to measure 3 1/2 cups. Dissolve gelatin in 2 cups boiling vegetable liquid. Add remaining liquid and vinegar. Add vegetables. Pour into shallow dish. Chill until firm. Serve with salad dressing. Yield: 8-10 servings.

Miriam Loe, DeSabla 762

EVERLASTING SALAD

3/4 c. sugar
1/2 c. wine vinegar
1/4 c. cider vinegar
1/2 c. oil
1 tsp. each salt and pepper
1 can French-style green beans
1 can petite peas
1 can whole kernel white corn
1 c. chopped green pepper
1 c. chopped celery

1 c. chopped onion
1 sm. can chopped pimento

Combine first 6 ingredients and 1 tablespoon water in saucepan. Bring to a boil; cool. Add remaining ingredients. Marinate, tightly covered, for 24 hours.

Inez Jensen, Los Banos 79

SHOE PEG CORN AND VEGETABLE SALAD

1 c. sugar
3/4 c. white vinegar
1/4 c. oil
1 tbsp. salt
1 tsp. pepper
1 16-oz. can Shoe Peg corn, drained
1 16-oz. can French-style green beans, drained
1 12-oz. package frozen peas, cooked
1 sm. jar chopped pimento
1 c. chopped onion
1 c. chopped green pepper

Combine sugar, vinegar, oil, salt, 1 tablespoon water and pepper in saucepan. Bring to a boil; cool. Pour over vegetables in bowl. Marinate in refrigerator overnight or longer. Yield: 6 servings.

Lydia Linn, Hemet-San Jacinto 693

RUTH'S LAYERED VEGETABLE SALAD

2 c. cottage cheese
2 tbsp. mayonnaise
1 tsp. salt
1/2 tsp. white pepper
1 tbsp. grated onion
1 head Boston lettuce, chopped
1 1-lb. can sliced beets, drained
1 cucumber, thinly sliced
1 lg. Bermuda onion, thinly sliced into rings
2 lg. tomatoes, peeled, thinly sliced

Combine first 5 ingredients in bowl; mix well. Layer lettuce, 3 tablespoons cottage cheese mixture, beets, cucumber, onion rings and tomatoes in glass salad bowl with straight sides. Top with remaining cottage cheese mixture. Garnish with chives. Yield: 8 servings.

Ruth Hunter, Rough and Ready 795

MARY'S LAYERED VEGETABLE SALAD

1 head lettuce, chopped
2/3 c. chopped celery
2/3 c. chopped green peppers
2 bunches green onions
  and tops, chopped
1   10-oz. package frozen green
  peas, thawed
2 c. mayonnaise
2 tsp. sugar
1   4-oz. package grated
  American cheese

Layer all ingredients in bowl in order given. Chill, covered with foil, for 24 hours. Yield: 15-21 servings.

Mary L. Horder, Rincon Valley 710

BROWN RICE SALAD

3/4 c. Smucker's grape jelly
1/2 c. fresh lemon juice
1/4 c. olive oil
2 tbsp. dried mint leaves
1/2 tsp. salt
1 c. brown rice, cooked

1 c. chopped parsley
2 cucumbers, peeled, seeded, chopped
1 c. chopped red radishes
1/2 c. chopped green onions
Lg. lettuce leaves

Combine grape jelly, lemon juice, olive oil, mint and salt in blender container. Process until smooth. Layer rice, parsley and half the cucumbers in straight-sided 1 1/2-quart glass bowl. Pour dressing on top. Chill for several hours to overnight. Add remaining chopped vegetables; toss to mix. Serve on lettuce-lined plates. Yield: 6-8 servings.
Note: May substitute 1 cup bulgur cooked in 2 cups boiling water for 15 minutes for brown rice. Mixture may be served in rolled lettuce leaves and eaten as finger food.

Photograph for this recipe on opposite page.

RICE SALAD

1 c. rice, cooked
6 tbsp. olive oil
3 tbsp. vinegar
1 tsp. salt
1 1/2 tsp. pepper
1 tsp. tarragon
1/2 c. chopped red or green pepper
1/4 c. chopped parsley
1/4 c. chopped onion
1 sm. cucumber, chopped

Combine hot rice and mixture of olive oil, vinegar, salt, pepper and tarragon in bowl. Fold in red pepper, parsley and onion. Chill, covered, overnight. Add cucumber just before serving; toss to mix. Yield: 6 servings.
Note: May store in refrigerator for several days.

Audrey Frankford, Loomis 638

UNUSUAL RICE SALAD

2 pkg. chicken-flavored rice mix
2 6-oz. jars marinated artichoke hearts
1/2 c. chopped green pepper
1 sm. bunch green onions, sliced
8 to 10 Spanish olives, sliced
2/3 c. mayonnaise

Cook rice according to package directions, omitting butter. Drain artichokes, reserving marinade. Add to rice with green pepper, green onions and olives. Add mixture of reserved marinade and mayonnaise; mix well. Chill in refrigerator. Yield: 10-12 servings.

Dorothy McConnell, Los Banos 79

RICE CURRY SALAD

1 pkg. chicken Rice-A-Roni
2 or 3 green onions, sliced
1 sm. green pepper, chopped
8 stuffed green olives, sliced
2 6-oz. jars marinated artichoke
    hearts, chopped
1/2 tsp. curry powder
1/2 c. mayonnaise

Cook Rice-A-Roni according to package directions, omitting butter and browning. Cool. Add onions, green pepper and olives. Drain artichoke hearts, reserving liquid. Combine reserved liquid with curry powder and mayonnaise in bowl. Add with artichoke hearts to rice; mix well. Chill in refrigerator.
Yield: 12 servings.
Note: May add 1 cup chopped chicken, turkey, ham or shrimp.

Kathleen Ponte, French Camp-Lathrop 510

SPINACH-RICE SALAD

1 c. rice, cooked
1/2 c. Italian salad dressing
1 tbsp. soy sauce
2 c. chopped fresh spinach
1/2 c. sliced celery
1/2 c. sliced green onions and tops
1/3 c. crisp-fried crumbled bacon
1/2 c. chopped radishes

Combine slightly cooled rice with mixture of salad dressing and soy sauce; mix well. Chill, covered, in refrigerator. Add remaining ingredients; mix well. Yield: 6-8 servings.

Bertha Monroe, Bayside 500

RICE-VEGETABLE SALAD

3 c. cooked rice, cooled
1 1/2 c. sliced celery
1 10-oz. package green peas, cooked
1/4 c. minced onion
1/2 c. diced pimento
1 c. cubed American cheese
1 c. mayonnaise
1 tsp. lemon juice
1/2 tsp. salt
1/2 tsp. pepper

Combine all ingredients in bowl; toss lightly. Serve in lettuce cups. Garnish with sliced hard-boiled egg and tomato wedges.

Nadine Olson, Kingsburg 679

MACARONI SALAD

2/3 c. vinegar
1 c. sugar
2 c. mayonnaise
2 lg. carrots, chopped
1 lg. green pepper, chopped
1 lg. onion, chopped
1 8-oz. package curly
  macaroni, cooked

Bring vinegar and sugar to a boil in saucepan; cool. Add mayonnaise; mix well. Combine with vegetables and macaroni in bowl. Let stand for 12 hours. Yield: 20 servings.

Aleta Paul, Lake Francis 745

FROG EYE PASTA SALAD

1 c. sugar
2 tbsp. flour
1/2 tsp. salt
1 3/4 c. pineapple juice
2 eggs, beaten
1 tbsp. lemon juice
1 16-oz. package ocini de pepe
1 tbsp. oil
2 tsp. salt
3 11-oz. cans mandarin oranges, drained
2 20-oz. cans crushed pineapple, drained
1 carton whipped topping
1 c. miniature marshmallows (opt.)
1 c. coconut (opt.)

Combine sugar, flour and 1/2 teaspoon salt in saucepan. Stir in pineapple juice and eggs. Cook over medium heat until thickened, stirring constantly. Stir in lemon juice; cool. Cook pasta in 3 quarts boiling water in saucepan with oil and 2 teaspoons salt for 9 to 10 minutes or until just tender. Rinse with cold water; drain. Combine with cooked mixture in bowl; mix well. Chill overnight. Add remaining ingredients; mix lightly. Chill. Yield: 25 servings.
Note: May store, covered, in refrigerator for 1 week.

Josie Manfrina, Lompoc 646

BETTY'S PASTA SALAD

1 head broccoli, chopped
1 carton fresh mushrooms, chopped
1 green onion, chopped
1 can ripe olives
1 12-oz. jar marinated artichoke
  hearts, chopped
2 pkg. Italian salad dressing
  mix, prepared

1 12-oz. package jumbo shell
  macaroni, cooked
3 tomatoes, chopped
2 avocados, chopped

Combine first 5 ingredients and salad dressing in bowl. Marinate for 2 to 3 hours. Add macaroni; mix well. Add tomatoes and avocados just before serving.

Betty L. Kelley, Apple Valley 593

BOILED COLESLAW DRESSING

2 eggs, slightly beaten
1 tsp. prepared mustard
1/2 tsp. salt
1/4 c. packed light brown sugar
1/2 c. cider vinegar

Combine all ingredients and 1/2 cup water in saucepan. Cook until thickened, stirring constantly. Chill in refrigerator.
Note: Combine 3 tablespoonfuls per 1 cup coleslaw in bowl; mix well. Store remaining dressing in refrigerator.

Edna Cox, La Avenida 655

ONION SALAD DRESSING

1 med. onion, chopped
1/2 c. sugar
1 tsp. dry mustard
1 tsp. salt
1/3 c. vinegar
1 c. oil

Combine onion, sugar, mustard and salt in blender container. Process until blended. Add vinegar and oil alternately, processing after each addition.
Note: Use a red onion for pink color.

Mary Cupp, American River 172

LOW-CALORIE
ROQUEFORT DRESSING

2 c. lite salad dressing
1 pkg. Roquefort cheese, softened
1 pkg. blue cheese, crumbled
1/2 pt. nondairy sour cream
1/4 tsp. garlic salt
1/4 c. lemon juice (opt.)

Combine all ingredients in bowl. Beat with wire whisk until blended. Chill, covered, for 2 days. Serve on salads or cooked vegetables.

Margie Westmoreland, Morro Bay 749

VEGETABLES & SIDE DISHES

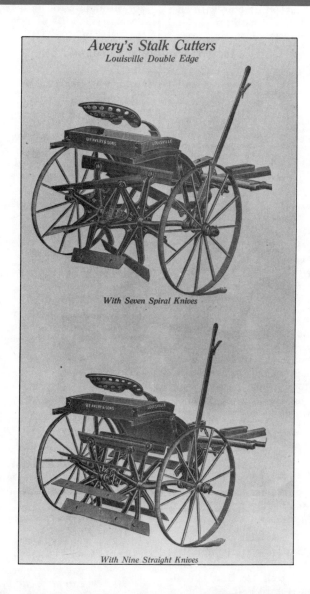

Avery's Stalk Cutters
Louisville Double Edge

With Seven Spiral Knives

With Nine Straight Knives

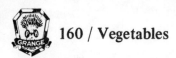

ARTICHOKE NIBBLES

2 jars marinated artichoke hearts
1 sm. onion, chopped
1 clove of garlic, minced
4 eggs, beaten
1/4 c. fine bread crumbs
1/4 tsp. salt
1/8 tsp. each pepper, oregano
1/8 tsp. Tabasco sauce
1/2 lb. sharp Cheddar cheese, grated
1 tbsp. minced parsley

Drain 1 jar artichoke hearts. Combine with undrained artichokes, onion and garlic in skillet. Saute for several minutes. Combine eggs, crumbs and seasonings; mix well. Add sauteed vegetables, cheese and parsley; mix well. Pour into greased 7 x 11-inch baking dish. Bake at 350 degrees for 30 minutes or until set. Cut into 1-inch squares.

Dottie Grace, Feather River 440

JERUSALEM ARTICHOKE PATTIES

2 c. sliced mushrooms
1 med. onion, sliced
1 clove of garlic, minced
1/4 c. oil
1 carrot, grated
2 c. grated artichokes
1 c. whole wheat flour
2 eggs, lightly beaten
Soy sauce, cayenne pepper or hot
    sauce to taste
Oil for frying

Saute mushrooms, onion and garlic in 1/4 cup oil in skillet. Combine with carrot, artichokes, flour, eggs and seasonings in bowl; mix well. Drop by rounded tablespoonfuls into 1/8-inch hot oil in skillet. Flatten into patties with back of spoon. Cook until lightly browned on both sides. Yield: 20-24 patties.

Viola Holmes, North Fork 763

LIMA BEAN CASSEROLE

1 16-oz. package frozen lima beans
1 16-oz. can boiled onions
1 can cream of chicken soup
Grated cheese

Cook beans according to package directions until almost tender. Combine with onions and soup in casserole. Top with cheese. Bake at 350 degrees for 20 minutes or until heated through.

Jane Staggs, Rainbow Valley 689

STRING BEANS AL CRUDO

1 med. onion, sliced
2 tbsp. oil
1 sm. can tomatoes
1/2 tsp. salt
Pepper to taste
1 lb. string beans
1/4 c. stock
1 tsp. chopped parsley

Saute onion in oil in skillet. Add tomatoes, salt, pepper and beans. Cook, covered, over low heat for 40 minutes or until tender, adding stock as necessary. Add parsley just before serving.

Anna Compagnoni, Ripon 51

CHEESE-TOPPED GREEN BEAN CASSEROLE

3 c. young green beans
1 clove of garlic, minced
1 med. onion, minced
1 sm. green pepper, chopped
1/4 c. chopped pimento
3 tbsp. butter
1 8-oz. can tomato sauce
1 tsp. Tabasco sauce
1 c. shredded Cheddar cheese

Cook beans in a small amount of water in saucepan until tender-crisp; drain. Saute garlic, onion, green pepper and pimento in butter in skillet for 5 minutes. Stir in tomato sauce, Tabasco sauce and beans. Pour into 1-quart casserole; sprinkle with cheese. Bake at 350 degrees for 25 minutes. Yield: 4 servings.

Photograph for this recipe on opposite page.

THREE-BEAN CASSEROLE

1 c. finely chopped celery
1 1/2 c. chopped onions
2 tbsp. bacon drippings
1 6-oz. can tomato paste
1/2 c. packed brown sugar
1 env. spaghetti sauce mix
2 tbsp. prepared mustard
1 tsp. garlic salt
2 tbsp. vinegar
2 1-lb. cans large lima beans, drained
1 1-lb. can kidney beans, drained
1 1-lb. can pork and beans in
    tomato sauce
8 slices crisp-fried bacon, crumbled

Saute celery and onions in bacon drippings in skillet. Add 1 cup water, tomato paste and next 5 ingredients; mix well. Bring to a boil. Combine beans and bacon in 3-quart casserole. Add sauce; mix well. Bake, uncovered, at 350 degrees for 1 hour, adding a small amount of water if necessary to prevent dryness.

Fern Kias, San Dimas 658

VERNON ROSE'S RED BEANS

1 lb. dried red beans
1/2 lb. ground beef
1/2 lb. bacon, chopped
1 lg. onion, chopped
3 cloves of garlic, chopped
1 can tomato sauce
1/2 tsp. each cumin, cayenne pepper
*   and chili powder*
1/2 tsp. each cinnamon, nutmeg,
*   cloves and allspice*
Salt to taste

Soak beans in water to cover overnight. Cook until tender. Brown ground beef and bacon in skillet. Add onion, garlic, tomato sauce and seasonings. Simmer for 15 minutes. Stir into beans. Simmer until of desired consistency.

Vina J. Weathers, Capay 461

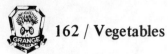

SPECIAL OCCASION BRUSSELS SPROUTS

2   10-oz. packages frozen
    Brussels sprouts
1/2 c. sliced almonds
2 tbsp. butter
1/8 tsp. thyme
1 can cream of chicken soup

Cook Brussels sprouts in a small amount of water in saucepan until just tender; drain well. Brown almonds in butter in skillet, stirring constantly. Add thyme and soup; mix well. Heat to serving temperature. Pour over hot Brussels sprouts.

Exean Freeny, Fieldbrook 771

THELMA'S RICE AND BROCCOLI CASSEROLE

1 c. uncooked rice
1 can cream of celery soup
1 sm. jar Cheez Whiz
2   10-oz. packages frozen chopped broccoli
1 c. cornflake crumbs

Combine first 4 ingredients in bowl; mix well. Pour into casserole. Top with crumbs. Bake at 325 degrees for 1 hour or until rice is tender. Yield: 6 servings.

Thelma Jardine, Estrella 488

NELLIE'S BROCCOLI AND RICE CASSEROLE

2 bunches broccoli
2 onions, chopped
1 stick margarine
2 cans cream of chicken soup
1 lg. jar Cheez Whiz
1 c. milk
2 c. minute rice

Cook broccoli in unsalted water in saucepan until just tender. Saute onions in margarine in skillet until tender. Do not brown. Add soup, Cheez Whiz and milk; mix well. Layer broccoli, rice and cheese mixture in casserole. Bake at 350 degrees for 1 hour or until bubbly.

Nellie Jones, New Era 540

ELLEN'S BROCCOLI CASSEROLE

2   10-oz. packages frozen broccoli
2 eggs, beaten

1 can cream of mushroom soup
1 c. mayonnaise
1 c. grated Cheddar cheese
1/4 c. chopped onion
Dash of pepper

Cook broccoli using package directions; drain well. Place in buttered casserole. Combine eggs, soup, mayonnaise, cheese and onion; mix well. Pour over broccoli. Sprinkle with pepper. Bake at 350 degrees for 30 minutes.

Ellen Cox, Yucaipa 582

NIPPY CABBAGE WEDGES

1 med. head cabbage
3 tbsp. butter, melted
2 tbsp. flour
1/2 tsp. French's onion salt
1 c. milk
1 egg yolk
1 tbsp. French's prepared yellow mustard
2 tsp. lemon juice

Cut cabbage into 6 wedges. Cook, covered, in a small amount of boiling water in saucepan until tender-crisp. Blend butter, flour and onion salt in saucepan. Blend in milk and egg yolk. Cook over medium heat until thickened, stirring constantly. Add mustard and lemon juice; mix well. Spoon sauce over well-drained cabbage wedges. Yield: 6 servings.

Photograph for this recipe on page 164.

RED DOT CABBAGE

4 c. coarsely shredded cabbage
1/2 tsp. caraway seed
1 tbsp. margarine
2 frankfurters, sliced into 1/4-in. rounds

Stir-fry cabbage and caraway seed in margarine in skillet for 2 minutes. Add frankfurters. Cook, covered, for 3 to 5 minutes, stirring twice. Yield: 2-4 servings.

Vivian W. Tuttle, Millville 443

VERA'S CARROT CASSEROLE

2 c. rice, cooked
3 c. ground carrots
1 c. peanut butter
2 c. milk

2 eggs
1 onion, ground
1/2 tsp. sage
1 tsp. salt

Combine all ingredients in bowl; mix well. Pour into greased 9 x 13-inch baking dish. Bake at 350 degrees for 1 hour. Serve with favorite gravy.

Vera I. Blakeley, Yucaipa Valley 582

CARROTS IN ORANGE SAUCE

3 tbsp. margarine, melted
1/2 c. sugar
1 1/2 tbsp. cornstarch
3 tbsp. frozen orange juice
*   concentrate, thawed*
Salt to taste
4 servings hot cooked carrots

Blend first 3 ingredients in saucepan. Stir in orange juice concentrate and 1 cup water gradually. Cook until thickened, stirring constantly. Add salt to taste. Let stand for several hours to overnight. Serve over hot cooked carrots. Yield: 4 servings.

Edythe Koerzendorfer, Keyes 524

HOLIDAY CARROT RING WITH PEAS

2 c. mashed cooked carrots
2 eggs, lightly beaten
1/2 tsp. salt
2 tbsp. sugar
1/4 c. evaporated milk
1   10-oz. package frozen peas, cooked

Combine all ingredients except peas in bowl; mix well. Pour into well-greased 1-quart ring mold. Place in pan of water. Bake at 350 degrees for 45 minutes or until knife inserted in center comes out clean. Unmold on serving plate. Fill center with cooked peas. Garnish with parsley sprigs. Yield: 6-8 servings.

Ava DeRousse, Waterford 553

MARINATED CARROTS

5 c. sliced carrots
1 med. onion, sliced
1 green pepper, sliced

1 c. sugar
1 can tomato soup
1/2 c. oil
1/2 c. vinegar
1 tsp. prepared mustard
1 tsp. Worcestershire sauce
1 tsp. each salt, pepper

Cook carrots in water in saucepan until tender-crisp; drain and cool. Combine with onion and green pepper in bowl. Mix remaining ingredients in bowl. Pour over vegetables. Marinate, covered, for 12 hours. Drain. Yield: 12 servings.

Mary A. Trick, Hessel 750

CALIFORNIA DEEP-FRIED CAULIFLOWER

1 head cauliflower, separated
*   into flowerets*
1 to 2 c. milk
1 to 2 c. flour
1 egg, beaten
2 tbsp. milk
1/2 tsp. salt
1 pkg. cornflake crumbs
2 to 3 qt. oil for deep frying

Drain cauliflower well. Dip each floweret in milk. Place in flour in plastic bag; shake until well coated. Dip in mixture of egg, 2 table-spoons milk and salt; roll in crumbs to coat, pressing firmly over surface if necessary. Deep-fry in 375-degree oil for 1 1/2 to 2 minutes or until golden brown. Drain on paper towels. Serve immediately or keep warm in 350-degree oven for 5 to 10 minutes. Yield: 6-8 servings.

Loleta Kalsbeek, Winnetka Center 668

CAULIFLOWER-CHEESE BAKE

1 head cauliflower, broken into flowerets
1 c. evaporated milk
Dry bread crumbs
Salt andpepper to taste
Cheddar cheese, grated

Cook cauliflower in water in saucepan until just tender; drain. Place in baking dish. Pour evaporated milk over cauliflower. Layer crumbs, seasonings and cheese over top. Bake at 350 degrees for 30 minutes. Yield: 6 servings.

Dorothy Lisenbee, Ripon 511

CHEESE-CROWNED CAULIFLOWER

1 med. head cauliflower
1/4 c. mayonnaise
1 tbsp. French's prepared yellow mustard
1/4 tsp. salt
1/2 c. grated Cheddar cheese

Trim outer leaves from cauliflower. Place in boiling salted water in saucepan until tender but firm; drain. Place in shallow baking dish. Combine mayonnaise, mustard, salt and cheese in bowl; mix well. Spoon over cauliflower. Bake at 400 degrees for 10 to 15 minutes or until golden brown. Yield: 6 servings.

Photograph for this recipe on page 171.

BARBARA'S CORN CASSEROLE

2 cans cream-style corn
1 c. cracker crumbs
1/3 c. melted butter

Alternate layers of corn, crumbs and butter in greased 2-quart baking dish until all ingredients are used. Bake at 400 degrees for 30 minutes or until bubbly. Yield: 6-8 servings.

Barbara Hunt, Yucaipa Valley 582

VERNA'S CORN CASSEROLE

1 med. onion, chopped
1 med. green pepper, chopped

1/4 c. margarine
2 eggs, beaten
1   8 1/2-oz. package corn bread mix
1 can cream-style corn
1 can whole kernel corn
2 c. yogurt
1 c. (or more) shredded Cheddar cheese

Saute onion and green pepper in margarine in skillet. Combine eggs and corn bread mix in large bowl; stir until just blended. Add corn; mix well. Pour into buttered 10 x 15-inch baking dish. Spoon sauteed vegetables over batter. Beat yogurt until creamy; spread over top. Sprinkle with cheese. Bake at 350 degrees for 45 minutes. Yield: 8-12 servings.
Note: May substitute sour cream for yogurt.

Verna Webb, Greenhorn 384

CORN-CHEESE BAKE

1   16-oz. can cream-style corn
1/3 c. flour
1   3-oz. package cream cheese, cubed
1/2 tsp. onion salt
1   16-oz. can whole kernel corn, drained
1/2 c. shredded Swiss cheese
Buttered crumbs (opt.)

Mix cream-style corn and flour in saucepan. Add cream cheese and onion salt. Heat until cheese is melted, stirring constantly. Add remaining ingredients except crumbs; mix well. Pour into buttered casserole. Top with crumbs. Bake at 400 degrees for 30 minutes or until bubbly. Yield: 6-8 servings.

Eleanor H. Chase, Banner 627

CORN CUSTARD MEXICANA

1 tbsp. chopped pimento
2 tbsp. chopped celery
2 eggs
2 c. sour cream
1   4-oz. can chopped green chilies
2 c. fresh corn
1/2 c. cornmeal
1/2 c. melted margarine
1 tsp. salt
1 c. grated Monterey Jack cheese

Combine all ingredients in large bowl; mix well. Pour into greased 2-quart casserole. Bake, covered, at 350 degrees for 45 minutes or until browned.

Lynn Buchanan, Waterford 553

CORN PUDDING

2 eggs, beaten
1 tbsp. flour
3 tbsp. butter
1/3 c. sugar
1 c. milk
1 tbsp. vanilla extract
1/2 tsp. salt
1   16-oz. can corn, drained

Combine all ingredients except corn in bowl; mix well. Stir in corn. Pour into greased 2-quart casserole. Bake at 400 degrees for 40 minutes. Yield: 6 servings.

Kate Myers, Ceres 520

SCALLOPED CORN

1 can whole kernel corn
1 can cream-style corn
1   8-oz. carton sour cream
1/2 c. melted butter
2 eggs, beaten
1 pkg. corn bread mix
Salt and pepper to taste
1 c. shredded Cheddar cheese

Combine all ingredients except cheese in bowl; mix well. Pour into buttered baking dish. Bake at 350 degrees for 25 to 30 minutes. Top with cheese. Bake for 10 minutes longer.

Jean Cockran, Fair Valley 752

FRIED CUCUMBERS

4 med. cucumbers, sliced
1 lg. onion, thinly sliced
1 tbsp. shortening
1/2 tsp. salt
1/4 tsp. pepper
3 tbsp. vinegar
1 tbsp. sugar
3 tbsp. sour cream
1 tsp. flour

Brown cucumbers and onion in shortening in skillet. Add salt and pepper. Cook over medium heat until tender. Add vinegar and sugar. Simmer for several minutes. Add sour cream. Simmer for several minutes longer. Add flour. Cook until thickened, stirring constantly. Pour into serving dish. Yield: 4 servings.
Note: May fold in crisp-fried crumbled bacon just before serving. Serve hot or cold.

Barbara L. White, Lompoc 646

LINDA'S STUFFED MUSHROOMS

12 lg. mushrooms
2 to 3 tbsp. melted butter
Salt to taste
Pepper to taste
2 tbsp. minced green
    onion tops
1/2 to 1 tbsp. flour
1/2 c. heavy cream
2 tbsp. minced fresh parsley
1/4 c. grated Swiss cheese

Wash mushrooms; pat very dry. Remove and chop stems. Dip caps in melted butter; arrange in baking dish. Sprinkle with salt and pepper. Saute stems and green onion tops in remaining butter in skillet for 5 minutes. Sprinkle with flour. Cook for 1 minute, stirring constantly. Add cream. Cook until thickened, stirring constantly. Add salt, pepper and parsley. Spoon into mushroom caps. Top each with 1 teaspoon Swiss cheese. Bake at 375 degrees for 10 minutes or until lightly browned.

Barbara Clark, Feather River 440

STUFFED EGGPLANT

2 med. eggplant
1 1/2 lb. ground beef
1/4 c. chopped onion
1/4 c. chopped green pepper
1/4 clove of garlic, chopped
1 1/4 tsp. Tabasco sauce
1 tsp. salt
1/4 c. oil
1 1/2 c. cooked rice
1 tsp. lemon juice

Slice eggplant into halves; scoop out and chop pulp. Saute eggplant pulp, ground beef, onion, green pepper, garlic, Tabasco sauce and salt in oil in skillet until eggplant is lightly browned. Add rice; mix well. Spoon into eggplant halves. Place in greased baking dish. Bake at 375 degrees for 30 minutes. Sprinkle with lemon juice. Serve immediately. Yield: 4 servings.

Photograph for this recipe on opposite page.

EGGPLANT PATTIES

1 lg. eggplant
1 med. onion
1 green pepper
1 clove of garlic
2 eggs, beaten
Salt and pepper to taste
1 1/2 c. butter cracker crumbs

Cube unpeeled eggplant. Cook in a small amount of water in saucepan until tender; drain. Grind eggplant, onion, green pepper and garlic. Combine with eggs, salt, pepper and crumbs in bowl; mix well. Shape by 1/4 cupfuls into patties. Brown on both sides in shortening in skillet.

Elmer Carlson, Kingsburg 679

BAKED ONION LOAF

2 c. buttermilk baking mix
1 can French-fried onions
1 1/2 c. Monterey Jack cheese
4 eggs
1 can cream of onion soup
Dash each of salt and pepper

Combine baking mix and 1/2 cup water in bowl; mix well. Pat into baking dish. Sprinkle half the onions and cheese over dough. Combine eggs, soup and salt and pepper in bowl; mix well. Pour into prepared pan. Top with remaining onions and cheese. Bake at 375 degrees for 25 minutes.

Kaye Windsor, Anderson 418

CHEESY ONION PIE

4 c. thinly sliced onions
1 tbsp. margarine
2 c. shredded sharp cheese
1 unbaked 9-in. pie shell
3 eggs
2/3 c. half and half
1 tsp. salt
1/4 tsp. pepper
6 tomato slices

Saute onions in margarine in skillet until golden brown. Alternate layers of onions and cheese in pie shell, ending with cheese. Combine eggs, half and half, salt and pepper in bowl; beat lightly. Pour over layers. Bake at 400 degrees for 25 minutes. Arrange tomato slices on top. Bake for 5 minutes.

Fern Willman, Mt. Lassen 417

WHITNEY'S ONION PIE

3 c. sliced white onions
2 tbsp. butter
Salt and pepper to taste
1 1/2 c. crushed soda crackers
1/2 c. melted butter
1 1/2 c. hot milk
2 eggs, beaten
1/2 lb. Cheddar cheese, grated

Saute onions in 2 tablespoons butter in skillet. Season with salt and pepper. Layer cracker crumbs, 1/2 cup butter and sauteed onions in 9 x 13-inch baking dish. Combine milk and eggs in skillet. Add cheese. Heat until cheese is melted, stirring constantly. Pour over onions. Bake at 350 degrees for 1 hour.

Wilbalee Clark, Sisquoc 651

FRIED ONION RINGS

4 lg. red onions
1 c. milk
2 c. flour
1 c. buttermilk
2 c. cracker crumbs
Oil for deep frying

Slice onions 1/4 inch thick; separate into rings. Dip in milk; coat with flour. Dip in buttermilk; coat with mixture of cracker crumbs and a small amount of flour. Deep-fry until golden brown.

Viola DeMoss, Kingsburg 679

MARINATED BLACK-EYED PEAS

2/3 c. oil
5 tbsp. red wine vinegar
2 onions, chopped
1 c. chopped parsley
2 cloves of garlic, crushed
2 tsp. basil
1 tsp. oregano
1/2 tsp. dry mustard
1/2 tsp. pepper
Dash of red pepper flakes
1 pkg. frozen black-eyed peas, cooked
Green pepper rings

Combine first 10 ingredients in bowl; mix well. Drain peas well. Pour marinade over warm peas; toss to mix. Chill, tightly covered, overnight. Line platter with green pepper rings. Spoon marinated peas into center. Yield: 12 servings.

Mary Ann Chase, Alturas 406

STUFFED GREEN PEPPERS

4 med. green peppers
1 1/2 lb. ground beef
1/4 c. chopped onion
1/4 c. chopped green pepper
1 1/4 tsp. Tabasco sauce
1 tsp. salt
1 1/2 c. cooked rice

Remove tops from peppers; scoop out seed. Parboil in boiling water in saucepan for 15 minutes; drain. Cook ground beef, onion, chopped green pepper, Tabasco sauce and salt in skillet until green pepper is tender, stirring frequently. Add rice; mix well. Fill each pepper with about 3/4 cup filling. Place peppers upright in greased baking dish. Bake at 375 degrees for 30 minutes or until peppers are tender. Serve hot or cold. Yield: 4 servings.

Photograph for this recipe on page 166.

CHILI RELLENO SQUARES

2 4-oz. cans mild green chilies,
thinly sliced
3 c. shredded Monterey Jack cheese
1 1/2 c. grated sharp Cheddar cheese
2 eggs
2 tbsp. milk
1 tbsp. flour

Seed chilies for milder flavor if desired. Alternate layers of cheeses and chilies in greased

9-inch square baking pan, beginning and ending with cheese. Combine remaining ingredients in bowl; mix well. Pour over layers. Bake at 350 degrees for 1 hour. Cut into small squares. Serve warm. Yield: 3 dozen.

Daphne Craig, Independent 470

CHILI PEPPER CASSEROLE

2 7-oz. cans chopped mild green chilies
1 lb. Cheddar cheese, grated
2 c. milk
1/2 c. flour
2 eggs
1 tsp. salt

Alternate layers of chilies and cheese in greased 1 1/2-quart casserole. Combine remaining ingredients in bowl; mix well. Pour over layers. Bake at 350 degrees for 45 minutes or until golden brown. Yield: 6 servings.
Note: May be served cold.

Margaret Almstrom, Napa 307

GREEN CHILI ENCHILADA CASSEROLE

10 corn tortillas
1 sm. onion, finely chopped
2 tbsp. butter
1 4-oz. can chopped green chilies
1 can cream of chicken soup
1/2 soup can evaported milk
1/2 lb. longhorn cheese, grated

Soften tortillas in hot oil in skillet; drain. Saute onion in butter in skillet. Add chilies, soup and evaporated milk. Cook until heated through, stirring constantly. Alternate layers of tortillas and sauce in greased 1-quart casserole. Sprinkle cheese on top. Bake at 350 degrees for 30 minutes or until bubbly.

Peggy L. Houk, Sebastopol 306

RUTH'S CHILES RELLENOS

1 6-oz. can whole green chilies, sliced
1 1/2 tsp. (heaping) flour
1/4 lb. Monterey Jack cheese, grated
1 6-oz. can whole green chilies, sliced
1/4 lb. butter, sliced
1 1/2 tsp. (heaping) flour

1/4 lb. Monterey Jack cheese, grated
4 eggs, beaten
1/2 c. (or more) milk

Layer first 3 ingredients in greased 6 x 10-inch casserole. Layer 1 can chilies, butter, 1 1/2 teaspoons flour and 1/4 pound cheese on top. Pour mixture of eggs and milk over layers. Add enough additional milk to nearly fill casserole. Bake at 350 degrees for 1 hour or until set.

Ruth Finney, Riverbank 719

CHILES RELLENOS CASSEROLE

1 c. half and half
2 eggs
1/3 c. flour
3   4-oz. cans whole green chilies
1/2 lb. Monterey Jack cheese, grated
1/2 lb. sharp Cheddar cheese, grated
1   8-oz. can tomato sauce

Beat half and half with eggs. Add flour; mix until smooth. Split chilies; rinse to remove seed. Drain on paper towels. Combine cheeses. Reserve 1/2 cup for topping. Alternate layers of remaining cheese, chilies and egg mixture in 1 1/2-quart casserole. Pour tomato sauce over top. Sprinkle with reserved cheese. Bake at 350 degrees for 1 1/4 hours. Yield: 4 servings.

Vinita J. Moore, Concow 735

HOLIDAY POTATO BAKE

1 c. chopped onion
1/4 c. butter
1 can cream of celery soup
1   16-oz. carton sour cream
4 lb. potatoes, cooked, peeled, chopped
1 1/2 c. shredded Cheddar cheese
1/2 c. cornflake crumbs
3 tbsp. melted butter

Saute onion in 1/4 cup butter in skillet; remove from heat. Add soup and sour cream; mix well. Combine potatoes, cheese and soup mixture in bowl; mix well. Pour into greased 9 x 13-inch baking dish. Chill, covered, overnight. Top with crumbs. Drizzle 3 tablespoons melted butter over top. Bake at 350 degrees for 1 hour. Garnish with pimento strips and parsley.

Rita F. Bradley, Sierra Valley 466

POTATO CASSEROLE A LA SYBIL

1/4 c. butter
1 can cream of chicken soup
1 pint sour cream
8 med. potatoes, cooked, grated
1 1/2 to 2 c. shredded Cheddar cheese

Heat butter and soup in saucepan. Blend in sour cream. Stir into potatoes. Place in 9 x 13-inch baking dish. Top with cheese. Bake at 350 degrees for 1 hour. Yield: 8 servings.

Sybil W. Green, Fairfax 570

BAKED SLICED POTATOES

4 lg. baking potatoes
1/4 c. melted butter
1/4 c. oil
2 cloves of garlic, minced
1/2 tsp. salt
1/2 tsp. thyme

Slice unpeeled potatoes 1/4 inch thick. Place overlapping slices in buttered baking dish. Brush slices with mixture of butter and oil. Pour remaining mixture over top. Sprinkle with garlic, salt and thyme. Bake at 400 degrees for 25 to 30 minutes or until potatoes are tender and browned at edges. Serve immediately.

Lorna Polasek, Humboldt 501

ALICE'S POTATO PUFFS

3 tbsp. margarine
1/2 tsp. (or more) seasoned salt
1/2 c. sour cream
1/4 c. milk
2 3/4 c. mashed potato flakes
2 eggs, slightly beaten
3 tbsp. melted margarine
6 1/3 tbsp. fine dry bread crumbs
1/2 tsp. poultry seasoning

Combine 1 cup water, 3 tablespoons margarine and seasoned salt in large saucepan. Bring to a boil; remove from heat. Stir in sour cream, milk and potato flakes. Let stand until liquid is absorbed; mix lightly. Cool slightly. Add eggs; mix well. Shape by 2 1/2 tablespoonfuls into balls. Roll in 3 tablespoons melted margarine; coat with mixture of crumbs and poultry seasoning. Arrange on buttered baking sheet. Bake at 400 degrees for 15 minutes.

Alice Capen, American River 172

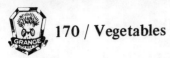

HASSELBACK POTATOES

8 sm. baking potatoes
1/2 c. butter
1/2 tsp. salt
1/4 tsp. onion salt
1/2 tsp. paprika
2 tbsp. bread crumbs
1/2 c. shredded Cheddar cheese

Cut unpeeled potatoes into 1/8-inch slices 3/4 through. Place each potato on foil square; separate to resemble fan. Drizzle with butter; sprinkle with seasonings. Wrap tightly; place on baking sheet. Bake at 350 degrees for 45 minutes. Open foil; shape into cup around potato. Sprinkle with mixture of crumbs and cheese. Bake for 15 minutes longer.

Irene L. Cool, El Camino 462

MARY'S POTATO CASSEROLE

6 med. potatoes
1 can cream of chicken soup
1 16-oz. carton sour cream
1 1/2 c. grated Cheddar cheese
1/4 c. chopped onion
Salt and pepper to taste

Cook unpeeled potatoes in boiling water until almost tender; cool. Peel and grate potatoes. Combine with remaining ingredients in bowl; mix well. Pour into greased 2-quart casserole. Chill overnight. Bake at 350 degrees for 45 minutes. Yield: 6-8 servings.

Wanda Rector Arbuckle, Millville 443

POTATO AND CHEESE BAKE

1 16-oz. carton sour cream
1 can cream of chicken soup
1/2 c. melted butter
2 green onions, chopped
Salt and pepper to taste
1 2-lb. package frozen hashed
  brown potatoes
1 1/2 c. grated Cheddar cheese

Blend sour cream, soup and butter in bowl. Add green onions and salt and pepper to taste. Layer half the potatoes, half the soup mixture and 3/4 cup cheese in 9 x 13-inch baking dish. Repeat layers. Bake at 350 degrees for 1 hour. Garnish with additional green onions. Yield: 8-10 servings.

Marietta Ewert, Rough and Ready 795

ROADSIDE POTATOES

1 c. milk
1 1/2 tsp. flour
1 tsp. salt
Dash of Tabasco sauce
1 lg. onion, chopped
4 med. potatoes, peeled, grated
1/4 lb. Cheddar cheese, grated

Combine first 5 ingredients in blender container. Process until smooth. Mix with potatoes and cheese. Pour into greased 8-inch baking pan. Bake at 350 degrees for 1 1/4 hours or until golden. Yield: 6 servings.

Billie Stenstrom, Lake Francis 745

GOLDEN-CAPPED TOMATOES

6 med. tomatoes
Salt and pepper to taste
1/4 c. mayonnaise
1 tbsp. French's prepared yellow mustard
1 tsp. instant minced onion
1/2 tsp. sugar
2 tbsp. fine cracker crumbs

Cut thin slice from stem end of each tomato. Place cut side up in shallow baking dish; sprinkle with salt and pepper. Combine remaining ingredients in bowl. Spoon over cut surface to cover. Bake at 400 degrees until topping is lightly puffed. Yield: 6 servings.

Photograph for this recipe on page 171.

SPINACH CASSEROLE

1/2 lb. thin spaghetti
1 10-oz. package frozen
  chopped spinach
1/4 c. melted butter
1/2 lb. Monterey Jack cheese, grated
2 tbsp. chopped onion
1 c. sour cream

Cook spaghetti according to package directions until just tender. Cook spinach according to package directions for 3 minutes. Combine spaghetti, spinach and remaining ingredients in bowl; mix well. Pour into 8 x 10-inch baking dish. Bake at 325 degrees for 20 minutes. Yield: 6-8 servings.

Mildred Seale, Mt. Lassen 417

SPINACH CUSTARD

1 sm. onion, chopped
1 clove of garlic
1 pkg. frozen spinach, thawed
3 eggs, beaten
1/2 tsp. each salt and pepper

1 c. shredded Monterey Jack cheese
1/4 c. cottage cheese

Combine all ingredients in greased 1 1/2-quart baking dish; mix well. Bake at 400 degrees for 40 minutes or until set. Yield: 6 servings.

Stella Hammer, Bernardo 506

PRALINE YAM CASSEROLE WITH ORANGE SAUCE

2 16-oz. cans Louisiana yams, drained, mashed
2 eggs
1/4 c. packed dark brown sugar
2 tbsp. butter, melted
1 tsp. salt
1/2 c. pecan halves
1/4 c. packed brown sugar
3 tbsp. melted butter

Combine first 5 ingredients in bowl; mix well. Pour into 1-quart casserole. Arrange pecans over top. Sprinkle with 1/4 cup brown sugar; drizzle 3 tablespoons butter over all. Bake at 375 degrees for 20 minutes.

ORANGE SAUCE

1/3 c. sugar
1 tbsp. cornstarch
1/8 tsp. salt
1 tsp. grated orange rind
1 c. orange juice
1 tbsp. lemon juice
2 tbsp. butter
1 tbsp. Grand Marnier
3 dashes of angostura bitters

Blend first 6 ingredients in saucepan. Bring to a boil over medium heat, stirring constantly. Remove from heat. Stir in butter and remaining ingredients. Serve over yam casserole.

Photograph for this recipe on opposite page.

DEEP-FRIED ZUCCHINI

1 1/2 c. flour
1/2 can beer
3 med. zucchini, sliced into thin strips
Oil for deep-frying

Combine flour and beer in bowl; mix well. Let stand at room temperature for 3 hours. Dip zucchini into batter. Deep-fry until golden brown; drain. Serve with cheese sauce or ranch dressing.

Patricia Avila, Sacramento 12

JAPANESE-STYLE ZUCCHINI PATTIES

1/4 c. flour
1/4 c. cornstarch
1/2 c. biscuit mix
1/4 c. Parmesan cheese
1/4 tsp. garlic salt
Dash of pepper
1 egg, beaten
2 c. thinly sliced sm. zucchini
1/2 c. thinly sliced onion
1/2 c. shredded carrot
Oil for frying

Combine dry ingredients in bowl. Add mixture of egg and 1/4 cup cold water; mix well. Add vegetables. Let stand for 5 minutes; mix well. Drop by spoonfuls into 1/4-inch 375-degree oil. Flatten with spoon. Fry until golden brown. Drain on paper towels. Serve warm with soy sauce and mustard. Yield: 18-20 servings.

Yoshiko Harter, Chico 486

ZUCCHINI A LA LEWIS

6 med. zucchini
1 lg. onion, chopped
6 slices bacon, chopped
1 can tomato sauce
1 c. cubed sharp Cheddar cheese
Salt and pepper to taste

Cut zucchini into 1-inch cubes. Boil until tender. Brown onion and bacon in skillet. Add tomato sauce; mix well. Add cheese. Combine zucchini, sauce and seasonings in casserole; mix well. Bake at 375 degrees for 30 minutes. Yield: 6 servings.

Ruth Lewis, Yucca 736

SOUR CREAM AND ZUCCHINI CASSEROLE

4 c. chopped zucchini
1 c. chopped onion
1 c. sour cream
1 can cream of chicken soup
2 c. grated carrots
1 pkg. corn bread stuffing mix
1 stick butter, melted

Steam zucchini until tender; drain. Mix with onion, sour cream, soup and carrots in bowl. Mix stuffing mix and butter. Layer half the stuffing mixture, all the zucchini mixture and remaining stuffing mixture in 9 x 13-inch baking dish. Bake at 350 degrees for 30 minutes or until carrots are tender. Yield: 8-10 servings.

Mary Alice Conner, Keyes 524

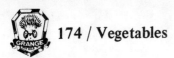

JUNE'S ZUCCHINI CASSEROLE

2 lb. zucchini
1/2 lb. pork sausage
1 med. onion, chopped
1 clove of garlic, chopped
1 c. bread crumbs
1 1/2 tsp. salt
1/2 tsp. pepper
2 tbsp. chopped parsley
2 eggs, separated
1/2 c. grated cheese

Cook zucchini in boiling water in saucepan until tender. Drain and chop. Saute sausage, onion and garlic in skillet. Combine zucchini, sausage mixture, crumbs, seasonings and egg yolks in bowl; mix well. Fold in stiffly beaten egg whites gently. Pour into buttered casserole. Top with cheese. Bake at 325 degrees for 50 minutes. Yield: 6 servings.

June McMillan, Whitesboro 766

ZUCCHINI SICILIANA

2 slices bacon, chopped
2 cloves of garlic, chopped
1/2 med. onion, chopped
3 5-in. zucchini, sliced
Salt and pepper to taste
Oregano to taste
Dash of cinnamon (opt.)

Saute bacon in skillet for several minutes until partially cooked. Add garlic and onion. Saute until lightly browned. Add zucchini and seasonings; mix well. Cover tightly. Shake skillet several times. Do not remove cover. Cook for 2 minutes. Uncover. Cook for 1 minute longer or until of desired tenderness, stirring gently. Do not overcook.

Ella Iantosca, Berryessa 780

NAN'S ZUCCHINI SOUFFLE

2 c. grated zucchini
3 eggs, beaten
15 soda crackers, crushed
Garlic salt to taste
Grated cheese
Onion salt to taste

Combine all ingredients in bowl; mix well. Pour into greased casserole. Bake at 350 degrees for 45 minutes.

Nan Larson, Humboldt 501

GEORGIA'S ZUCCHINI SOUFFLE

2 lb. zucchini
2 lg. onions
1/4 c. oil
3/4 c. cracker crumbs
3/4 c. grated cheese
1 egg, beaten
1/2 c. milk
Salt and pepper to taste

Coarsely grind zucchini and onions. Saute in oil in skillet for 15 minutes. Do not brown. Combine with half the crumbs and half the cheese. Pour into buttered 9 x 12-inch baking dish. Pour mixture of egg and milk over zucchini. Sprinkle with salt and pepper. Top with remaining cheese and crumbs. Bake at 350 degrees for 30 to 40 minutes or until set.
Yield: 8-10 servings.

Georgia Hunt, Hesperia 682

ZUCCHINI FINGER FOOD

4 eggs, beaten
Pinch of garlic powder
1/2 tsp. each salt, basil
1/2 tsp. dried parsley
1/2 c. oil
1/2 c. grated cheese
1/2 c. biscuit mix
1 onion, chopped
2 c. grated zucchini

Combine all ingredients in bowl; mix well. Pour into greased 7 x 10-inch baking pan. Bake at 350 degrees for 30 minutes or until browned. Cut into squares; serve hot. Yield: 12 servings. Note: May be frozen.

Glatys Montgomery, Orangevale 354

FRESH VEGETABLE GHIVETCH

2 potatoes, peeled, cubed
2 carrots, peeled, sliced
1/2 head cauliflower, broken
    into flowerets
2 stalks celery, chopped
1/2 lb. mushrooms, sliced
2 onions, chopped
1 red pepper, chopped
1 clove of garlic, chopped
1 13 3/4-oz. can chicken broth
2 tsp. salt
1/8 tsp. pepper
2 tbsp. chopped fresh dill

Combine all ingredients in bowl; mix well. Spoon into greased 2-quart casserole. Bake, covered, at 350 degrees for 1 hour. Yield: 8 servings.

Hazel T. Ivey, Banner 627

BULGUR WHEAT PILAF

3 tbsp. butter
1 c. bulgur wheat
2 tbsp. instant minced onion
2 tbsp. parsley flakes
2 beef bouillon cubes
1/2 tsp. garlic salt
1/2 tsp. basil
1/2 tsp. oregano

Melt butter in 2-quart saucepan. Add remaining ingredients. Cook over low heat until lightly toasted, stirring constantly. Add 2 cups water. Simmer, covered, for 30 minutes or until bulgur is tender. Yield: 4 servings.

Dorothy Ratcliff, Millville 443

HOMINY CASSEROLE

1 lg. can white hominy
1 can Cheddar cheese soup
1 can green chilies, chopped
1 sm. can pimento, chopped
Salt and pepper to taste
Grated cheese

Combine hominy, soup, chilies, pimento and seasonings in bowl; mix well. Pour into greased 1-quart casserole. Sprinkle cheese over top. Bake at 350 degrees for 1 hour. Yield: 8 servings.

Viola DeVries, Elbow Creek 733

SAUSAGE-CRACKER DRESSING

1 lb. pork sausage
1/2 c. butter
4 lg. celery stalks, chopped
1 lg. onion, chopped
10 c. coarsely crushed soda crackers
1/2 c. milk
3/4 tsp. rosemary
1/2 tsp. pepper

3 eggs
Cooked chopped turkey giblets
3/4 c. giblet broth

Brown sausage in skillet. Remove sausage with slotted spoon. Add butter to pan drippings. Saute celery and onion in butter mixture until tender. Remove from heat. Add remaining ingredients; mix well. Yield: Enough for 14 to 16-pound turkey.

Charlotte Harrell, Montgomery 442

TURKEY DRESSING

3/4 lb. ground beef
3/4 lb. sausage
4 stalks celery, chopped
1 onion, chopped
1/2 c. chopped parsley
3/4 c. melted butter
2 loaves French bread, cubed
2 qt. milk
Salt, pepper, sage and poultry
*   seasoning to taste*

Brown ground beef and sausage in skillet, stirring until crumbly; drain. Saute celery, onion and parsley in butter in skillet until tender. Combine all ingredients in large bowl; mix well. Pour into greased casserole. Bake at 350 degrees for 1 hour. Yield: 15 servings.
Note: May stuff turkey if desired.

Virginia West, Feather River 440

BETTY'S RING OF PLENTY

1 1/2 c. cooked sm. elbow macaroni
1 c. cubed sharp Cheddar cheese
1 c. soft white bread crumbs
1 tbsp. minced parsley
3 tbsp. minced pimento
1 tbsp. minced onion
3 tbsp. melted shortening
1 tsp. salt
1/8 tsp. pepper
1 c. milk, scalded
1 egg, well beaten

Combine all ingredients in bowl in order given; mix well. Spoon into greased 10-inch ring mold. Place in pan of hot water. Bake at 375 degrees for 35 minutes. Unmold on serving plate. Yield: 8 servings.

Betty Hackett, Turlock 573

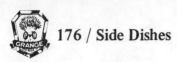

MACARONI RING OF PLENTY

1/2 c. cooked macaroni
1 c. chopped cheese
1 c. cubed bread
1 tbsp. minced parsley
3 tbsp. minced pimento
3 tbsp. melted shortening
1 tbsp. minced onion
1 c. milk, scalded
1 egg, well beaten
1 tsp. salt
1/8 tsp. pepper

Combine all ingredients in bowl; mix well. Spoon into greased ring mold. Bake at 350 degrees for 45 minutes. Unmold on serving plate.

Marjorie Smith, Goat Mountain 818

CRUSTLESS QUICHE

1 tbsp. butter
3 eggs, beaten
1 c. shredded cheese
1 tsp. Worcestershire sauce
8 slices crisp-fried bacon, crumbled
1 can French-fried onions
1 c. sour cream

Melt butter in 9-inch pie plate. Combine remaining ingredients in bowl; mix well. Pour into pie plate. Bake at 325 degrees for 25 minutes. Yield: 6-8 servings.

Mable Williams, Kingsburg 679

EGG FOO YUNG

2 tbsp. flour
1 tsp. salt
4 eggs, well beaten
2 tbsp. instant onion
1 c. bean sprouts, drained
1/2 c. shortening
1 tsp. cornstarch
1 tbsp. oil
1 tsp. sugar
1 tsp. soy sauce

Combine first 3 ingredients in bowl; mix well. Add onion and sprouts; mix well. Brown 1/4 cup at a time in hot shortening in skillet; drain. Combine cornstarch and 1 cup water in saucepan. Add remaining ingredients; mix well. Cook until thickened, stirring constantly. Serve over Egg Foo Yung. Yield: 1 dozen.

Betty Higgs, Rio Linda 403

MICROWAVE BROWN RICE

1 c. short grain brown rice
2 tbsp. butter
1/2 tsp. salt

Combine rice, butter, salt and 2 1/4 cups water in 2-quart glass casserole. Microwave, covered, on Medium for 30 minutes. Let stand, covered, for 30 minutes. Yield: 8 servings.

Leta Gale, Dos Palos 541

MY FAVORITE PILAF

1 c. broken vermicelli
1/4 c. butter
1 c. rice
3 c. chicken broth
Salt and pepper to taste

Brown vermicelli in butter in skillet. Add rice and broth; mix well. Simmer, tightly covered, until moisture is absorbed. Season with salt and pepper. Yield: 6 servings.

Betty Goeringer, Madera 783

LONG GRAIN RICE PILAF

1 handful No. 47 orzo
2 tbsp. butter
1 13 3/4-oz. can chicken broth
1 c. long grain rice
1/2 to 1 tbsp. salt

Brown orzo in butter in skillet. Add broth and rice. Bring to a boil. Add salt; mix well. Simmer, tightly covered, for 20 minutes. Let stand, partially covered, for 5 minutes. Yield: 6-8 servings.

Louise Daniels, Empire 521

PORK-FRIED RICE

1 c. chopped pork
1/2 c. chopped onion
1/2 c. green onions
1 tbsp. oil
1/2 c. chopped celery
1/4 c. shredded carrot
Salt and pepper to taste
5 eggs, beaten
3 tbsp. oil
2 to 3 c. steamed rice
1/4 c. cooked green peas

Brown pork and onions in 1 tablespoon oil in skillet. Add celery and carrot; mix well. Cook until tender-crisp. Season with salt and pepper. Scramble eggs in 3 tablespoons oil in large skillet. Add rice; mix well. Add pork mixture. Cook for 5 minutes, stirring constantly. Top with peas. Yield: 6 servings.

Rose Saberniak, Ripon 511

MOLLIE'S RICE PILAF

1/2 c. chopped onion
2 tbsp. oil
1 1/3 c. rice
1 c. chicken stock

Saute onion in oil in skillet for 2 minutes. Add rice; mix well. Spoon into 1 1/2-quart casserole. Add stock and 1 1/2 cups water; mix well. Bake, covered, at 350 degrees for 25 minutes. Fluff with fork. Yield: 4 servings.

Mollie S. Holten, Orland 432

PEPPER-RICE CASSEROLE

3 c. cooked rice
1/2 c. chopped onion
1/4 c. chopped celery
1/4 c. chopped green pepper
1 sm. can jalapeno peppers, chopped
1 c. milk
3 eggs, beaten
1/4 c. oil
1 tbsp. chopped parsley
Salt and pepper to taste
1/2 c. grated cheese

Combine all ingredients except cheese in bowl; mix well. Pour into greased 9 x 12-inch baking dish. Sprinkle cheese on top. Bake at 250 degrees for 2 hours. Yield: 8-10 servings.

Maxine Barlow, Escalon 447

ZUCCHINI AND RICE WITH SAUSAGE

1 lb. sausage
1 1/2 c. minute rice
3 c. sliced zucchini
1/2 c. thinly sliced onion
1 16-oz. can stewed tomatoes

1 tsp. prepared mustard
1 tsp. garlic salt
Dash of pepper
1 c. grated sharp Cheddar cheese

Brown sausage in large skillet. Drain, reserving 2 tablespoons pan drippings. Add rice, zucchini and onion. Cook until lightly browned, stirring constantly. Stir in tomatoes, 1 cup hot water, mustard, garlic salt and pepper. Bring to a boil. Simmer, covered, for 5 minutes. Stir in cheese. Heat until cheese melts.

Clara Johnson, Empire 521

AL'S MEATLESS VEGETABLE SOUP

4 lg. carrots, sliced
2 med. potatoes, cubed
1 lg. onion, chopped
2 1/2 c. chopped celery
2 c. mashed tomatoes
1 sm. green pepper, chopped
Dash of rosemary
1/2 tsp. Beau Monde seasoning
1/2 tsp. cumin (opt.)
Salt and pepper to taste
1 tsp. parsley flakes
1 bay leaf
Dash of garlic powder
1/4 c. margarine

Combine all ingredients and 1 quart water in saucepan. Simmer for 1 hour. Remove bay leaf. Simmer for 1 to 2 hours longer. Add additional water or tomatoes to make of desired consistency if necessary. Yield: 6 servings.

Alfred J. Benish, Trinity River 458

LIMA BEAN SOUP

1 lb. dried lima beans
1 med. onion, finely chopped
1 stalk celery, finely chopped
1 can tomato soup
6 slices bacon, finely chopped
Salt and pepper to taste

Soak beans in 3 quarts water overnight. Add onion, celery and soup. Bring to a boil over medium heat. Simmer for 1 1/2 hours or until beans are tender, stirring frequently and adding additional water if necessary. Brown bacon in skillet; drain. Add to soup mixture with salt and pepper.

Erma Pritto, Sonora 705

BROCCOLI SOUP

2 10-oz. packages frozen
chopped broccoli
3 c. chicken broth
1/3 c. minced onion
4 tsp. butter
1/2 tsp. salt
2/3 c. chopped peeled potatoes
1/4 tsp. each marjoram, thyme
1 c. whipping cream

Combine all ingredients except cream in saucepan. Cook, covered, for 15 to 20 minutes or until vegetables are tender. Puree mixture in blender. Cool. Stir in whipping cream just before serving. Serve hot or cold garnished with crumbled crisp-fried bacon. Yield: 8 servings.

Dorothy Wurst, Fonbloom 602

CREAM OF BROCCOLI SOUP

3 c. chopped fresh broccoli
1/4 c. instant minced onion
Salt to taste
1 1/2 c. chicken broth
3/4 c. half and half
1 can cream of potato soup
1 soup can milk
1 1/2 tsp. curry powder

Steam broccoli with onion and salt in broth in saucepan until tender. Combine with half and half in blender container. Process until pureed. Add soup, milk and curry powder. Blend until smooth. Store in refrigerator for 4 to 5 days or freeze if desired.

Ethel Lesher, Mt. Lassen 417

CABBAGE SOUP

1 qt. chicken broth
1 c. sliced potato
1 c. sliced onion
1 c. sliced cabbage
2 chicken bouillon cubes

Combine all ingredients in saucepan. Cook until vegetables are tender. Yield: 8-10 servings.

Mary L. Marshall, Morro Bay 749

CREAM OF CAULIFLOWER SOUP

1 lg. onion, chopped
2 tbsp. butter
2 14-oz. cans chicken broth

2 med. carrots, sliced
1 med. head cauliflower, cut
into flowerets
1 c. half and half
1/8 tsp. nutmeg
Salt and pepper to taste
1 tbsp. chopped parsley
1 c. grated yellow cheese

Saute onion in butter in 3-quart saucepan for 5 minutes. Add broth. Bring to a boil. Add carrots and cauliflowerets. Simmer, covered, for 7 minutes or until tender. Puree a small amount at a time in blender. Combine puree, half and half and seasonings in saucepan. Bring to a simmer. Serve with parsley and cheese.
Yield: 12 servings.

Neva Clark, Feather River 440

GAZPACHO

1 1/2 c. tomato juice
1 beef bouillon cube
1 tomato, chopped
1/4 c. chopped cucumber
2 tbsp. chopped green pepper
2 tbsp. chopped onion
2 tbsp. wine vinegar
1 tbsp. oil
1/2 tsp. salt
1/2 tsp. Worcestershire sauce
3 drops of Tabasco sauce

Heat tomato juice to boiling point in saucepan. Add bouillon cube. Stir to dissolve. Stir in remaining ingredients. Chill for several hours. Pour soup into cups. Sprinkle with additional chopped tomato, chopped cucumber, chopped green pepper, chopped onion and herbed croutons. Yield: 3-4 servings.

Dorothy Glassey, Apple Valley 593

GOOD FLU SOUP

2 tbsp. garlic, chopped
2 tbsp. onion, chopped
A small amount of margarine
1 can chicken noodle soup
2 tbsp. apple cider vinegar

Saute garlic and onion in margarine in 2-quart saucepan. Add soup and 1 soup can water. Simmer until heated through. Add vinegar; mix well. Yield: 2-3 servings.

Eva Borchers, Chico 486

MINESTRONE SOUP

1 sm. zucchini, cubed
2 stalks celery, chopped
1 carrot, chopped
2 green onions, chopped
1 tsp. salt
1/4 tsp. pepper
1/2 tsp. garlic salt
1 clove of garlic, pressed
1 tbsp. oil
1/4 c. chopped parsley
3 tbsp. butter
1 16-oz. can tomatoes, mashed
1 16-oz. can kidney beans
1/2 c. Sherry
1/4 c. elbow macaroni
4 or 5 leaves chard, chopped
Parmesan cheese

Combine first 12 ingredients and 2 1/2 cups water in 3-quart saucepan. Mash 3/4 of the beans. Add all beans to saucepan. Simmer for 1 hour. Add Sherry, macaroni and chard. Simmer for 12 minutes. Serve with Parmesan cheese. Yield: 6-8 servings.

Ann Ehrig, Ripon 511

MOCK MINESTRONE SOUP

1/2 lb. ground beef
1 med. onion, chopped
2 tbsp. oil
1 can tomato soup
1 can old-fashioned vegetable soup
1 can bouillon
1 16-oz. can pinto beans
2 lg. handfuls very thin spaghetti

Brown ground beef and onion in oil in skillet, stirring until crumbly. Combine soups, bouillon and beans in saucepan. Bring to a boil. Add ground beef mixture. Bring to a boil. Add spaghetti. Cook for about 10 minutes or until spaghetti is tender. Serve with hot garlic bread. Yield: 8-10 servings.

Maggie M. Miller, Hemet-San Jacinto 693

CHEESE SOUP

6 stalks celery, chopped
6 carrots, chopped
1/2 c. chopped onion
1 10-oz. package frozen peas
1 can chicken broth
1 16-oz. jar Cheez Whiz, melted
1 stick butter, melted
Flour

Cook celery and carrots in 6 cups water in saucepan until tender. Add onion and peas. Simmer for 30 minutes. Add broth. Stir in cheese. Blend butter with enough flour to make soft paste. Add to soup. Cook until thickened, stirring constantly. Yield: 6-8 servings.

Sheila Burns, Quartz Hill 697

FAMOUS PALOUSE SPLIT PEA SOUP

1 c. split peas
1 ham bone
3 tbsp. chopped onion
6 sprigs of parsley
1 sprig of thyme
6 sprigs of green celery leaves
8 peppercorns, crushed
Salt to taste
2 tbsp. butter
1 1/2 tbsp. flour
2 c. milk, scalded

Rinse and soak split peas in cold water overnight. Drain. Cover with 3 quarts water. Add ham bone, onion, parsley, thyme, celery, peppercorns and salt to taste. Bring to a boil. Simmer until peas are tender. Remove ham bone; strain soup mixture through fine sieve. Keep warm. Melt butter over low heat in saucepan. Blend in flour. Do not brown. Stir in milk gradually. Cook until slightly thickened, stirring constantly. Combine both mixtures. Bring to a boil several times, stirring frequently. Serve with croutons.

Marjorie Long, Montgomery 442

FRANK-POTATO CHOWDER

1 5 5/8-oz. package dry scalloped
*   potato mix*
1 10-oz. package frozen
*   mixed vegetables*
4 frankfurters, sliced
3 c. milk
Parmesan cheese

Combine potato mix, vegetables and 3 cups water in saucepan. Simmer for 15 minutes, stirring occasionally. Add frankfurters and milk. Simmer for 10 minutes longer. Serve with cheese. Yield: 6-8 servings.

Lynne Fagundes, American River 172

THE BREAD BOARD

Serving freshly baked bread is a truly satisfying experience. Bring out a steaming, crusty loaf of whole wheat bread, and you're bound to get more "ooh's" and "aah's" than the fanciest flaming dessert or an elaborate entree.

Fortunately, once you learn the basics of bread making, you'll see how easy it really is. If this is your first time, you'll appreciate the easy quick breads that don't require rising or kneading. Then, move on to yeast, sourdough and unleavened breads for more creative baking. And if you really want to be a hit hostess, try serving homemade hamburger buns at your next cookout!

QUICK BREADS

Using baking powder, baking soda, air, sourdough or steam for leavening, quick breads can be made on the spur of the moment. They rise in the oven during baking and emerge as piping hot delights.

It's important to stir, not beat, quick breads just long enough to mix the ingredients. After baking, cool on a rack, wrap, and store in an airtight container or serve immediately while still warm.

YEAST BREADS

Who would have thought the wonderful aroma coming from the kitchen on bread baking day is really the expansion of gases released by the yeast's action, and gluten stretching in the wheat?

But that's only the beginning step in creating perfect yeast breads. Kneading comes next — to spread the gluten throughout the dough and thoroughly blend ingredients. There's a proper way to knead dough, but don't worry about perfecting your technique at first. Just do the best you can.

When You Need To Knead . . .

1. Place dough on a floured board, flatten out lightly.
2. Pull a corner towards you with fingers close together.
3. Then, press down and forward with the heels of your hands.
4. Give dough a quarter turn and repeat — continuing about ten minutes — until the dough is smooth and elastic.
5. Kneading's complete when small bubbles appear under the surface.

BREAD BAKING TIPS

- Rather than making large loaves of bread, shape small, individual loaves for two and three member families.
- Most sweet breads freeze well. Be sure and let cool thoroughly — preferably overnight — before freezing.
- All baking powder breads improve if allowed to stand at room temperature for 20 minutes before being placed in oven.
- Shortcut quick breads can be made with prepared biscuit mix.
- Grease finger tips before starting to knead.
- The choice of pan affects the crust. Glass, dark tin and dull aluminum pans produce a thick crust.
- Glass and enamel pans require a lower temperature.
- Milk, cream or butter, used in the recipe or brushed on at the end of the baking period, gives a good, over-all brown color.
- For a glazed crust, brush the top with an egg wash near the end of baking time.
- To keep the crust soft, brush with butter after the bread is baked and removed from pan.
- To test for doneness: Notice if the loaf has shrunk from the sides of the pan or test by tapping the top of the loaf and listening for a hollow sound.
- If you heat chopped fruits and nuts for sweet bread mixtures, dust with flour before adding to the dough. Fruits and nuts will not sink to the bottom of the pan.
- For variety, don't use bread pans when baking. Instead, shape free-form loaves on cookie sheets.
- Save wrappers from butter and margarine and use later to grease pans for cakes and breads, or for greasing potatoes before baking. Store wrappers in the freezer to use when needed.
- When substituting one yeast for another, remember: one packet dry yeast is equivalent to 3/5-ounce package compressed yeast.
- It's better to use too much yeast than too little. The dough will simply rise faster.
- The richer the recipe is with shortening and sugar, the more yeast will be needed for the dough to rise.
- Use ingredients at room temperature; cold ingredients slow yeast action.
- Scald, then cool milk, before adding to dough to destroy any organisms which might interfere with yeast action.
- If you have trouble getting whole grain breads to rise, use a little extra yeast. After you get the feel of kneading breads, reduce the amount of yeast.
- Old bread — especially if it has nuts, fruit or sugar in it — makes excellent bread pudding.
- Cool breads before slicing.
- Slice loaves before freezing.
- When you slice homemade bread, save the crumbs. Store in a covered container in the freezer until needed.

Then, Let the Dough do its Thing . . .

1. Place the dough in a greased bowl; turn to grease the surface so when dough rises, it does not dry out.
2. Cover dough with a towel and place in warm place (80-85 degrees), free from drafts.
3. Let rise until doubled in bulk (1 to 1 1/2 hours).
4. Punch dough down.

Now, Get it into Shape!

LOAVES

1. With knife, divide dough into loaf-sized portions. Shape into ball; then flatten into rectangle, carefully squeezing out gas bubbles.
2. Roll into loaf shape, tucking the ends under.
3. Place into greased loaf pan, seam side down. Let rise until doubled in bulk. Bake according to recipe instructions.

ROLLS

Parker House Rolls

Roll dough out to about 1/2-inch thickness. Cut with a biscuit cutter. Using the dull edge of a knife, crease the round of dough to one side of the center. Brush with melted butter and fold large side over small side. Seal edges. Place about 1" apart on greased baking sheet. Cover and let rise until doubled in bulk. Brush top with melted butter.

Clover Leaf

Form dough into three small balls about the size of large marbles. Have melted butter on hand to dip balls into. Place three balls in each greased cup of a muffin pan. Allow dough to rise until doubled in bulk.

Pan Rolls

Form dough into balls about one-third the size of a desired baked roll. Place balls about 1/4" apart in a shallow baking pan. Cover and let rise until doubled in bulk. Brush with melted butter.

Crescent

Dough should be divided into three equal parts and rolled into a circle about 10-12" in diameter. Each circle is then cut into pie-shaped pieces. Roll each pie-shaped piece beginning with the larger end and sealing the small end. Place about 2" apart on a baking sheet. Be sure the point of the dough is underneath. Curve each rolled pie-shaped piece to form a crescent. Cover rolls and let rise until doubled in bulk. Brush with melted butter.

WHAT WENT WRONG . . .	. . . AND WHY
Bread and biscuits are dry	Too dry mixture; too slow baking; or over-handling (To remedy, dip quickly in milk, bake for a few minutes; serve hot.)
Bread is very open and has uneven texture	Too much liquid or over-handling in kneading
Gray crumb; slightly heavy taste	Over-rising or over-fermentation
Strong yeast smell from baked bread	Too high proportion of yeast or over-rising
Tiny white spots on the crusts	Too rapid rising; dough not covered properly
Crust has bad color	Too much flour used in shaping
Small flat loaves	Old yeast; not enough rising or rising much too long; too hot an oven
Heavy compact texture	Too much flour worked into bread when kneading; insufficient rising time; oven temperature too hot
Coarse texture	Too little kneading
Crumbly bread	Too much flour, under-mixing; oven temperature too cool
Yeasty sour flavor	Too little yeast; rising time too long
Fallen center	Rising time too long
Irregular shape	Poor technique in shaping
Surface browns too quickly	Oven temperature too hot
Bread continues to rise too long and is porous in the center and upper portion of the loaf	Oven temperature too cool
Overall poor texture, color, flavor and volume	Inferior flour

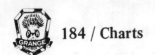

EQUIVALENT CHART

WHEN RECIPE CALLS FOR:		YOU NEED:
BAKING ESSENTIALS	2 c. butter	1 lb.
	4 c. all-purpose flour	1 lb.
	4 1/2 c. sifted cake flour	1 lb.
	1 square chocolate	1 oz.
	1 c. semisweet chocolate pieces	1 6-oz. package
	4 c. marshmallows	1 lb.
	2 2/3 c. brown sugar	1 lb.
	2 2/3 c. confectioners' sugar	1 lb.
	2 c. granulated sugar	1 lb.
	3 c. tapioca	1 lb.
CEREAL AND BREAD	1 c. fine dry bread crumbs	4-5 slices
	1 c. soft bread crumbs	2 slices
	1 c. small bread cubes	2 slices
	1 c. fine cracker crumbs	24 saltines
	1 c. fine graham cracker crumbs	14 crackers
	1 c. vanilla wafer crumbs	22 wafers
	1 c. crushed cornflakes	3 c. uncrushed
	4 c. cooked macaroni	1 8-oz. package
	3 1/2 c. cooked rice	1 c. uncooked
DAIRY	1 c. freshly grated cheese	1/4 lb.
	1 c. cottage cheese	1 8-oz. carton
	1 c. sour cream	1 8-oz. carton
	1 c. whipped cream	1/2 c. heavy cream
	2/3 c. evaporated milk	1 sm. can
	1 2/3 c. evaporated milk	1 tall can
FRUIT	4 c. sliced or chopped apples	4 med.
	1 c. mashed banana	3 med.
	2 c. pitted cherries	4 c. unpitted
	3 c. shredded coconut	1/2 lb.
	4 c. cranberries	1 lb.
	1 c. pitted dates	1 8-oz. package
	1 c. candied fruit	1 8-oz. package
	3 to 4 tbsp. lemon juice plus 1 tsp. grated rind	1 lemon
	1/3 c. orange juice plus 2 tsp. grated rind	1 orange
	4 c. sliced peaches	8 med.
	2 c. pitted prunes	1 12-oz. package
	3 c. raisins	1 15-oz. package

WHEN RECIPE CALLS FOR:	YOU NEED:
MEATS 4 c. diced cooked chicken	1 5-lb. chicken
3 c. diced cooked meat	1 lb., cooked
2 c. ground cooked meat	1 lb., cooked
NUTS 1 c. chopped nuts	4 oz. shelled
	1 lb. unshelled
VEGETABLES 2 c. cooked green beans	1/2 lb. fresh or 1 16-oz. can
2 1/2 c. lima beans or red beans	1 c. dried, cooked
4 c. shredded cabbage	1 lb.
1 c. grated carrot	1 lg.
1 4-oz. can mushrooms	1/2 lb. fresh
1 c. chopped onion	1 lg.
4 c. sliced or diced raw potatoes	4 med.
2 c. canned tomatoes	1 16-oz. can

COMMON EQUIVALENTS

1 tbsp. = 3 tsp.
2 tbsp. = 1 oz.
4 tbsp. = 1/4 c.
5 tbsp. + 1 tsp. = 1/3 c.
8 tbsp. = 1/2 c.
12 tbsp. = 3/4 c.
16 tbsp. = 1 c.
1 c. = 8 oz. or 1/2 pt.
4 c. = 1 qt.

4 qt. = 1 gal.
6 1/2 to 8-oz. can = 1 c.
10 1/2 to 12 -oz. can = 1 1/4 c.
14 to 16-oz. can (No. 300) = 1 3/4 c.
16 to 17-oz. can (No. 303) = 2 c.
1-lb. 4-oz. can or 1-pt. 2-oz. can (No. 2) = 2 1/2 c.
1-lb. 13-oz. can (No. 2 1/2) = 3 1/2 c.
3-lb. 3-oz. can or 46-oz. can or 1-qt. 14-oz. can = 5 3/4 c.
6 1/2-lb. or 7-lb. 5-oz. can (No. 10) = 12 to 13 c.

ABBREVIATIONS

Cup . . . . . . c.
Tablespoon . . . . . tbsp.
Teaspoon . . . . . tsp.
Pound . . . . . lb.
Ounce . . . . . oz.
Package . . . . . pkg.

Gallon . . . . . gal.
Quart . . . . . qt.
Pint . . . . . pt.
Dozen . . . . . doz.
Large . . . . . lg.
Small . . . . . sm.

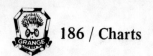

SUBSTITUTION CHART

	INSTEAD OF:	USE:
BAKING	1 tsp. baking powder	1/4 tsp. soda plus 1/2 tsp. cream of tartar
	1 tbsp. cornstarch (for thickening)	2 tbsp. flour OR 1 tbsp. tapioca
	1 c. sifted all-purpose flour	1 c. plus 2 tbsp. sifted cake flour
	1 c. sifted cake flour	1 c. minus 2 tbsp. sifted all-purpose flour
DAIRY	1 c. buttermilk	1 c. sour milk OR 1 c. yogurt
	1 c. heavy cream	3/4 c. skim milk plus 1/3 c. butter
	1 c. light cream	7/8 c. skim milk plus 3 tbsp. butter
	1 c. sour cream	7/8 c. sour milk plus 3 tbsp. butter
	1 c. sour milk	1 c. sweet milk plus 1 tbsp. vinegar or lemon juice OR 1 c. buttermilk
	1 c. sweet milk	1 c. sour milk or buttermilk plus 1/2 tsp. soda
SEASONINGS	1 tsp. allspice	1/2 tsp. cinnamon plus 1/8 tsp. cloves
	1 c. catsup	1 c. tomato sauce plus 1/2 c. sugar plus 2 tbsp. vinegar
	1 clove of garlic	1/8 tsp. garlic powder OR 1/8 tsp. instant minced garlic OR 3/4 tsp. garlic salt OR 5 drops of liquid garlic
	1 tsp. Italian spice	1/4 tsp. each oregano, basil, thyme, rosemary plus dash of cayenne
	1 tsp. lemon juice	1/2 tsp. vinegar
	1 tbsp. prepared mustard	1 tsp. dry mustard
SWEET	1 2/3 oz. semisweet chocolate	1 oz. unsweetened chocolate plus 4 tsp. sugar
	1 1-oz. square chocolate	3 to 4 tbsp. cocoa plus 1 tsp. shortening
	1 c. honey	1 to 1 1/4 c. sugar plus 1/4 c. liquid OR 1 c. molasses or corn syrup
	1 c. granulated sugar	1 c. packed brown sugar OR 1 c. corn syrup, molasses or honey, minus 1/4 c. liquid

CANDY CHART

PRODUCT	TEST IN COLD WATER*	DEGREES F. ON CANDY THERMOMETER			
		SEA LEVEL	2000 FEET	5000 FEET	7500 FEET
FUDGE, PENUCHE, FONDANT	SOFTBALL (can be picked up but flattens)	234°- 240° F.	230°- 236° F.	224°- 230° F.	219°- 225° F.
CARAMELS	FIRM BALL (holds shape unless pressed)	242°- 248° F.	238°- 244° F.	232°- 238° F.	227°- 233° F.
DIVINITY, TAFFY AND CARAMEL CORN	HARD BALL (holds shape though pliable)	250°- 268° F.	246°- 264° F.	240°- 258° F.	235°- 253° F.
BUTTERSCOTCH, ENGLISH TOFFEE	SOFT CRACK (separates into hard threads but not brittle)	270°- 290° F.	266°- 286° F.	260°- 280° F.	255°- 275° F.
BRITTLES	HARD CRACK (separates into hard and brittle threads)	300°- 310° F.	296°- 306° F.	290°- 300° F.	285°- 295° F.

* Drop about 1/2 teaspoon of boiling syrup into one cup water, and test firmness of mass with fingers.

QUANTITIES TO SERVE 100

Baked beans . . . . .5 gallons
Beef . . . . 40 pounds
Beets . . . . 30 pounds
Bread . . . . 10 loaves
Butter . . . . 3 pounds
Cabbage for slaw . . . . 20 pounds
Cakes . . . . .8 cakes
Carrots . . . . 33 pounds
Cauliflower . . . . 18 pounds
Cheese . . . . 3 pounds
Chicken for chicken pie . . . . 40 pounds
Coffee . . . . 3 pounds
Cream . . . . 3 quarts
Fruit cocktail . . . . 1 gallon
Fruit juice . . . . .4 No. 10 cans
Fruit salad . . . . 20 quarts
Ham . . . . 40 pounds
Hamburger . . . . .30 to 36 pounds
Ice cream . . . . .4 gallons
Lettuce . . . . .20 heads

Loaf sugar . . . . 3 pounds
Meat loaf . . . . 24 pounds
Milk .6 gallons
Nuts . . . . 3 pounds
Olives . . . . 1 3/4 pounds
Oysters . . . . 18 quarts
Pickles . . . . .2 quarts
Pies . . . . .18 pies
Potatoes . . . . 35 pounds
Potato salad . . . . 12 quarts
Roast pork . . . . 40 pounds
Rolls . . . . .200 rolls
Salad dressing . . . . 3 quarts
Scalloped potatoes . . . . .5 gallons
Soup .5 gallons
Tomato juice . . . . .4 No. 10 cans
Vegetables . . . . .4 No. 20 cans
Vegetable salad . . . . 20 quarts
Whipping cream . . . . 4 pints
Wieners . . . . 25 pounds

CAKE BAKING GUIDE

WHAT WENT WRONG . . .	WHY . . .	
	Butter-Type Cakes	Sponge-Type Cakes
Cake falls . . .	Too much sugar, liquid, leavening or shortening; too little flour; temperature too low; insufficient baking.	Too much sugar; over-beaten egg whites; under-beaten egg yolks; use of greased pans; insufficient baking.
Cake cracks or humps . . .	Too much flour or too little liquid; overmixing; batter not spread evenly in pan; temperature too high.	Too much flour or sugar; temperature too high.
Cake has one side higher . . .	Batter not spread evenly; uneven pan; pan too close to side of oven; oven rack or range not even; uneven oven heat.	Uneven pan; oven rack or range not level.
Cake has hard top crust . . .	Temperature too high; overbaking.	Temperature too high; overbaking.
Cake has sticky top crust . . .	Too much sugar or short-ening; insufficient baking.	Too much sugar; insufficient baking.
Cake has soggy layer at bottom . . .	Too much liquid; under-beaten eggs; shortening too soft; undermixing; insufficient baking.	Too many eggs or egg yolks; underbeaten egg yolks; undermixing.
Cake crumbles or falls apart . . .	Too much sugar, leaven-ing or shortening; under-mixing; improper pan treatment; improper cooling.	
Cake has heavy, compact quality . . .	Too much liquid or short-ening; too many eggs; too little leavening or flour; overmixing; temperature too high.	Overbeaten egg whites; underbeaten egg yolks; overmixing.
Cake falls out of pan before completely cooled . . .		Too much sugar; use of greased pans; insufficient baking.

INDEX

PHOTOGRAPHY CREDITS

California Milk Advisory Board; California Almond Growers Exchange; California Honey Advisory Board; Cling Peach Advisory Board; Lindsay Olive Growers; California Dried Fig Advisory Board; The J. M. Smucker Company; Ocean Spray Cranberries, Inc.; Karo Corn Syrup; United Fresh Fruit and Vegetable Association; Fleischmann's Margarine; R. T. French Company; American Dry Milk Institute, Inc.; Diamond Walnut Kitchen; Ralston Purina Company; Evaporated Milk Association; National Live Stock and Meat Board; United Dairy Industry Association; Washington State Apple Commission; Campbell Soup Company; National Macaroni Institute; National Fisheries Institute; Ruth Lundgren, Ltd.; Knox Gelatine, Inc.; California Raisin Advisory Board; National Dairy Council; The McIlhenny Company; and Louisiana Yam Commission.

ORDER INFORMATION

ADD TO YOUR COOKBOOK COLLECTION
OR GIVE AS PERFECT GIFTS

FOR ORDERING INFORMATION

WRITE TO:

CALIFORNIA STATE GRANGE
2101 Stockton Blvd.
Sacramento, California 95817

OR CALL:

1-916-454-5805